Judging War, Judging History

Stanford Studies in Human Rights

Judging War, Judging History

Behind Truth and Reconciliation

Pierre Hazan

Translated by
Sarah Meyer de Stadelhofen

Stanford University Press
Stanford, California

Stanford University Press
Stanford, California

Judging War, Judging History was originally published in French in 2007 under the title
*Juger la guerre, juger l'histoire: Du bon usage des commissions vérité et de la justice
internationale* © 2007, Presses Universitaires de France.

Printed in the United States of America on acid-free, archival-quality paper

Library of Congress Cataloging-in-Publication Data

Hazan, Pierre.
    [Juger la guerre, juger l'histoire. English]
    Judging war, judging history : behind truth and reconciliation / Pierre Hazan ;
translated by Sarah Meyer de Stadelhofen.
        p.   cm. — (Stanford studies in human rights)
    Includes bibliographical references.
    ISBN 978-0-8047-6955-6 (cloth : alk. paper)—
    ISBN 978-0-8047-6956-3 (pbk. : alk. paper)
    1. Transitional justice.   2. Human rights.   3. International criminal
courts.   4. Truth commissions.   5. Justice, Administration of—Political
aspects.   I. Title.   II. Series: Stanford studies in human rights.
    JC571.H363   2010
    323.4'9—dc22   2009044478

Typeset by Westchester Book Group in 10/14 Minion Pro

To the Alexandrias of yesterday, today, and tomorrow
To my mother and to the memory of my father

Contents

Acknowledgments

MY RESEARCH INTO the policies of punishment and pardon is a long-ripening fruit. Beginning in 1992, I (first, due to circumstances, then rapidly by choice) reported as a journalist on the birth and the action of the international criminal courts in the former Yugoslavia and Rwanda; the criminal charges against Chad's ex-dictator, Hissène Habré; the work of the Equity and Reconciliation Commission in Morocco; and the debates—often vehement—on the punishment of the crimes against humanity committed in Sudan, Afghanistan, Uganda, Sierra Leone, Cambodia, Iraq, and Somalia, after visiting those countries. My role as UN correspondent in Geneva for two newspapers, *Libération* (Paris) and *Le Temps* (Geneva), enlightened me on the political and ideological issues in our world and on the international agenda.

Progressively, I felt a need to study these events in a more profound way. Consequently, I submitted a proposal to write a doctoral thesis on these events in the Political Science Department of the University of Geneva. I thank the members of the department for accepting my proposal, which was the basis for this book. I thank, in particular, Pierre Allan, the director of my thesis, as well as the members of my jury, Stanley Hoffmann (Harvard University), Alexis Keller, and William Ossipow and Robert Roth (Geneva University), who have encouraged me in this project.

These acknowledgments would be incomplete if I did not mention the institutions that have supported me: the Human Rights Program (HRP) of Harvard Law School and, in particular, its clinical director, James Cavallero, and the founder and then director, Henry Steiner, who welcomed me warmly as a fellow between January and August 2006; and the United States Institute of Peace (USIP), in Washington, D.C., which welcomed me as a Senior Fellow from October 2006 to July 2007. USIP was, in particular, a place of exceptional intellectual stimulation. I would also like to mention Virginia Bouvier and John Crist, of the Jennings Randolph Fellowship program, who were of invaluable assistance, as well as my research assistant, Eric Smucker, who combines unusual efficiency with a great sense of humor. My writing also reflects my work on the International Criminal Tribunals, which I carried out for a research project at the Swiss National Foundation for Scientific Research (FNRS) under the direction of Pierre Allan and Robert Roth. I would like also to thank Paul Garapon, director of the Presses Universitaires de France (PUF), who supported this project from the beginning.

It would be impossible to mention here all the people who have counted in my intellectual evolution and who have given me their perspectives and points of view. These discussions have enriched me, even if I have not always agreed with the analyses. I would like to cite first Antoine Garapon, General Secretary of l'Institut pour les Hautes Etudes pour la Justice (IHEJ), in Paris, whose intellectual stimulation, availability, and openness of mind have been a great support. I would also like to thank Georges Abi-Saab, Pamela All, Louise Arbour, Eileen Babbitt, Dan Bar On, Judy Barsalou, Cherif Bassiouni, Reda Benjelloun, Gilad et Keren Ben Nun, Mo Bleeker, Rony Brauman, Reed Brody, Mauro Bottaro, Antonio Cassese, Andrew Clapham, Luigi Condorelli, Adama Dieng, Béatrice Le Frapper de Han, Mark Freeman, Eric Goldstein, Maria Jose Guembe, Philip Grant, Suleyman Guengueng, Roy Gutman, Fabienne Hara, Priscilla Hayner, Benjamin Herzberg, Marie Heuzé, Deborah Isser, Gorka Espiau Idoiaga, Louis Joinet, Neil Kritz, Samy Ketz, Michael Ignatieff, Richard Goldstone, Siegi Hirsch, Tim Kelsall, Leila Kilani, Abdeslam Maghraoui, Haim Malka, Juan Mendez, Peter Maurer, Frédéric Mégret, Nicolas Michel, Laurel Miller, Bernard Millet, Jean-David Levitte, Jürg Lindenmann, Jamie O'Connell, Diane Orentlicher, Carla del Ponte, Mona Rishmawi, Habib Rijab, Christian-Nils Robert, Naomi Roht-Arriaza, Anne-Marie La Rosa, François Sergent, Hugo Slim, Rosalind Shaw, James Snyder, Eric Sottas, Henry Steiner, Ruti Teitel, Kimberly Theidon, Peter Uvin, Detlev Vagts, Patricia Wald, Lars Waldorf, Harvey Weinstein, Driss el Yazami, Valentin Zellweger, and Paul van Zyl.

I thank *Libération* and *Le Temps*, as well as the Swiss Broadcasting Company (TSR), the Franco-German ARTE channel, a friendly acronym (for once) which stands for Association Relative à la Télévision Européenne, and the production company Article Z for having shown such confidence in me for all these years. Thank you, too, to the Swiss Federation of Journalists for supporting this project. Finally, I would like to thank Sarah Meyer de Stadelhofen for her superb work translating this book into English and for her great sense of humor; and Françoise Globa-Quiquerez for translating many English quotes for the French version of this work.

Having completed this work, I understand why writers offer special thanks to their wives. I thank Emmanuelle, as well as my children, for their understanding for the hours, months, and years of work that went into this manuscript. I thank Emmanuelle all the more for having encouraged, supported, and intellectually accompanied me on this journey.

The word "truth" makes me uncomfortable. The word "truth" still tips the tongue. I hesitate at the word. I am not used to using it. Even when I type it, it ends up as either "turth" or "trth." I prefer the word "lie." The moment the lie raises its head I smell blood. Because it is here where the truth is closest.

—Antjie Krog, member of the South African
Truth and Reconciliation Commission

Instead of the whole truth, however, the reader will find moments of truth, and only by means of these moments can this chaos of horror and evil be articulated. These moments arise unexpectedly, like oases in the desert. They are anecdotes, revealing in their brevity what truth is about.

—Hannah Arendt

Prologue
The Human Selection

"I DON'T WANT to play Doctor Mengele," said Beat.

All wars are absurd; this one was particularly absurd. It was autumn 1993. A few kilometers away, the Muslims and Croats of Bosnia fought as allies against the Serbs. Here, in Mostar, they fought each other.

I was in Bosnia-Herzegovina with delegates of the International Committee of the Red Cross (ICRC), on a mission for which they were ill prepared: select and free five hundred prisoners out of some fifteen hundred being held in a cave formerly used as an arms depot by the Yugoslav army.

Some Western governments, through political pressures (that is, the United States, Germany, Austria, and the Vatican), had obtained permission from the Bosno-Croatian authorities to free some of the prisoners of this camp. Beat, a doctor in his mid-fifties who had recently retired from a career in the Basle chemical industry, was on his first mission for the Red Cross. This decent, ordinary man found himself in charge of this life-or-death selection process.

The obvious choice was to free the most desperately ill. To identify the weakest men, Beat opted for a quantitative approach based on body mass index.[1] The ICRC delegates wondered how the prisoners would react: Would they understand why they were being weighed and measured? Would they rebel, sensing that a selection was under way? No, the prisoners did not react at all. For two or three mornings, after breakfast, we entered this sinister camp, with our scales and our yardsticks, where we spent the day conscientiously weighing and measuring the prisoners. The front line was a dozen kilometers away; distant shelling formed the backdrop of our work. Drunken soldiers arrived from the front in broken-down Yugos and insulted our interpreters. Impassively, we carried out our administrative and physical task of selection, man by man. We had managed to find a few small wooden tables: one of us could sit to write while a second measured and a third weighed the prisoners. In that way, we would be more comfortable at our task.

When we had determined the five hundred men who were to go free, the head of the ten-person delegation took the list to the camp. It was at this moment that I understood civil war. Guards and prisoners had grown up together: everyone knew almost everything about everybody else—at least, they knew the all-important fact of who (through personal fortune, or from family members with jobs in Switzerland, Austria, or Germany, and so on) would be able to get together a few thousand deutschmarks to buy freedom. The camp commander, a plump, unpleasant little man, refused to free those who were "worth anything." Should we accept his terms, or should we continue to demand freedom for the weakest, risking that no prisoners would be freed and that they would all die? Standing in the middle of the camp, the ICRC delegates debated, while the guns thundered in the distance. The head of the delegation argued that we had to save the lives we could, even if it meant taking liberties with principles; the delegation's lawyer insisted that we had to stick to our principles, because to yield would compromise any future possibility of freeing the weakest prisoners. Finally, the camp commander himself put an end to the debate: none of the prisoners, whether they were "worth anything" or not, would go free. The ICRC buses left the camp, empty.

In about two hours I was in Split, a peaceful seaside town on the Adriatic coast. In Split, people drank wine; girls laughed; the war seemed a world away. But I could not forget the starving men whom I had weighed and measured for the past three days or the insane futility of this exercise: a chair, a table, a scale, a yardstick, the men filing past, the lives that hung in the balance. I felt unclean. Who was I to choose among men? Questions jumbled up in my mind. When faced with extreme circumstances, what decisions were the least unjust? Have I, who had weighed so many prisoners, any idea of the "weight" of international law that was supposed to protect them? Would it ever be possible for these men—prisoners and their guards—to live together again? What account must we—humanitarians, diplomats, or journalists—give of our personal responsibility? Can society rebuild after such a disaster?

These questions were still in my mind a year later when I went to Rwanda after the genocide there.[2] I met survivors who seemed to float in the air and converse with ghosts, priests whose faith was forever shaken, and men who had become murderers by an accident of history that taught them to deny their crimes forever. I heard the word *reconciliation* repeated ad infinitum, the mantra of the new Rwandan authorities, the UN agencies, the International Criminal Tribunal Rwanda (ICTR), and the nongovernmental organizations (NGOs). But, above all, I assessed the crushing task of reconstructing any kind of social fabric in a nation whose prisons overflowed with more than 120,000 men accused of being the cogs of this appalling killing machine and whose institutions were devastated, resources exhausted, security compromised, and population traumatized and divided; it was a place where democracy was still to be born.

And yet, there was a ray of hope. On 16 October 1998, a Spanish judge filed charges against former Chilean dictator Augusto Pinochet and, suddenly, the impunity of dictators no longer seemed a foregone conclusion. Even in Chad, Pinochet's house arrest in faraway England sent out a shock wave. At considerable risk, the victims of former dictator Hissène Habré had covertly recorded the testimonies of hundreds of victims in the improbable hope that one day their former dictator, now known as the "African Pinochet," would also be brought to judgment.[3] I was struck by the determination of these victims to take charge of their own destinies, to see justice rendered.

Like many of my generation, I was fascinated by the resurgence of moral rhetoric in politics and international relations; by the debate on the comparable merits of pardon versus punishment; by the oxymoron of international justice delivered not after the crimes, but during the time of war; and by the presumed morality of the new Truth and Reconciliation Commissions. However, slowly but surely, my enthusiasm for these mechanisms of justice became tempered. I saw their constructive potential, for both victims and society, but also their limits. As Julie Mertus puts it: "No charges can be filed for the destruction of souls, the loss of childhood and the breaking of dreams."[4]

Of course, I knew, as we all do, that governments do not always live up to their own laws. The politicizing and manipulation of justice are not in themselves surprising, but they take on a stronger dimension now that the courts can intervene almost immediately after the crime is committed. This intervention raises the immediate political stakes for establishing the "truth" about a massacre and organizing a response even before the judges can decide the case. I happened to witness the first attempt at international justice in real time following the massacre of Racak in Kosovo in January 1999. Each of the four principal protagonists—Serbs, Albanian Kosovars, Americans, and French— tried to impose their own versions of the facts, according to their respective interests for blocking, speeding, or justifying intervention by the prosecutor of the International Criminal Tribunal for the former Yugoslavia (ICTY), as well as NATO military intervention against Serbia. History was now expected to render justice, even as the events unfolded before our eyes. I was disturbed by this and by certain side effects of this new politics of punishment and pardon. Yes, the victims had been given a central role, and it would be difficult not to rejoice that people who had been so humiliated and cast aside should at last receive public recognition. But this inversion of roles also had its perverse side.

Commenting on the trial of Klaus Barbie, which began in 1987, Jean-Michel Chaumont put his finger on the "competition for victimhood" that seeks to differentiate those deported for racial reasons from those deported as Resistants.[5] The question was put crudely during the trial of the former head of the Gestapo in Lyon: Were we, decades later, to sort through those unfortunate passengers who traveled in the same cattle cars toward the death camps? Were we to separate the victims of war crimes—crimes for which the statute of limitations had expired—from the victims of imprescriptible crimes against humanity? If so, in which category should we put Jewish Resistants? The French Court of Cassation settled the matter by widening the definition of crimes against humanity. But this rivalry among victims had revealed both the desire for recognition on the part of people who have been profoundly humiliated and the symbolic stakes involved in establishing a "hierarchy of victims."

This hierarchy, appearing in its first form during the Klaus Barbie trial, would take on a disturbing global dimension. It was as if even victimhood could not escape the rules of capitalism and neoliberal globalization: a spotlight on the suffering of some, oblivion for others. I would see for myself this competition at the Third UN Conference Against Racism, about which I will say more later. The victim's suffering contributes to the dehumanization of his adversary. There is nothing new in this, of course, but in the context of the ethnic conflicts of the end of the twentieth century and beginning of the twenty-first, it holds a singularly alarming resonance.

So, with experiences stretching over fifteen years and with hopes tempered by concern, I began my research into the evolution of the values and norms of societies confronted with mass crimes. I took on this work because I was con-

vinced that today, more than ever, the politics of memory determine the construction of our common destiny. I also hoped that it would be a way to stay
true to the voices and faces who shared with me their suffering and their
hopes, a way of showing respect to the unknown destinies of men and women
dragged into the torment of war.

Introduction

AT THE END of the twelfth century, the Christian world invented the concept of Purgatory, a holding chamber between Hell and Paradise. In Purgatory, the souls leaving earth could be purified of their sins, if they repented, and then enter eternal life. The historian Jacques Le Goff observes that the creation of Purgatory brought about the modification of the Christian imagination: "To change the geography of the Beyond, that is, the universe, to modify the time of the after-life, thereby, the clash between terrestrial, historical and eschatological time, the time of existence and the time of waiting, is to work a slow but essential mental revolution. It is, literally, to change life itself."[1]

Several centuries later, in response to geopolitical upheaval linked to the end of the Cold War, a new place appeared, not on the spiritual plane but on the political: transition. As in Purgatory, this new space was also about confession, judgment, and, sometimes, repentance. As in Purgatory, it held the promise of possible salvation.

With the birth of this intermediary world, the topography of the Cold War yielded ground to a new political geography. The collapse of the Soviet Union buried the bipolar world and, with it, the metaphor of international relations as a chess game between two implacable enemy camps. In the new era, international politics was no longer a "zero-sum game." The cynical thinking of Realpolitik was dropped in favor of the optimism of political liberalism. The fall of the Berlin Wall raised the hope that democracy was now possible for all nations. Multilateralism, the renewal of the United Nations (free at last of the Great Powers' paralyzing veto), human rights, democracy, humanitarian action—these were the key phrases of an era whose denizens wondered aloud how to make best use of the "peace dividend." As Ariel Colonomos notes, "The congenital evangelism of liberalism gets the upper-hand of the negative anthropology of realism."[2] At the end of the 1990s, one of the theories in fashion was to interpret the rise of political and economic liberalism as the end of ideological conflicts, as political economist Francis Fukuyama puts it in his 1992 best-seller entitled (no less) *The End of History and the Last Man*.[3] However, the genocide of the Tutsis in Rwanda in 1994 and the politics of ethnic cleansing in the former Yugoslavia and elsewhere quickly put an end to this hope.

The exhilaration of the immediate post–Cold War era, nevertheless, unleashed profound dynamism marked by the renewal of the Wilsonian ideal[4] updated for the 1990s. The idea of political and moral progress and social transformation was at the heart of the new system of thinking. Imported from the Anglo-Saxon world, a new term, *transitional justice*, consecrated this shift in perspective. But this new term was misleading, for it was not justice but societies themselves that were in transition after periods of repression, crimes against humanity, and genocide.

The term *transitional justice* first appeared in 1992, coined by law professor Ruti Teitel.[5] It was an idea whose time has come. That same year, under the auspices of a U.S. foundation, Charter 77, some fifty participants from twenty-one countries—in particular, the ex-Communist regimes of Central and Eastern Europe, post-apartheid South Africa, and the ex-dictatorships of South America—met for two days in Salzburg to reflect on the challenge that united them: how to organize politically, judicially, symbolically, and culturally during the crucial period of transformation from an oppressive regime to democracy. What social and legal norms had to be introduced to manage this intermediary time of transition that, in many ways, resembled a new Purgatory?[6]

To their surprise, despite the differences of their individual national contexts, the participants of the Salzburg meeting found that they all faced similar challenges. This discovery contributed to the new idea of transitional justice— that, in spite of radically different historical situations, societies coming out of extreme situations shared "tools" that favored "reconciliation." This conviction, both instrumental and ethical, was popularized by Archbishop Desmond Tutu, president of South Africa's Truth and Reconciliation Commission: "Tools new and old, foreign and domestic, but above all practical and effective to design a reconciliation process appropriate to a particular set of circumstances."[7] From Capetown to Kigali, Belgrade to Belfast, common "tools" were employed to dampen the flames of war and persecution: truth commissions, international or semi-international criminal courts, memory laws, individual or collective reparation, public expressions of repentance, the opening of archives, political and institutional reforms, the rewriting of history books, and commemorative ceremonies and laws.[8]

It is these institutions and practices that today make up transitional justice. Ruti Teitel defines the term as "a conception of justice associated with periods of political change, characterized by legal responses to confront the wrongdoings of repressive predecessor regimes."[9] But what about transitional justice's ideological foundation? What is this brave idea that pretends to "reconcile" societies? Transitional justice rests on an ambitious gamble that the politics of punishment and pardon can curb violence. If crimes against humanity, by definition, *unleash* men, then transitional justice will accomplish the path in reverse by restoring social ties and a political community.

Transitional justice establishes a period both "before" and "after" the crime. It marks the beginning of a new era, although its ambition is not to erase the past but, on the contrary, to integrate the stain of the crime into the heart of society. Transitional justice proposes a myth in the sense intended by Paul Ricoeur:[10] first, it identifies the wrong; then, it invites judicial or extrajudicial institutions to take account of the tragedy before proposing its resolution. This process leads to public recognition of the crime and, if possible, the criminal's confession carries the promise of social change and gives new life to the old dream of redemption from Evil. Was it any surprise, then, that the face-off of torturers and victims during the public hearings of South Africa's Truth and Reconciliation Commission should fascinate public opinion far beyond its borders?

In the era of globalization, the politics of punishment and pardon offer themselves not only as the answer to barbarity—an answer that is acceptable to the United Nations, a number of states, and NGOs—but also as the vector for creating democratic society. Transitional justice is both the product and the agent of a revolution that is not only judicial but also cultural and psychological. In one sweep, transitional justice modifies the political practices involved in conflict resolution, national reconciliation, and the commemoration of mass crimes. By elaborating collective identities and new national mythologies, it raises the "threshold of expectation"; it mobilizes public opinion and the media and sets off passionate debate about democracy and impunity, restorative and criminal justice, the imperatives of justice, and the imperatives of peace. Transitional justice lays the ground rules of truth, justice, reconciliation, construction of democracy, and a state of law. It introduces terms, often of religious or psychoanalytic inspiration and totally foreign to the vocabulary of the Cold War, to the political lexicon: reconciliation, truth, punishment, pardon, repentance, catharsis. The court, as institution and metaphor, becomes the new center of international relations.

To better grasp the extent of these changes, Chapter 1 of this book retraces the genesis of the politics of punishment and pardon after 1945. Chapter 2 analyzes the construction of the idea of transitional justice and its rise in power.

The toolbox of transitional justice has become all but obligatory in the process of reestablishing peace, democracy, and regional stability. In fifteen years, the creation of some thirty truth commissions, as well as many criminal courts, both semi-international and international, has reconfigured the architecture of the international system. But what are its limits, contradictions, ambiguities, and, more important, its results? To what degree has transitional justice paid off as a way to curb violence? Chapters 3, 4, and 5 put transitional justice to the test by looking at three recent examples.

Chapter 3 examines the UN conference in Durban in September 2001. This meeting was the most ambitious attempt ever made on a global scale to put the memory of mass crimes—that is, slavery and colonization—to rest. I will explore the political and ideological clash between the African and Arab-Islamic side, on one hand, and the West, on the other. I will consider, in particular, the symbolically charged controversy that pits the Holocaust as a unique event against multiple "holocausts," as well as the stakes involved in the definition of crimes against humanity and in the demands for reparation by the countries and NGOs of the Southern Hemisphere, particularly (but not limited to) those from Africa. In Chapter 4, I will look at the work of the first Truth and Reconciliation Commission created in the Arab-Islamic world, Morocco's Equity and Reconciliation Commission (ERC).

I will examine how local actors may take over a truth commission and attempt to use it for their own political goals. Last, but not least, through the International Criminal Court's charges against the leaders of the Lord's Army in Uganda, in Chapter 5 I will examine the virulent debate on the nature of the International Criminal Court (ICC): Is it an expression of true universalism or merely Western imperialism in new clothes?

At the crossroads of politics, law, ethics, psychology, and religion, transitional justice challenges all social actors, for it poses fundamental questions about the nature of societies trying to awaken from the nightmare of war and repression. Above all, the questions it poses are essential for each of us.

Chapter 1

The Genesis of Transitional Justice

THE WEST'S HANDLING of Nazi crimes was the womb from which the concept of transitional justice was born. It provided transitional justice's legitimacy, constructed its moral and legal arguments, and outlined what would become, decades later, the institutions, values, and practices of transitional justice. With its ambiguities and limits, the handling of these crimes marked the conceptual leap over the abyss of mass crimes and sought to refound political communities by setting up a new authority.

World War II has never been as topical as it has been since the fall of the Berlin Wall. The racial persecutions of the Third Reich have been retroactively interpreted in the West as the foreshadowing of post–Cold War ethnic cleansing—notably, the Bosno-Serbian camps, the massacres of Srebrenica, and the genocide of the Tutsis in Rwanda. Faced with this extreme violence against civil populations in many places on the planet, destabilizing entire regions, there was urgent need for political actors as a whole (in particular, NGOs and certain UN agencies, as well as the UN Security Council) to check the destructive forces and reestablish social links in torn-apart societies. Many governments take as example the politics of punishment and measures of reparation against the Nazis, as well as strategies of commemoration elaborated after 1945. Thus, in the 1990s, political and judicial decisions made over several decades in different countries and with no direct link between them (except those linked as Nazi crimes) gave rise to a coherent response to mass crimes and spread globally. They represented the attempt to recreate authority, in the same way that the Nuremberg trials, along with the creation of the United Nations, were acts of self-recreation by the international system.

To understand the establishment of policies of punishment and pardon in the 1990s, we must analyze their origins. As we shall see, the fact that transitional justice was born of a Western historical experience would have heavy consequences in the competition for victimhood decades later.

In awarding a central place in history to World War II and the genocide of the Jews, the West took on the three roles of justice: (international) judge (that is, the United States), victim (that is, the European Jews and the Jewish state, which made itself spokesman for the millions of dead), and criminal (that is, Nazi Germany).[1] The symbolic triad of justice was reconstituted, and the speeches, norms, and practices of what decades later became known as transitional justice were developed. The experience was significant in that a multitude of actors were mobilized, sometimes thousands of kilometers from one another, and the staging and recounting of the war and the Nazi crimes served to reestablish political communities.

The United States, the first conceiver of the international criminal court, understood the symbolic and political stakes perfectly. With the Allied military tribunals in Nuremberg and Tokyo, it affirmed its moral authority and, simultaneously, its preeminence in the new world order. West Germany initiated a policy of repentance and reparation because it was the sine qua non condition imposed by the United States in the 1950s for rejoining the world community. The Jewish state emphasized the victim ethos to reinforce its legitimacy against hostility from the Arab world and a part of the Third World. International criminal justice, reparations, expressions of repentance, and commemoration policy—everything that we will see again in the 1990s—were put in place. The treatment—judicial, political, and commemorative—of the Nazi crimes represented this conceptual leap that would announce the new approach to mass crimes.

The Nuremberg Trials, or How to Legitimize the New World Order

The history of the Nuremberg trials illustrates that this unprecedented experience succeeded above and beyond all hopes. In terms of transition, the trials embodied the passage from one political organization of the world to another. Criminal justice played an essential role: for the first time, the courts were charged symbolically with defining and legitimizing the new world order. This era, which the Germans called "Year Zero," also applied, although differently, to the rest of the world. The Nuremberg trials put a stop to any pretense that "nothing happened." Crimes had been committed and this irrefragable reality preserved the uniqueness of the event. The refounding of a democratic order had a history—that of Nazi violence—which the Allied military tribunals were charged with writing. By the recognition and legitimacy given them, they established authority, and, at the same time, by modifying the values, perceptions, and expectations of society and by redirecting political action, they catalyzed evolution in the normative structure of the international system.

U.S. attorney Robert Jackson was fully conscious of this challenge of establishing authority that was not merely the reflection of a triumphant United States and the justice of the victors. His response was to transform this difficulty into a moral obligation "before History" imposed on the "civilized world."[2] The victor is not only he who wields the sword; having met this challenge, he redoubles his efforts to meet this new task, becoming the third party of justice—in this case, the International Court, the Just. The Nuremberg trials thus introduced an essential player who would reappear almost a half-century later: the international criminal judge.[3] It was this moral authority, whereby the United States was intricately linked with the idea of Good, to which Robert Jackson referred in the first words of his opening speech to the International Military Tribunal at Nuremberg: "That four great nations, flushed with victory and stung with injury stay the hand of vengeance and voluntarily submit their captive enemies to the judgment of the law is one of the most significant tributes that Power has ever paid to Reason."[4]

At the same time, by positioning itself as the champion of law, the United States put itself in a difficult position. It could no longer distance itself from the rules and values that it formulated without paying the political price for this betrayal. Decades later, the Bush Administration realized this fact at its own cost—the loss of support of international opinion and of its European allies—when it wished to free itself from the Geneva Conventions and international humanitarian law. Jackson displayed astonishing foresight when he noted that the Nuremberg trials, as a normative process, would engage American authorities to a degree that they had never dared to imagine: "We must never forget that the record on which we judge these defendants today is the record on which history will judge us tomorrow. To pass these defendants a poisoned chalice is to put it to our own lips as well. We must summon such detachment and intellectual integrity to our task that this Trial will commend itself to posterity as fulfilling humanity's aspirations to do justice."[5]

Through the few images released, public opinion—except that of Germany until the 1960s—absorbed a sanitized vision of the Nuremberg trials. The crimes of the Third Reich were so monstrous, the proof so undeniable, the price of victory so heavy that, besides the defendants and a large segment of German opinion, few objected to this purified, oversimplified presentation. As several members of the tribunal explained to the public, the hearings were a formidable history lesson—indeed, "the greatest history lesson the world has ever known," according to U.S. prosecutor Robert Kempner.[6] The lesson of Nuremberg was that, from that point on, the history of world crimes would be written by an international tribunal. Only a handful protested the trials; among them was the unrepentant fascist Maurice Bardèche, who in 1948 published *Nuremberg, ou la terre promise* and, in 1952, *Nuremberg II, ou les faux-monnayeurs*, two classics of French revisionism.[7] But the essential point was elsewhere: that the all-but-sacred enclosure of the court had been used to affirm a historical truth. With mixed success, this heritage would be echoed in the birth of the first international criminal courts in 1993 and 1994. Through the trial of mass murderers, an international judge would be charged with stating the terms of the new order and producing an official version of the facts and, thus, in part, writing history.

The force of the Nuremberg trials was inseparable from the purification rites that it put in place. Under the pressure of the U.S. prosecutor, justice became a never-before-seen face-off. To begin, Jackson set up a movie screen, marking the first use of film in a courtroom. Despite the fact that he had at his disposal all the proof left behind by the Nazis—hundreds of thousands of documents and hundreds of lawyers to go through them—Jackson had seen the footage taken in the concentration camps by Hollywood director John Ford, and he wanted to use it to confront the Nazi officials with their crimes. Jackson even moved up the film's showing by several weeks—to the fifth day of the trial—because the press corps was beginning to grow restless that nothing "newsworthy" was happening. Justice's spectacular dimension, in the literal sense of the term, intensified: the film brought the criminals face to face with their monstrous acts. The event was unprecedented and spectators scrutinized the Nazi officials' slightest expressions and movements while watching the horrifying images. The proof of Evil was indisputable and this evidence had purification value. The face-off between victims and former political and military VIPs now treated like criminals was unprecedented. When a survivor of Auschwitz, Claude Vaillant-Couturier, passed slowly in front of all of the accused

and stared with scorn at Hermann Göring, history rejoiced. This second en-
counter between victims and executioners restored moral order to a broken
world.

Nuremberg's remarkable pedagogic effect was, nevertheless, based on a
debatable legal construction. The prosecution built its entire strategy on the
debatable idea of "conspiracy to wage war" and "conspiracy to commit crimes
against humanity."[8] Historian Christopher Browning calls this "the Nuremberg vision": the idea, for example, that the genocide of the Jews was the product of a horrible war of aggression. This vision explained why Nazi acts of
persecution that occurred before the war were never prosecuted. The Allies
did not wish to create a potentially embarrassing precedent for themselves.
The manner in which they treated certain of their own minorities and peoples
living in their colonies was far from exemplary, and they did not wish to expose themselves to criticism.

For this reason, too, the "world's greatest history lesson"—the label given
to justice in Nuremberg—was also one of self-censorship. The construction of
the historical "truth" that came from Nuremberg underlined the will to use
the moral and legal register to political ends. All international criminal courts
and truth commissions had a dimension of political justice. To pretend that
an absolute barrier was possible between law and politics was as absurd as to
pretend to live without oxygen. The question was to know at what moment the
political agenda denatured that of justice. The Nazi crimes were so immense
that the liberties taken with the historical truth and the highly political organization of the charges counted for little.

We now know that the U.S. and British governments were well aware of
the fact that, at the very moment of the Nuremberg hearings, the USSR was
installing its own concentration camps in its occupation zone; in one of these
camps, Mühlberg am Elbe, of some 122,000 German prisoners never brought
to trial, 43,000 perished.[9] To avoid sinking into moral relativism, which would
have compromised the moral superiority of the liberal values contained implicitly in the charges, the Americans and British kept quiet about the division of Poland during the Nazi-Soviet Pact of 1939 and the Soviet-Finnish
War of 1939 (and the Allied bombing of Germany, which killed an estimated
600,000 people). Of the four charges contained in the act of accusation of 19
October 1945 (a common conspiracy to wage aggressive war, crimes against
peace, war crimes, and crimes against humanity), the British historian Richard Overy notes that at least one of the prosecuting states, "the Soviet Union,

was guilty on three of the four counts for acts it had willfully committed on its own behalf during the previous decade."[10]

The legal construction of the highly political contours of the definition of "crimes against humanity" was also debatable. The Allies wanted simultaneously to sanction the Nazis' extermination policy against the Jews and Gypsies while protecting themselves from the risk that similar charges might one day be brought against themselves. At the beginning of the Cold War, the United States feared being accused by the USSR for the lynchings and institutionalized discrimination against African Americans at home. The Soviets feared accusations for their treatment of certain ethnic groups, such as the Ukrainian kulaks or Chechens, then being deported to Siberia. The French and British had put down people seeking independence in their colonies.

On Armistice Day, 8 May 1945, the very symbol of peace and a return to democracy in Europe, the French army brutally started to repress an uprising in Setif, Algeria, causing, in the coming months and years, the deaths of tens of thousands of people. For the Allies in Nuremberg, the aim was to denounce an "order of barbarity" while carefully circling around it in order to avoid any risk of its backfiring. Thus, the charge of "crimes against humanity" was seldom invoked; its legal definition implied that the crime must be committed in the context of international conflict, thereby putting the Great Powers in the clear.[11] For this reason, the Allies refrained from judging Nazi leaders for "Kristallnacht," which took place in 1938, before the war, because they did not wish to set a precedent that could prove dangerous for themselves.

This point is central: the emergence of legal norms was directly influenced by the political and strategic needs of the Great Powers. "Crimes against humanity" became a criminal charge during the Nuremberg trials, but, in the phrase coined by French judge Donnedieu de Vabres, it "swooned by the window" until the end of the Cold War.[12] It was not in the interests of the Great Powers to extend its application during the East-West conflict, for they did not want their protégés or themselves to be judged. It was only after the fall of the Berlin Wall and the policies of "ethnic cleansing" in the former Yugoslavia that the concept of "crimes against humanity" would return in force. If the concept could reappear so forcefully, it was because, over the ensuing decades, the intellectual work supporting the idea of a crime against humanity had continued, announcing the end of an international system based on the Westphalian model of all-powerful national sovereignty. In the post–Cold War world, the Nuremberg trials have been used to justify the centrality of crimes against humanity.

Germany and the Politics of Repentance

West Germany was the source of all thinking on the reworking of collective identity. Intellectuals, principally existentialist philosopher Karl Jaspers, played a pioneering role in this process, clearing a path that would later be borrowed by German authorities: take stock of national identity, de-Nazify it, demilitarize it, metamorphose it, and, having done so, find a way toward "health" that leads to reintegration in the community of nations and normalization within Germany.

In his first university course of the postwar period, Karl Jaspers asked his fellow citizens to examine their consciences: "Our only chance for salvation lies in total frankness and honesty. . . . This path alone may save our soul from the life of a pariah. Whatever comes to us, we must see it come. This is a daring spiritual and political act on the edge of the abyss."[13] To this vision of redemption through individual responsibility was added the more political approach of Jaspers's former student Hanna Arendt, who challenges any idea of treating Hitlerism as a simple historical incident: "We can no longer afford to take that which was good in the past and simply call it our heritage, to discard the bad and think of it as a dead lead which by itself time will bury in oblivion. The 'subterranean' stream of Western history has finally come to the surface and usurped the dignity of our tradition."[14]

What proved decisive was that the reflection initiated by intellectuals became official state policy. In the construction of a new ethos for postwar Germany, there was a conjunction between the moral imperatives advanced by intellectuals and the pursuit of national interest. The United States was, in effect, set in making a gesture toward world Jewry[15] as the condition for Germany's return to full sovereignty. Thus, for both political and moral reasons, German Chancellor Konrad Adenauer put in place a policy of repentance and reparations, both moral and financial, toward both the survivors of the concentration camps and the state of Israel.

The U.S. government exported its values and norms (even if it sometimes refrained from applying them domestically); the government of the Federal German Republic (RFA) incorporated them and translated them into political acts (for example, reparations), out of strategic necessity before, very slowly, these values and norms were integrated into German culture. It is striking to note the degree to which the German government, initially out of constraint, has dealt with its past—in contrast to Austria, which continues to present itself purely as a victim of Nazism.

Having secretly negotiated the terms with the Israeli government and the representatives of the World Jewish Congress, Chancellor Adenauer gave a speech in the Bundestag (the German Parliament) on 27 September 1951 in which he recognized the suffering endured by the Jewish people and affirmed the German will to make moral and material reparations because, he said, the crimes had been committed in the name of the German people. Legally and politically, these reparations were unprecedented. They brought victims onto a scene previously reserved for states alone, in which reparations were made by a conquered state to the victor—for example, those laid out in the Treaty of Versailles. Never before had states willingly granted reparations to individual victims for suffering inflicted on a minority. With the birth of reparations for victims of crimes against humanity, a norm began to emerge.[16] Decades later, many victims would consider reparations for mass crimes a legitimate expectation. However, in the climate of the 1950s, the idea provoked the most violent controversy the Jewish state had known. The right-wing opposition leader, Menachem Begin, fiercely opposed reparations, going so far as to compare accepting German money to a "new genocide."[17] Posters for Begin's party insisted that "the blood of reparations soaks in Jewish blood."[18]

If reparations shocked many Israelis, a part of German society, for radically different reasons, also opposed both the policy of contrition and the Nuremberg trials. Positioning the government of the RFA as the successor to the Third Reich and, as such, responsible for Nazi crimes, met strong resistance at the heart of German society. Many of them felt they had already paid their debt during the Allied bombing raids, the Nuremberg trials, the loss of territory on Germany's eastern border, and the occupation, during which hundreds of thousands of women were raped by Soviet soldiers, and the German minorities were expelled from Czechoslovakia, Poland, and Hungary. They called for the release of war criminals, and American authorities finally acquiesced: in the context of the Cold War conflict with the Soviet bloc, the Americans discreetly freed the great majority of Nazi criminals, including those directly responsible for the extermination of tens of thousands of civilians.[19] If the Americans had not suspected that the Soviets would veto such a move, they probably would have freed any prisoners judged at Nuremberg who were still alive at that point. What now mattered was ensuring that the German population would fight with the "free world" against the USSR. At the beginning of the 1950s, behind the Adenauer government's rhetoric of Germany's moral responsibility, addressed to an international audience, the political reality of German society asserted itself against the United States, Great Britain, and France.

Chancellor Adenauer, then, executed two policies: one designed to satisfy public opinion at home and the other to reintegrate his country in the international arena. Nevertheless, Germany had established a new language in the recognition of mass crimes. This rhetoric, in its many forms, would become the great laboratory of transitional justice. Reparations, multiple expressions of repentance, and multiple procedures of commemoration symbolized the break with the past, the tangible materialization of a fundamentally different Germany.

A new ritual had been put in place; on 7 December 1970, it intensified with the meditation of Chancellor Willy Brandt before the monument commemorating the uprising of the Warsaw ghetto.[20] Brandt's silent kneeling changed the perception of Germany more effectively than any number of speeches. The fact that Willy Brandt himself opposed Nazism during wartime strengthened the symbolism of the act. This silent kneeling coming from such a man struck many and foreshadowed the public apologies that would be pronounced by heads of state and government in the post–Cold War era.

Even if inspired initially by strategic motives, the German government's policy of commemoration and repentance gradually infused the collective conscience of German society, eventually participating in the country's rebuilding and reunification in 1989. Berlin, the capital of reunified Germany, carries in its architecture the memory of World War II through monuments and memorials that recall the past. German society's identity has been modified by the values and norms imposed on it by the postwar United States. In turn, Germany has created and exported practices of transitional justice: reparations, expressions of repentance, the building of memorials, the rewriting of history books, the visits of schoolchildren to concentration camps—practices that other countries have borrowed and adapted to the circumstances of their own history.

Personified by a variety of actors, many countries in the post–Cold War world demonstrated the idea of nation-building from the same ethical insistence on assessing the full extent of crimes committed, the same political will to rework the national ethos through policies of commemoration, and the same need for "normalization" by acquiring the "certificate of respectability" in the international community through reparations and big gestures. But often these acts were carried out with the same reticence and ambiguity as shown in the German experience, foreshadowing the tensions between ethical and strategic imperatives that countries engaged in the process of transition would demonstrate decades later. Thus, as much by its philosophy as by its form, the German experience has defined transitional justice's theoretical framework and has been a part of its modus operandi.

The Awakening of Jewish Memory and the Insistence on Imprescriptibility

At the beginning of the 1960s, the statute of limitations for Nazi war crimes and crimes against humanity mobilized Jewish institutions as well as intellectuals. As a result of the pressure they brought to bear, the idea of imprescriptibility, heretofore unknown in law, became a feature of the new definition of crimes against humanity. Crimes against humanity would take on a stronger resonance with the passage of time and the awakening of Jewish memory. One of the texts that marked this evolution, *L'Imprescriptible*, by French philosopher Vladimir Jankélévitch, places crimes against humanity outside of time where nothing, not even pardon, can affect them: "Pardon died in the death camps," Jankélévitch writes. He highlights a line by Paul Eluard, cutting in its radicalness: "There is no salvation on earth as long as we can pardon the executioners." He begins his book: "Has the time come to pardon or, at least, to forget? Twenty years are, apparently, enough for the unforgivable to become miraculously forgiven: a crime that is inexpiable until May 1965 suddenly ceases to be so at the beginning of June, as if by enchantment. And thus official and legal forgetting begins that night at midnight." Then Jankélévitch protests:

> This crime against nature, this unmotivated crime, this exorbitant crime is, thus, by definition, a "metaphysical" crime, and the perpetrators of this crime are not simple fanatics, nor blindly doctrinarian, nor merely abominably dogmatic: they are, in the proper sense of the word, monsters. When an act negates the essence of a man as man, the prescription that would absolve them in the name of morality itself contradicts morality. Is it not contradictory and even absurd to speak of pardon? To forget this gigantic crime against humanity would be a new crime against the human species.[21]

The only solution, the philosopher concludes, is to "pursue the criminals, as the judges of the Allied tribunal in Nuremberg have promised, to the ends of the earth." Jankélévitch was heard. The awakening of Jewish memory stimulated the international community. After all, there was consensus for punishing Nazi war criminals and their collaborators. Thus, between 1968 and 1972, the international community adopted different measures and introduced the principle of universal jurisdiction and imprescriptibility.[22] On 26 November 1968, the UN General Assembly adopted Resolution 2391, "The Convention on the Non-Applicability of Statutory Limitations to War Crimes and Crimes Against Humanity" (which entered into force on 11 November 1970). Resolution 2391 made imprescriptible war crimes, as "defined in the Statutes of the international military Tribunal of Nuremberg," as well as crimes against humanity, "whether committed in time of war or in time of peace" and "irrespective of the date of their commission."[23] On 3 December 1973, the General Assembly also adopted "The Principles of International Cooperation in the Detection, Arrest, Extradition and Punishment of Persons Guilty of War Crimes and Crimes Against Humanity."

This profusion of new norms, crystallized first around the Nazi crimes, generated its own political dynamic. It stimulated the UN General Assembly to adopt, on 30 November 1973, Resolution 3068, which stated that "Apartheid is a crime against humanity and inhuman acts resulting from the policies and practices of apartheid and similar policies and practices of racial segregation and discrimination . . . are crimes violating the principles of international law, in particular the purposes and principles of the Charter of the United Nations, and constituting a serious threat to international peace and security."[24]

Launched by Jewish institutions, the struggle against impunity, which became a priority of human rights organizations from 1989 on, thus originated in the particular context of World War II and, subsequently, in the condemnation of apartheid. By awarding a central place to the condemnation of crimes against humanity (especially, from the 1980s, with the trials of Paul Touvier, Klaus Barbie, and Maurice Papon in France), these precedents laid the groundwork for the growing litigiousness of international relations.

Israel, the Eichmann Trial, and
the Creation of a New National Ethos

Contemporary forms of commemoration originated in Germany; and the awakening of Jewish memory contributed to the growing litigiousness of international relations. But Israel's commemoration policy was also essential in setting up transitional justice. As in Germany's case, this commemoration policy responded to moral objectives—to maintain the memory of the dead—but also to strategic objectives. At the creation of Israel in 1948, the still-fresh memory of the genocide reinforced the Jewish state's legitimacy inside the international community and contributed to distracting public attention in the West from the expulsion of tens of thousands of Palestinians. The Zionist ethos put the new Jew, the "citizen-soldier," in opposition to the "Jews of the ghetto," who were the essence of the Diaspora condition and who allowed themselves to be "led like lambs to the slaughter."

In 1960 an Israeli commando's spectacular kidnapping of Adolf Eichmann, one of the principal architects of the "Final Solution" who had been living in Argentina, created the opportunity to revisit the Israeli policy of memory of World War ll. Israeli prime minister David Ben-Gurion used the Eichmann trial to cement the Israeli society in commemorating the martyrs of the millions of Jews killed by the Nazi. At the time, the Israeli state was only twelve years old and marked by tensions between citizens from Ashkenazi and Sephardic origins,[25] so Ben-Gurion saw the trial as an opportunity to develop a new national ethos. As in Germany, but even more willfully, Israel's policy of commemoration was designed to mould a collective identity. To the German experience of commemoration—building the image of a state that accepts moral responsibility for its past crimes—was added Israel's experience—building the image of victim, both for the reason mentioned above, but also and above all for the purposes of international politics.

In contrast to the trials in Nuremberg, the Eichmann trial, as prosecutor Gidéon Hausner explains, does not seek to "enrich the Library of History." It was rather a lesson for the present: both to educate the world about the genocide and to build the Israeli, "the new Jew," presumed to have radically broken with the Jew of the Diaspora and the spirit of submission that Zionist ethos attributed to him. To do so, Hausner called dozens of witnesses: "Only through the testimony of witnesses can the facts be portrayed to the court and made real to the people of Israel as well as to other peoples, in a way that mankind cannot recoil before the truth as one would recoil from a boiling cauldron, in such a way that one cannot distance oneself from this unbelievable and fantastic nightmare which emerges from Nazi documents."[26] Their testimony carried emotional weight that documents could not: "the immediacy of these first-person stories acts like a fire in the cold room of History," observes Geoffrey Hartman.[27]

The Nuremberg trials introduced footage of the camps and the testimonies of survivors. John Ford's film was additional documentary proof of Nazi barbarity, but it presented this proof in an objective and factual manner. In the same way, the survivors who testified were there to confirm the details of the charges. The job of the Nuremberg prosecutors was to establish judicial and historical truth, which for them was more or less the same thing.

The Eichmann trial brought a change of tone. Instead of the clinical and antiseptic description of the concentration machine and the Nazi extermination, it substituted a portrayal that attempted to reproduce the horror. The crimes no longer needed to be proven: the evidence was known to all. Historical truth had been solidly established. It was now a matter of making this evidence come alive. What mattered to Hausner and Ben-Gurion was that this material carried a symbolic charge—the power to evoke suffering and horror—that could contribute to the construction of a new Israeli national myth and the reaffirmation of the legitimacy of the Jewish state more effectively than any history book or UN resolution could. The Eichmann trial set a precedent that, decades later, would continue to inspire the international tribunals and, even more, the truth commissions. For, the latter, as for Ben-Gurion, the commemoration stakes were also, if not primarily, political.

Thus, in its own way, the Eichmann trial served the same purpose as the museum of Yad Vashem, the all-but-obligatory pilgrimage for visiting heads of state, which proposed granting Israeli nationality posthumously to the millions of Jews who had died in the Holocaust.[28] During the Eichmann trial, Ben-Gurion declared that Israel was "the heir of six million dead . . . , the sole heir. . . . If they had lived, the large majority of them would have come to live in Israel."[29] Revealingly, Eichmann was charged not only with "crimes against humanity" but also with "crimes against the Jewish people," because the prosecutor, responding to the demands of the Israeli Prime Minister, sought to emphasize the religious-nationalistic dimension of his victims. This approach received strong criticism: Ben-Gurion was accused of confiscating the Holocaust solely in the name of Israeli national interests.[30] In the escalating propaganda war with the Palestinians and the Arab world in general, Ben-Gurion and his successors used the memory of the Holocaust to "position" the Jewish state as history's ultimate victim. The Eichmann trial fit into the fierce battle for legitimacy between Israelis and Palestinians. The Israeli government compared the hostility of the Palestinians and the Arab world, in general, to Nazism. In 1981, Prime Minister Menachem Begin wrote to U.S. president Ronald

Reagan to justify the Israeli army's attack on Beirut as an attempt to "capture Adolf Hitler [that is, Yasser Arafat] in his bunker."[31] This deliberate blurring of Palestinian-Nazi was a mirror image of propaganda in the Arab world whereby Israel was labeled a "genocidal" state. This propaganda hit a record low point in December 2006 with the revisionist conference organized by Iranian president Mahmoud Ahmadinejad, who argued that the Holocaust was a "myth."

The escalation confused analysis, annihilated historical reality, and, finally, contributed to the loss of any sense of responsibility. On the other hand, it was most enlightening in terms of the political stakes of commemoration: in the construction of a new postwar German identity, as in the Israeli-Palestinian competition for victimhood, one of the essential objectives was to incarnate, in the eyes of world public opinion, the image of redemption through atonement for one's crimes or the promotion of one's martyrdom. In all cases, it was about winning points for one's moral posturing and the political justice of one's cause by leaning on the image of victim.

In the Israeli-Palestinian conflict, the victimization cult was transformed into an escalation of horror before an improbable tribunal of history: the Holocaust vs. Nakbah.[32] In a world where the rhetoric of human rights was so charged, the victim's helplessness had value as symbolic power.

With reason, Avishai Margalit and Bariel Morzkin note that "the process of how people are made to vanish has become a distinctive feature of postwar conceptions of what memory is."[33] Strategies of commemoration play an essential ideological role in the construction of national ethos as well as in the international public domain. In the context of the unipolar world of post-1989, the victim of crimes against humanity took a central place in the formulation of collective identity and formed the cultural and political base on which transitional justice was built.

If it was a historical event in the West that signed the birth certificate of transitional justice, it was also the West that, after 1945, brutally repressed the will for self-determination of colonized peoples. This simultaneity between the process to recognize the wounded dignity of victims and the conduct of repressive policies would have heavy consequences. For, if this scene in history throws light on the Jewish tragedy, it leaves aside, on the other hand, that of the colonized peoples. The victory over Nazism allowed Jews to reenter the category of "fellow man," but the peoples of the Third World remained outside "civilization." Evoking, in particular, the case of the Algerians and their struggle for independence, Pierre Vidal-Naquet notes: "The Algerians, whom we proclaimed French, were felt to be different and even 'inferior,' as colonized people have always been. . . . The crimes against humanity committed in Algeria have also had difficulty reaching the public conscience, including, for a long time, the conscience of historians."[34]

The wars of decolonization, which cost the lives of millions of men, women, and children, involved no process of reparation. As mentioned above, at the very moment when the Allies were vanquishing Nazi Germany, the French army bloodily repressed demonstrations for independence in Setif, with the deaths of thousands of people.

This ethnocentric reading of mass crimes was not new. In October 1904, General von Trotha proclaimed his "extermination order" for the Herero people of South-West Africa (now Namibia) in these terms: "I, the great general of the German army, send the following to the Herero people. . . . All Hereros must leave this country. . . . Any Herero found inside the German borders, with or without a gun, with or without livestock, will be shot. I will not except women or children: I will send them back to their people. I will shoot them. This is my decision for the Herero people."[35]

As extreme as von Trotha's order may sound, it expressed the hierarchical view of humanity then current.[36] John Stuart Mill, the English philosopher who was no doubt the most influential of the nineteenth century and a great liberal spirit, wrote: "To imagine that the same international customs and the same international rules of morality apply from one civilized nation to another, or between civilized and savage peoples, is a grave error which every statesman must avoid."[37] Even Alexis de Tocqueville shared this vision: "I believe that the right of war authorizes us to raze this country [Algeria] and that we should do so by destroying the crops at the moment of harvest, or continuously through rapid incursions, raids, with the objective of carrying off men and herds. . . . These acts are, in my opinion, unfortunate necessities to which anyone who must make war with the Arabs will be obliged to submit."[38]

In the same way that the nineteenth-century European powers built the foundations of international law on discrimination against colonized peoples, who were excluded from the benefits of protection of the laws of war, the premises of transitional justice excluded peoples who were colonized or in the process of decolonization. This difference of treatment is the original sin of transitional justice. In the 1990s, the effects of this ethnocentric reading of mass crimes would be felt.

ethnocentric basis of intl law

The Nuremberg trials and the commemoration policies in Germany and Israel and, in general, in the West thus created a new but complex dynamic. They simultaneously stimulated awareness of other crimes against humanity and forged new mechanisms for justice and financial compensation that would become generalized in the post–Cold War era. But they also contributed to creating a hierarchy of mass crimes, and this difference of treatment laid the foundation for the competition of victimhood, of which the UN conference in Durban in September 2001 was the most tangible manifestation.

The policies concerning the commemoration of Nazi crimes demonstrated the political stakes involved from the very beginning. They made up a complex pattern in the reformulation of national identity between geopolitical interests, the balance of power, and the values and norms of traditional justice. It is here that the moral and the political registers met in the 1990s.

Chapter 2

The Growing Strength
of Transitional Justice

TRANSITIONAL JUSTICE AROSE in a bloody century like a New Jerusalem. It pretends to offer answers for both past crimes and current violence. It promises to heal war-torn societies and reestablish democracy and the rule of law by rebuilding political communities, by correcting, moralizing, and repairing history through trials, commemoration duties, truth commissions, reparation, and memory laws (that is, law against the denial of the Holocaust and other crimes against humanity).[1] This is the hubris of transitional justice: the belief that law and the lessons of history can expel—if not mitigate—the violence in divided societies.

Transitional justice's rise in power is best seen in light of its three principal stages of growth. The first concurred with the waning of dictatorships: it began with the establishment of the truth commission in Argentina (1983) and ended with the creation of the Truth and Reconciliation Commission (TRC) in South Africa (1995). Transitional justice, at that point, concerned reconciliation within societies struggling to recover from bloody regimes. During the second period (1992–2001), the end goal was the same—to rebuild society politically and to pacify social relations—but the context was radically different. This second period was characterized by the multiplication of ethnic identity conflicts, with transitional justice seeking to curb violence by the use of law. The advent of the International Criminal Tribunal for the former Yugoslavia (ICTY, 1993) launched this important moment in the judicialization of international relations, which ended on 11 September 2001. The third period, that of post–September 11, has been marked both by the eclipse of transitional justice as a utopia for rebuilding societies but also, paradoxically, by the institutionalization and by the professionalization of its institutions and practices.

Separating transitional justice into its different periods highlights the dominant dynamics of each. For example, the period 1983–1995 was marked by two contradictory tendencies: optimism, due to the process of democratization that was then under way in dozens of countries, offset by the reality of genocide and ethnic cleansing. Restorative justice, of course, did not disappear in practice after 1995—indeed, the facts show that the creation of truth commissions was never more active than after the work of the South African TRC. But the dominant dimension of transitional justice, which up to 11 September 2001 had been restorative justice, became progressively the creation of criminal courts, themselves a product of the new reading by the West's Great Powers of the menace posed by destabilization of the international system.

Separating transitional justice into different periods also emphasizes its successive reorientation. It reveals what a purely instrumental vision—that of the "toolbox"—tends to hide: the ideological changes, the intervention of new actors, the role of the Great Powers—in a word, transitional justice's relation to politics. The concept of a "toolbox" has an unfortunate connotation in that it affirms that crimes against humanity—acts of genocide or massive violations of human rights—can be *managed* and *dealt with* by administrative science as if they were isolated details. This technocratic simplification, albeit seductive for politicians in that it offers the false promise of "turning the page," is based on an illusion. In fact, such crimes bring about the collapse of a political community. There is—there can be—no turnkey solutions that allow the rapid repair of broken strands of society; the process of social reconstruction must be counted in generations.

The Genealogy of the Concept of Transition

Transitional justice was formed from the aggregation of two vague, ill-defined notions: justice and transition. Numerous writers have noted the imprecision of the concept that suggests that societies evolve through predetermined phases, passing from dictatorship to a transitional period, before at last entering into the democratic Eden. How should the time of transition be defined? Is it the holding of elections? The adoption of a new constitution? The establishment of a multi-party system? Confronted with this difficulty, Cherif Bassiouni, chair of the drafting committee that wrote the ICC Statute in 1998, prefers to use the concept of *post-conflict justice*. But even this term raises problems.

What about cases in which—as Alex Boraine, vice-president of South Africa's Truth and Reconciliation Commission, mentioned at a symposium in 2004—a repressive state oppresses a part of its own population?[2]

The transition paradigm, born in the United States in the 1980s, seeks to explain the democratization process under way in various regions of the world: in Southern Europe (Greece, Spain, Portugal) from the mid-1970s; the end of the military regimes in Latin America and the liberalization process in certain Asian countries (in particular, the Philippines, in the 1980s); the collapse of the Communist regimes in Central and Eastern Europe in 1989 and the creation of fifteen new states on the ruins of the former USSR in 1991; and, in the years that followed, the dismantlement of apartheid in South Africa, the end of one-party regimes in Africa, and the liberalization movement in the Arab world.[3]

As early as the mid-1980s, U.S. president Ronald Reagan and his collaborators spoke of "democratic revolution on a global scale." Guillermo O'Donnell and Philippe Schmitter were among the first "transitologists" to theorize about this wave of democratization.[4] The transition paradigm imposed itself in the interpretation of new international realities that were offered as a way to make sense of the multiple and heterogeneous processes by which, almost simultaneously, states as different as Mauritania, Mongolia, and San Salvador were undergoing political liberalization, and some countries seemed to be "in transition."

In this new democratic world, politicians, human rights activists, former political prisoners, journalists, political analysts and priests across the continents have brought a common reflection to the question of violence committed by the agents of the state in former totalitarian regimes: "How should societies face their criminal past?"[5] Can we "sacrifice the quest for justice in the name of other social objectives, reconciliation?"[6] In 1988 the Aspen Institute held one of the first conferences on this theme. Titled "State Crimes: Punishment or Pardon," this gathering clearly announced the challenges of the time, calling for reflection on "the problems of a moral, political and legal order posed when a regime guilty of flagrant violations of human rights is followed by one more inclined to respect these rights."[7]

The key debate that still remains is the tension between the search for civil peace and the search for justice. Is it possible to create a state of law by blocking out earlier crimes? On the other hand, can the guilty be punished without endangering the fledgling democracy? In uniting the concept of justice with that of transition, transitional justice becomes the new era's paradigm: the tension between civilization and barbarity and its solution; the metamorphosis of societies, that is, the passage from dictatorship to democracy. Transitional justice will elaborate concrete solutions, establishing a compromise between the ideal of justice and political realism.

The Quest for Reconciliation

The Default Solution

Far beyond the borders of Latin America, Argentina's experience during the 1980s resonated with the political elite and human rights militants. The trials against the ex-leaders of the junta, then, the torturers, provoked such hostility from the military that they threatened the stability of the new government, raising fears of a new coup. On 24 December 1986, the Alfonsín government proclaimed the so-called end-all and due obedience amnesty laws; in 1990 President Carlos Menem completed them with a pardon for the heads of the junta. A complex relationship thus began, for if the application of criminal justice threatened to provoke a violent reaction from the outgoing elite, their impunity undermined the democratic legitimacy of the new authorities and weakened the construction of a state of law. Organizations of families of the "disappeared"—in particular the mothers and grandmothers of the Plaza de Mayo in Buenos Aires—put justice at the top of the political agenda. Stuck between the contradiction of preserving democracy and stigmatizing those responsible for the deaths of thousands of people, the governments of Argentina and Chile set up the first truth commissions worthy of the name. (The first truth commission had been set up in 1977 in Uganda under Idi Amin Dada. That same year, the International Committee of Jurists had presented a report to the United Nations estimating that between 25,000 and 250,000 people had been assassinated in Uganda since the coup d'état that brought Amin to power in 1971.)[8]

The idea of unveiling the "truth" about crime appears even more vital in that the military junta had carried out its repression in secret. The families of the disappeared in Latin America wanted to know what happened to their loved ones: Were some of them still alive? Where are they buried? Under what conditions were they murdered? Establishing the facts about the disappeared was imperative; with justice unlikely, the truth would be an option by default. In this way, the truth commissions were set up in Latin America.

They had the merit of preserving civil peace while giving a certain satisfaction to the families of the victims and in contributing to the establishment of the state of law.[9] But the South African experience would transform the view of the truth commission. No longer would it appear as a default solution but, on the contrary, as a positive choice, as much in moral terms as in political and strategic.

The Turning Point: The Promise of Restorative Justice

South Africa became the symbol of the new social engineering of transitional justice. Historically, its situation was scarcely different from that of Argentina or Chile: the former elite was determined to gain amnesty and the African National Congress (ANC) initially wished to go to trial; however, it did not want some of its own powerful militants to be judged. The generals who had protected Nelson Mandela during his secret negotiations with F. W. de Klerk, still in power, told Mandela that their indictment could lead to a very dangerous situation. The creation of the Truth and Reconciliation Commission (TRC) was the political compromise reached between these two contradictory demands, the demand for justice and the demand for amnesty. In a word, the South African TRC, as its name indicates, swore to produce "truth" and "reconciliation," and, thus, a future for all South Africans. The political genius of Nelson Mandela and the Truth and Reconciliation Commission were to transform this incapacity of rendering justice into the affirmation of a higher truth and justice. The South African message was, in essence, that restorative justice is more effective and more moral than criminal justice, for it produces both common values and a new collective identity, and, as a result, social consensus. Thus, the TRC's final report states that "even if the South African transition has occurred without amnesty agreement, if criminal prosecution has been politically feasible . . . , strengthening the restorative dimension of justice" helped to build a bridge between "the past of a deeply divided society characterized by strife, conflict, untold suffering and injustice and a future founded on the recognition of human rights, democracy and peaceful coexistence and development opportunities for all South Africans, irrespective of color, race, class, belief or sex."[10]

It is this social utopia that so captured the imagination of public opinion around the world, as well as that of many NGOs. Reed Brody, the advocacy director of the U.S. NGO Human Rights Watch, could only note that the world had become "besotted" with truth commissions, whatever their results: "It seems that because of South Africa, the international community has become blindly besotted with truth commissions, regardless of how they are established and whether they are seen as precursors or complements to justice or, very often now, as substitutes for justice."[11]

At a time when the world was experiencing the shocks of neoliberal globalization and witnessing images of war and misery in Africa, the discourse of pardon and reconciliation by those as charismatic as President Mandela and TRC president Archbishop Desmond Tutu was seductive. At the end of a century of genocide and mass crimes in the world, the South African TRC produced a rare commodity: hope for the reconciliation of mankind.

Three fundamental points separate the truth commissions of Argentina and Chile from that of South Africa and explain the latter's astonishing resonance: the amnesty-for-truth swap, the TRC's use of public hearings, and the position of the promoters of TRC concerning reconciliation.

The TRC relied, in effect, on a fundamental transaction between the perpetrators of political crimes and the state: a complete confession as a condition of amnesty. As Ronald Slye writes, the South African commission had put together "the most sophisticated amnesty undertaken in modern times, if not in any time, for acts that constitute violations of fundamental international human rights."[12] The supporters of the TRC insisted that the radical separation between amnesty and amnesia by which the truth commission operated produced social and political benefits that would be out of the reach of criminal proceedings. As evidence, they noted that the authorities and the families of the victims had obtained information and confessions from hundreds of agents of the state that could never have been obtained through a trial. They added that the truth commission also permitted the victims in countries of legal tradition of common law to escape brutal, if not traumatizing, cross-examination in the courtroom. In addition, the commissions provided a story about repression that was more nuanced than judicial truth, which turned around the guilty/victim polarity. As for the accused, the truth commissions' procedure of "naming and shaming" stained their reputations. Last, but not least, truth commissions were affordable for poor countries, in contrast to trials, which would be infinitely more costly.[13] It was assumed that the stigmatization of criminals and the "duty of memory" would guarantee that crimes were not repeated, with the implicit hypothesis that once the lessons of history were drawn, a state of law would follow. There was, in this, a naturalist representation of the sense of history.

The argument of its effectiveness was reinforced by the TRC's staging. Indeed, the TRC worked on two levels. On the first, it organized the production of historical as well as commemorative truth. In essence, the stakes were somewhat similar to those of the Eichmann trial: in South Africa, as in Israel, the creation of a new national myth. In this process, the victims held the key role. Twenty thousand of them testified in public hearings unprecedented in earlier commissions: a dramatic and trying face-to-face confrontation with the murderers of their loved ones—on television. The truth about political crime shown as a spectacle had several goals: first, it marked the break with the past; second, the reparation that the victims received in terms of social recognition was good for society. The term *reconciliation*, used previously by the partisans of amnesty to legitimize silence and, with it, impunity, had been rehabilitated by the new *doxa*. The principal goal of the TRC was social pacification.

In exchange for this sacrificial role, the gift of oneself to society—for the hearings exposed publicly the private suffering and torture—the victim was taken up by a support structure that was medical, psychological, and financial. The reestablishment of the dignity and psychic health of the victims was interpreted in terms of what was good for the nation. Their trauma was confused with that of society. Between the suffering body of the victim and the suffering of the state of society, an equation was drawn. The victims' "healing"—contested by some studies[14]—was proof that society as a whole had healed. An entire medical-social discourse reinforced this vision, affirming that the "healing" of trauma warded off the specter of civil war: "Healing can prevent future violence and facilitate reconciliation," states Eric Brahm.[15] Ervin Staub and Laurie Anne Pearlman go even further: "Reconciliation requires that victims and perpetrators come to accept the past and not see it as defining the future as simply a continuation of the past, that they come to see the humanity of one another, accept each other and see the possibility of a constructive relationship."[16]

In *Trauma and Recovery*, Judith Lewis Herman best captures this new *doxa*, which psychologically and socially justifies the work of the truth commission:

> The ordinary response to atrocities is to banish them from consciousness. Certain violations of the social compact are too terrible to utter aloud: this is the meaning of the word *unspeakable*. Atrocities, however, refuse to be buried. Equally as powerful as the desire to deny atrocities is the conviction that denial

does not work. . . . Remembering and telling the truth about terrible events are prerequisites both for the restoration of the social order and for the healing of individual victims.[17]

Mauro Bottaro puts it in anthropological terms: "In starting from the premise that each memory corresponds to a different truth, what is important is the freeing of 'speech in and of itself': speech that remembers, speech that reconstructs, speech that accuses, that pardons and that amnesties. Speech as a gift in return. Finally, speech that frees and that reconciles. Speech as a 'refounding instance.'"[18]

From this perspective, the expression of the memory of crimes in the public domain participated symbolically in the elaboration of a new social contract: in a word—but it is a key word in the vocabulary of transitional justice—reconciliation.

To this medical-social argument of the "national healing" was added the TRC's discourse articulated around a double sacredness: civic and religious. As a new social contract between the citizens of the state, the politics of pardon aimed to transform society: wounded souls leave or will someday leave the shadows of barbarity toward democratic dawn and national reconciliation. With the South African TRC, the truth commission was, for the first time, used as a lever for "nation building"; it was a voluntary approach to reinventing the identity as the "New South Africa," the "rainbow" nation. Simultaneously with the elaboration of a new nation to which blacks, whites, colored, and Indians could all adhere, the flags and hymns of the apartheid regime and the ANC converged, symbolizing the national reforging then under way. To this civic sacredness, TRC president Archbishop Desmond Tutu added a spiritual dimension: he linked Christian forgiveness and the African *ubuntu* to the goal of reconciliation, holding out the access to spiritual truth by the act of forgiveness, as seen in the title of his book, *There Is No Future Without Forgiveness*: "This third way [amnesty without oblivion] was consistent with a central feature of the African *Weltanschauung*—what we know in our languages as *ubuntu* in the Nguni group of languages, or *botho*, in the Sotho languages. . . . [U]*buntu* speaks of the very essence of being human. . . . It is to say: 'My humanity is caught up, is inextricably bound up in yours' or 'We belong in a bundle of life.'"[19]

Desmond Tutu fell back on the mysticism of Africanism to legitimize the TRC. Questions and criticism would be heard but would remain marginalized in the public domain. Some South African victims, sharing neither the faith nor the convictions of Desmond Tutu, objected to this mystic that claimed Africans preferred restorative to criminal justice. They thought of the world in political, not cultural, terms—that is, in the terms of individual opinion. The wife of Steve Biko, the black leader defenestrated at a police station, insists, "We all want reconciliation but with justice."[20] She went as far as the Constitutional Court—without success—to seek punishment for her husband's murderers.[21] This need for criminal justice was not the privilege of political militants. The vice president of the TRC, Alex Boraine, tells of the reaction of a South African widow to the testimony of her husband's murderer: "After learning for the first time how her husband had died, she was asked if she could forgive the man who did it. Speaking slowly, in one of the native languages, her message came back through the interpreters: 'No government can forgive.' Pause. 'No Commission can forgive.' Pause. 'Only I can forgive.' Pause. 'And I am not ready to forgive.'"[22]

To this anticultural criticism of the truth commission was added a political criticism that denounced, in particular, the fact that the TRC had investigated crimes committed under the laws of the apartheid regime but had not investigated the political, social, and cultural effects of its racist policies. Last but not least, the South African TRC was based on several fragile, if not debatable, hypotheses: truth leads to catharsis, which is always positive, and catharsis itself leads to "reconciliation." However, it is questionable to apply the concept of catharsis to an entire social body. In addition, empirical studies indicated that the factual "truth" of the crimes—assuming that it could be established— was not therapeutic for victims as a whole. As for reconciliation, if the development of the TRC meant that an entire society had to subscribe to the same moral opinion, did that not become a totalitarian goal?[23] All of these hypotheses indicated that the TRC discourse had imposed itself as self-evident.

The New Doxa

To consolidate peace in this new era, it was seen as necessary to elaborate the "truth" about the wrongs of the past in the public sphere. "Revealing is healing" was the slogan of the South African Truth Commission. It was also the approach of Chilean president Patricio Alwyn in 1989 when he set up the Rettig Commission (the truth commission named after its president): "To close our eyes to what has happened and to ignore it as if it was nothing will infinitely prolong a long-lasting source of pain, division, hate and violence at the heart of our society. Only enlightenment of the truth and a search for justice creates the moral climate indispensable to reconciliation and peace."[24]

This approach indicated the change in perception concerning strategies of national reconciliation. During the Cold War, amnesty was considered the catalyst for reunification *par excellence*, the price to pay for reestablishing the unity of a nation broken by war. No one interpreted it as a fermentation tank of hate and vengeance. This strategy for national reconciliation, Paul Ricoeur notes, had profound consequences on the writing of memory. Amnesty, he says, is a "judicial oversight, limited but with far-reaching consequences, in the sense that the stopping of a trial is the same as extinguishing the verbal expression of memory as if to say that nothing ever happened."[25] In the 1970s, President Charles de Gaulle even justified the banning of a French television documentary, *The Sorrow and the Pity* by Marcel Ophüls, in the name of national unity: "France does not need truth. . . . What we must give her is hope, cohesion and a goal."[26] De Gaulle was only expressing with brutal frankness the perception then current: in the Cold War atmosphere, national unity and reconciliation were to be achieved through silence. Whatever need the victims may have for justice and truth was simply set aside by the states and the United Nations.

With conviction, Freeman Dyson has expressed the philosophy of reconciliation that prevailed during the Cold War, namely, that reconciliation is achieved through amnesty. Interestingly, during World War II, Freeman Dyson was a British officer serving in the RAF bomber command, and he collaborated with the men who planned the bombing of Dresden, causing more than 35,000 civilian casualties, who were burned alive. "If we had lost the war," Dyson says, "those responsible might have been condemned as war criminals, and I might have been found guilty of collaborating with them." His analysis of reconciliation might be seen as a pro domo plea, but that does not affect the value of his argument:

> In my opinion, the moral imperative at the end of every war is reconciliation. Without reconciliation, there can be no real peace. Reconciliation means amnesty. It is allowable to execute the worst war criminals, with or without a legal trial, provided that this is done quickly, while the passions of war are still raging. After the executions are done, there should be no more hunting for criminals and collaborators. In order to make a lasting peace, we must learn to live with our enemies and forgive their crimes. Amnesty means that we are all

equal before the law. Amnesty is not easy and not fair, but it is a moral necessity, because the alternative is an unending cycle of hatred and revenge.

Dyson has a strong opinion about Werner von Braun. Serving in the German SS out of pragmatism, von Braun was one of the designers of the V1 rockets that fell on the English civilian population. After the war, however, he worked for the American intermediate range ballistic missile (IRBM) program before joining NASA, where he contributed to the success of the moon expedition. He received the 1975 National Medal of Science. The scientist never faced any criticism for his role during wartime. Dyson stresses: "I admire von Braun for using his God-given talents to achieve his visions, even when this required him to make a pact with the devil. . . . And I admire the United States Army for giving him a second chance to pursue his dreams. In the end, the amnesty given to him by the United States did far more than a strict accounting of his misdeeds could have done to redeem his soul and to fulfill his destiny."[27] Dyson's analysis reveals to which extent for decades reconciliation was equated with impunity.

As Argentinian lawyer Rodolfo Mattarollo describes it, during the Cold War, the fight against impunity was often "a true crossing of the desert";[28] or, as Louis Joinet, the UN's special rapporteur (expert) on impunity, says bluntly, it was "the era of the Law's pre-eminence over the victim."[29]

A half-century later, in the post–Cold War era, the prism was radically different. Transitional justice had reversed de Gaulle's and Dyson's approaches: the pact of silence, previously thought to be the guarantee of national unity and reconciliation, had been swept aside in favor of speech. There was a transfer of sacredness from state to victim. From now on, after periods of violence, the recomposition of national unity and reconciliation would come after the need for "truth." In his book *The Struggle Against Impunity*, Louis Joinet, who had played a major role in changing the attitude of the UN, quotes Geneviève Jacques, mirroring the new *doxa*: "Impunity represents the triumph of the lie, of silence, of oblivion. It aggresses and poisons the memory of each and every man as well as the memory of entire communities."[30] The medical metaphor had been reversed: the recounting of crimes did not open the wounds of a nation; it healed them. It is silence that, from now on, is considered the poisoner of societies.

To the initial tension between peace and justice was now added the tension between truth and justice. Truth was now thought to calm passions; criminal justice, however, threatened the fragile normalization process. This passage from silence to speech, from forgetting to the recounting of crimes, translated in the resurgence of a moral philosophy of international relations that sought to expel violence from history. The recognition of mass crimes, the stigmatization of its perpetrators, and the commemoration organized around special days were asserted, even to the point of giving them quasi-magical power, as acts of resistance and prevention of a potential return to barbarity.

In the same way that Marxism and *tiers-mondisme* had made "the damned of the earth" the engine for class struggle and revolution, transitional justice made victims its agents for national reconciliation. Society recognized their particular legitimacy and charged them with a mission: to participate in the elaboration of a new social pact between yesterday's dominant and downtrodden, thereby warding off the specter of civil war and legitimizing the rituals of justice destined to channel violence.

Traditionally, peace had been perceived as the end of the hostilities. However, this negative and minimal definition of peace as the opposite of war is no longer operational in a world where conflicts are essentially internal and civilians are targets. A cold peace between belligerents is merely a truce, for the political conditions that brought them to conflict may linger: the potential for hate and the thirst for revenge can at any moment ignite the tensions merely banked by a fragile peace accord. The imperative of survival calls people to move from cold to warm peace, the so-called thick peace, in the words of Pierre Allan and Alexis Keller: "Thick recognition implies full acceptance of the humanity of the other, including elements of human experience and their societal dimensions."[31] The act of pardon seeks to defuse the dynamics of confrontation. But this assumes that the roots of conflict have been politically treated. In this view, the public expression of crimes changes the social identity of the victim by recognizing his suffering in the public domain. In moving from knowledge to acknowledgment, Juan Mendez, the former Chilean political prisoner who became president of the International Center for Transitional Justice (ICTJ), sees the potential for transformation, not only of the victim, but also of society itself: "Knowledge that is officially recognized and which, by this fact, enters into the 'public cognitive sphere,' acquires a mysterious quality that it does not possess as a simple 'truth.' Official recognition at least allows the wounds to begin to heal."

This utopia of social reconciliation lies at the heart of the *doxa* of transitional justice and takes on an international dimension. Transitional justice has been built on the opposition inherited from the Cold War between, on one hand, civil and political rights and, on the other, economic, social, and cultural laws. The product of political liberalism, it has privileged the first to the detriment of the second.[32] This is how the South African TRC built itself as a model of democratic transition until, under the shock of ethnic cleansing, the founding principles of transitional justice were profoundly revised.

From the Politics of Pardon to the Politics of Punishment

The utopic period of social reconciliation was linked to the accelerated exit of repressive regimes. Transitional justice was interpreted as an exceptional response by states undergoing political change. Against the backdrop of state collapse and the proliferation of internal conflicts marked by mass violence against civilians, the paradigm of transition was swept away. The name *transitional justice* remained, but it was only a throwback to the optimism at the end of the Cold War. A new political dynamic was now in place.

Genocide in Rwanda (1994); the massacres in Srebrenica (1995); Liberian president Charles Taylor's cruelty to his own people and to those of Sierra Leone (1989–2003); the recruitment of child soldiers and the destruction carried out by the Lord's Resistance Army, which terrorized 2 million Ugandans in the north of that country (1988–present); the massacres in Chechnya (1994–1996)—together these events indicated the new world disorder. In the context of the period following the fall of the Berlin Wall, the persecution of civilian populations was not only morally shocking; it was interpreted by Western hegemony as a threat to regional stability and international security. Attracting attention to the destabilizing potential of these conflicts for the North, British prime minister Tony Blair emphasized: "We cannot turn our backs on conflicts and the violation of human rights in other countries if we still want to be secure."[33]

Faced with this challenge, Western governments and the major NGOs defending human rights responded not only by condemning the perpetrators of the crimes, but also by leaning on this condemnation to create a new body of norms to curb violence: new rules, new procedures, new judicial institutions. Brick by brick and, at first, like a rapid response to individual crises, a new architecture for an international system was built. In the same way that national dynamics in Argentina, Chile, and South Africa catalyzed a movement that would take on an international dimension, the system of collective security that took form during the 1990s did not initially respond to an overall plan. The creation of two international criminal courts for the former Yugoslavia and Rwanda in 1993 and 1994, respectively, were also only immediate responses to serious crises.

Nevertheless, this gradual normative process generated its own internal dynamic by creating a bureaucracy and new norms, which contributed in turn to underpinning the legitimacy for the spreading and globalizing of the judicial process of international relations. It fascinated the media and public opinion, whose interest could be measured in the multitude of news reports, documentaries, articles, and debates on the theme. In the few years between 1993 and 1998, international justice emerged on the international scene. The International Criminal Court's (ICC) August 2005 report to the UN General Assembly clearly expressed this new mechanism for collective security: "The Court is the centrepiece of an emerging system of international criminal justice which includes national courts, international courts and hybrid tribunals with both national and international components. These institutions of criminal justice are also closely linked to efforts to establish and maintain international peace and security."[34]

This system of collective security, which checked the all-powerful states, was based on the idea that there are norms so fundamental that they transcend national interests. As Antonio Cassese, president of the first international criminal tribunal (ICTY), writes, there is "the belief in a core of universal values (peace, respect for human rights, self-determination of people) that all members of the international community must respect. In other words, alongside national interests and reciprocal relations among States, there also exist common interests and concerns that transcend each single State and unite the whole of mankind."[35] In Cassese's eyes, these norms justify the supremacy of international criminal courts over national courts: the reign of reason incarnated in international law is supposed to immobilize Gulliver in its threads.

The years 1998–1999 were a critical time whereby transitional justice ceased to be interpreted uniquely as an exceptional phenomenon destined for a few states on the fast track to democratization; instead, it became formalized in a judicial system that was increasingly constraining. The policies of pardon, however, did not disappear—the South African Truth and Reconciliation Commission was at the height of its prestige—but it was only one of the two poles of transitional justice, side by side with the policies of punishment in full development. In the future the toolbox of transitional justice would seek less to manage past crimes than to stop actual crimes from being committed. From that point on, the Messiah would enter through the door of law.

Ameriglobalization

During the brief period of post–Cold War exhilaration, a few governments of nations in transition to democracy and a handful of organizations of victims and the families of "disappeared" were agents of change. By sheer determination, the mothers and grandmothers of the Plaza de Mayo in Buenos Aires succeeded in putting the question of the disappeared and the struggle against impunity at the top of the political agenda. In the period linked to the multiplication of internal conflicts, new actors took up the fight. These were the Western powers, in particular the United States, as well as the principal Western NGOs in defense of human rights—Human Rights Watch based in New York, the International Federation of Human Rights in Paris, and Amnesty International in London. There was a convergence of interests, even of philosophy, between the Clinton Administration, which came to power in 1993, and these NGOs, for the architects of the United States' new strategic doctrine intended to make human rights one of the pillars of the country's foreign policy, as outlined in a 1996 document from the Office of the National Security Adviser: "Promoting democracy does more than foster our ideals. It advances our interests because we know that the larger the pool of democracies, the better off we, and the entire community of nations, will be. Democracies create free markets that offer economic opportunity, make for more reliable trading partners and are far less likely to wage war on one another."[36]

Obviously, the reality of American policy was not as homogeneous as these lines suggest. With no national interests at stake, the United States opposed UN intervention in the Rwandan genocide in 1994 and stalled on intervening in the former Yugoslavia. But the potential for regional destabilization generated by these conflicts forced the Clinton Administration to realize that a response to mass crimes had become a priority.[37] The extension of international criminal law would become an axis of the Clinton Administration, to the point that the United States became an inescapable actor in the criminalization of international relations. Certainly, France was at the origin of the creation of the ICTY in 1993, but it was the United States that supported the ICTY politically, financially, and judicially, allowing it to develop. The United States was also the main architect of the International Criminal Tribunal Rwanda (ICTR) in 1994, after having opposed UN military intervention during the genocide.

The United States was also, with the British, a main political supporter of the Special Tribunal for Sierra Leone in July 2001. In spite of reticence by Congress and the Pentagon, President Clinton signed the Statute of the International Criminal Court on 31 December 2000.[38] The United States alone spent more than $500 million in support of international criminal courts over a dozen years.[39]

This process of extending criminal law was the fruit of American policy, which itself produced a new type of diplomacy—judicial diplomacy—marked in 1997 by the creation within the Clinton Administration of a new diplomatic function—ambassador for war crimes. This new function was rapidly imitated first by the government of Tony Blair, who created the post of coordinator for war crimes at the Foreign Office, and then by Norway, the Netherlands, and Denmark. This institutionalization of judicial diplomacy was significant of the evolution under way: world disorder was no longer seen uniquely in terms of military threats; now it was seen through a legal and moral prism that conditioned U.S. response, as shown in the analysis of David Scheffer, the first U.S. ambassador for war crimes:

> We live in a world where entire populations can still be terrorized and slaughtered by nationalist butchers and undisciplined armies. We have witnessed this in Iraq, in the Balkans, and in central Africa. Internal conflicts dominate the landscape of armed struggle today, and impunity too often shields the perpetrators of the most heinous crimes against their own people and others. As the most powerful nation committed to the rule of law, we have a responsibility to confront these assaults on humankind. One response mechanism is accountability, namely to help bring the perpetrators of genocide, crimes against humanity, and war crimes to justice. If we allow them to act with impunity, then we will only be inviting a perpetuation of these crimes far into the next millennium. Our legacy must demonstrate an unyielding commitment to the pursuit of justice.[40]

The rise in power of international criminal justice depended, thus, on the political weight of the American superpower and the attractiveness of the cultural model of the "benevolent hegemon." This policy of judicialization—to be examined in more detail—sought to criminalize the enemy and to place him on the side of evil. But it cannot be summed up in a purely instrumental reading of law. The Clintonian discourse stuck to profoundly moral values. It assumed a vision of history whereby the recognition of debts of blood was a prerequisite for the normalization of the relationships between states and even within states. Thus, in addition to supporting the development of the ICC, the Clinton Administration was the first government to practice "repentance diplomacy" and to become involved in reparation for victims, which would become a dominant trait of transitional justice. Indeed, President Clinton's policy became almost the norm for heads of state, to the point that Nigerian writer Wole Soyinka, who won the Nobel Prize for literature in 1986, noted that "the world seems seized by a frenzy of apology."[41]

Clinton publicly apologized on a number of occasions, an act unprecedented at this level of power. He repented for the United States' abandonment of the Tutsis during the genocide of 1994, for U.S. support of South American military dictatorships, for his country's responsibility in the deportation and enslavement of millions of Africans, and for the racist medical experiments at Tuskegee in which hundreds of African Americans with syphilis were deliberately left without treatment. After Clinton, it became almost impossible to keep track of public apologies. Numerous heads of state and governments, the UN secretary-general, the pope, and many others would in turn take inspiration from Clinton's example and repent for acts that had happened sometimes several centuries earlier.

Prime Minister Tony Blair apologized for British handling of the Irish famine of 1840. The Queen of England apologized to the Maoris of New Zealand for the Crown's breaking the Treaty of Waitangi in 1840 and stealing their land, as well as to Indians for the Amritsar Massacre of 1919. Pope John Paul II asked the Jews for forgiveness for Christian anti-Semitism and apologized to Muslims for the Crusades, as well as to "his Orthodox brothers" for the schism in the fourteenth century. In the document *Memoria e riconciliazone: la chiesa e le colpe del passato*, edited by the Commissione Teologica Internazionale, the Catholic Church considered asking repentance for the burning of heretic Giordano Bruno in Rome's Campo dei Fiori on 17 February 1600. The U.S. Senate apologized for the internment of Japanese Americans during World War II, to the Hawaiians for disposing of their queen, and, more recently, to African Americans for having never made lynching a crime. The indigenous peoples of America, Australia, and Canada received apologies, then reparations, for the theft of their land and the inhumane treatment inflicted on them. In 1998 the Swiss government officially apologized for turning back Jewish refugees at its borders during World War II. The Japanese government proffered token excuses and, indirectly, equally token sums for Japanese soldiers' treatment of Korean "comfort women" during the war. UN Secretary-General Kofi Annan apologized for his organization's moral responsibility in failing to intervene in the massacres of Srebrenica and the genocide in Rwanda. President Jacques Chirac apologized for France's "inextinguishable debt" to Jews deported with the assistance of French authorities. American and British private money rebuilt the famous Church of Our Lady in Dresden, destroyed by the U.S. Air Force and the RAF during World War II, with the Duke of Kent leading the British delegation for the first service. In 2007 the descendants of General Lothar von Trotha, the German officer responsible for the mass killings of the Hereros in Namibia in 1904, met the representatives of the Herero people to seek pardon and express deep shame over their ancestor's actions. In 2008 the government of Australia apologized for the suffering and past injustices committed against the Aborigine population.

In addition to judicial diplomacy and repentance diplomacy, the Clinton Administration gave support at the highest levels in 1997 to the claims of the World Jewish Congress (WJC) concerning the Swiss banks and their unscrupulous handling of assets belonging to Jews killed in the Holocaust. Undersecretary Stuart Eizenstat, former president of the Federal Reserve Bank Paul Volcker, and Secretary of State Madeleine Albright were directly involved in finding an accord with the Swiss banks.[42] The Clinton Administration's support of the WJC was marked by the organization of an unprecedented international conference, where the question of reparations was raised concerning events that took place a half-century earlier. The negotiations with the Swiss banks concluded in 1998 with an agreement before an American judge that awarded $1.25 billion to survivors and heirs. But, above all, this process of reparations contributed to the emergence of language, values, and norms that would trigger an avalanche of claims from other groups persecuted in the past and would turn against the very countries who were directly or indirectly the source of this legal and political evolution (that is, the United States and Israel, as the major American Jewish organizations played the predominant role in this evolution).

To capture the essence of this spirit of repentance, Jacques Derrida coined the term *latinoglobalization*,[43] meaning a cultural Christianization of the world according to forms of the Roman Catholic Church. It is true that transitional justice contains the ideas of fault, sin, confession, repentance, and atonement. But, even more than latinoglobalization, we could speak of *Ameriglobalization*, for judicialization and the psychoanalyzing and moralizing of social relations are powerful traits of American culture. At the moment when the

United States was winning the Cold War and becoming the sole superpower, it actively exported its "soft power," its culture, values, norms, and judicial organization.

It was, for example, American law that inspired the rules and functioning of the international criminal tribunals. Following are two examples with highly symbolic stakes. During the setting of the rules for the ICTY, the judges trained in the European legal tradition attempted to introduce judgment in absentia but were overruled by judges from the common law tradition, who considered trials in absentia to be a parody of justice. If the latter were able to impose their view, it was because the United States, as a superpower, was able to export its norms. Similarly, they were able to use plea bargaining, which came from the American interdisciplinary law and economics movement (as well as from scientific current) that judged judicial institutions in terms of results.[44] According to this view, every criminal trial carries risk for both parties. To reduce these risks, it suffices for the two parties to agree to pay a price, such as a fine or a sentence.[45]

Clearly, the development of the transitional justice toolbox was based, in part, on U.S. policy during the 1990s and, not surprisingly, also reflected a certain strain of American politics incarnated in Wilsonianism. The overlap of the political and the utilitarian-moral constituted one of the powerful features of American society. It referred back to a philosophy of social engineering accompanied by a concern for performance; to the conviction that all problems, including the "management" of war crimes, had managerial solutions; to the extreme litigiousness of American society; and to its immediate staging as well as to its puritanical vision of society. It also reflected the methods of social organization of American society and the weight passed on to the "moral entrepreneurs," the NGOs.

Although the United States was the principal architect of this process of judicialization, it no longer controlled it. The creation of the ICC posed the principle of superiority of international law over politics, and, while such a principle may be compatible with the process of European construction, it is much less so with that of the U.S. government, which has no intention of allowing its sovereignty to be curtailed by international judges. Paul Kahn observes that "the real sin of the United States is to believe in itself as a political entity, when the new world order is to be an order of law."[46] In fact, the United States was one of seven countries to oppose the creation of the ICC, a court against which the Bush Administration determinedly waged war.

In the past, the European powers brought education and religion to their colonies. Today, the West exports its concepts of justice and the universal: the setting of legal and social norms has always been an attribute of power, drawing the line between just and unjust, good and evil. The West, in particular the United States, built the postwar international order on the democratic legitimacy granted by its victory over Nazism, symbolized by the justice rendered by the Allied military tribunals at Nuremberg. This was the image projected by the alliance of force and virtue. The West, triumphant winner of the Cold War, reformulated its *mission civilisatrice* through international criminal justice. The centrality of crimes against humanity played an essential role in this logic.

The NGOs, the New Entrepreneurs of Norms

The major NGOs have also played an important role in this process of judicialization of international relations. The NGOs are the untiring advocates of international criminal justice, of the diplomacy of repentance, and reparations for the victims of crimes against humanity. They are part of the international community's neo-Kantian vision of universal values defended by supranational legal institutions. In *L'espace public*, Jürgen Habermas explains how publicity campaigns were born in the eighteenth-century salons, with the political effectiveness of the public domain "directed against the secret practices characteristic of the prince."[47] Two centuries later, the scene has changed only in the details: the salon has become the international public space and the NGOs are the new actors in the development of transitional justice. They affirm new values, set new rules for behavior, stigmatize those who transgress them, denounce the silence of the prince, and drive out the lies of the state by "speaking the truth." The NGOs are the self-appointed moral sentinels of the new international order. They reaffirm the message carried by the new tribunals: "States are still the main players on the international scene, [but] individuals are and should increasingly be the focus of international relations: States should primarily act as their representatives."[48]

The effectiveness of the international NGOs lies in the convergence of interests that tie them to the Western governments. They are the missionaries of humane globalization.[49] They constructed the selling points of international criminal justice, made the struggle against the impunity of war criminals one of their priorities in the 1990s, and succeeded in mobilizing public opinion, a number of governments, and the United Nations. Through their activism, they have made the struggle against impunity a moral absolute, affirming with conviction that only the criminalization of the perpetrators of such crimes will stop their repetition.

Their fight against impunity was expressed in their mobilization of two thousand NGOs from the Northern and Southern Hemispheres to create the International Criminal Court at the Rome Conference in 1998. They also played an important role in the charges filed against Augusto Pinochet, who was placed under house arrest in England after his incrimination by a Spanish judge, Baltasar Garzón. "The Pinochet effect" was a key moment, says Naomi Roht-Arriaza.[50] Pinochet's arrest came a mere three months after the end of the conference in Rome, where the ICC Statute was elaborated. The extraordinary take-off of international justice reinforced the development of transnational criminal justice. Under pressure of victims filing charges and the major human rights NGOs that supported them, the courts in Spain, France, Switzerland, and Belgium called for the ex-dictator's extradition. After five hundred days of house arrest, Augusto Pinochet was freed, under the pretext that he suffered from "mild dementia." But this legal drama, which mesmerized public opinion, marked a turning point. For the militants of human rights and the associations of victims in dozens of countries, a window of opportunity had been opened.

The Pinochet effect set off a chain reaction on several continents. Naomi Rhot-Arriaza captures their essence:

> The Pinochet cases established the legitimacy of transnational prosecutions based on both universal and passive personality jurisdiction, at least under some circumstances. They showed that the existing universal jurisdiction laws could actually be used, and touched off a new willingness by advocates and courts to use them. They made clear that there are some limits on the immunity of government officials when hauled before national courts accused of international crimes, even if we still debate exactly where those limits are. They strengthened the idea that proper accountability for such crimes is the business of justice everywhere, and that domestic laws enshrining unfair trials or shielding perpetrators are subject to outside scrutiny and cannot per se bind foreign courts. They yielded landmark jurisprudence in the highest national courts of a handful of countries, jurisprudence that both draws from international courts and ideas and feeds back into them.[51]

Indeed, the Pinochet affair resonated substantially. Dozens of charges were filed in Chile, and judges who had been fearful began to open investigations.

In Latin America, the British precedent provided a legal basis for contesting the amnesty laws adopted a few years earlier in several countries. The incrimination of Pinochet motivated the most important NGOs involved in human rights, in particular Human Rights Watch, to make international criminal justice their strategic priority in autumn 1998.[52]

In the name of universal jurisdiction, Human Rights Watch brought charges against another deposed dictator, Chad's Hissène Habré, who was at that time in exile in Senegal, but the supreme court of Senegal decided that the country lacked jurisdiction to judge him. Human Rights Watch reopened the file in Belgium and managed to get Hissène Habré charged in 2005. In February 2003, the International Federation of Human Rights filed the first criminal charges before the ICC against the president of Congo, Ange-Félix Patassé. A Swiss NGO with the eloquent name Trial (Track Impunity Always) launched accusations against Tunisia's former minister of the interior, who was suspected of being responsible for torture, while he was on a visit to Switzerland.

The Pinochet affair stimulated Belgian authorities to adopt the law of universal jurisdiction in 1999. Adopted unanimously in the Senate, across political lines, this law abolished one of the basic criteria of the exercise of the law—territoriality—in the name of saving humanity. It was a Copernican revolution for the field of law. Although the law would lose its most progressive aspects on 30 January 2003, it allowed Belgian courts to judge the perpetrators of torture, war crimes, and crimes against humanity, even when neither the victim nor the executioner had the slightest link to Belgium. This law, which infuriated the United States and which soon proved to be unmanageable (within a few months, some fifteen lawsuits were filed against acting heads of state for crimes against humanity), well indicated society's faith in the 1990s in almighty law.[53]

The NGOs' effectiveness in setting norms today functions as a three-stage rocket. First, these "entrepreneurs of norms" use their power to denounce, discredit, and isolate those who violate human rights, and then they push democratic governments to act. Through a strategy of guilt—the "law of din" so dear to Bernard Kouchner—they track scandals, denounce the guilty, and absolve the victim's image. They use public opinion as a lever to push democratic governments into action. They begin by trying in front of public opinion those who, according to them, transgress norms, even if it means overplaying their hand on occasion. Thus, during the Bosnian War, the NGO Doctors of the World (Médecins du Monde) conducted a poster campaign that compared Milosevic to Hitler. In a world where one's reputation, name, brand—be it that of state, institution, or society—is a commodity, the NGOs present the case before the court of public opinion. They organize the staging of scandal, hoping that the court of opinion will provide a favorable climate for, depending on the circumstances, unleashing a mechanism of solidarity, political intervention, or judicial reparation. To this end, they become moral guardian, referee, and mediator to states that have developed a niche market in international relations, such as Switzerland, Sweden, Norway, and Canada. These countries generally have a Protestant culture; they are not Great Powers and they do not drag behind themselves a colonial past. In short, they have no traditional interests to protect, as in the case of France or Great Britain.

Second, the NGOs work for the universal adoption of these norms, supported by international organizations and the states. The latter see a political interest in taking a moral position. In the name of the effectiveness of their message and action, the NGOs fashion a Manichean environment: on one side, the guilty (the criminals); on the other, the innocent victims. This simplistic message holds both to Louis Pasteur's adage, "Tell me neither who you are, nor your story; I only want to know what you are suffering from,"[54] and to the rules of television: "No exposé of a problem without also stating its solution: if the problem is a sick child, the solution is the doctor shown treating him. Off-screen doesn't exist: the country, social and political conditions of violence, etc. Nothing exists except what is shown on the small screen. The image ratifies the rhetoric and stages it."[55] The NGOs stage the victim and his executioner, affirming the need to restore lost dignity to the first and to stigmatize the behavior of the second. In this distribution of roles, the victim and the executioner exist only through the criminal act. They have neither past nor future. History, except for that of the crime, does not exist. The political and social causes of violence are mere backdrop, all but insignificant. They are reduced to the name of a country, a dot on the world map flashed at the spectators.

In the final stage, according to this approach, the states as a whole progressively adopt these norms. The resistant actors are subject to "strategic bargaining." If they accept the rules of the international community, they will have the right to the rewards of respectability (access to loans from the World Bank and the International Monetary Fund [IMF], as well as the right to apply for membership in the European Union [EU]). If they refuse, they pay the price of their isolation. The cooperation of the countries of the former Yugoslavia with tribunal at The Hague perfectly illustrates this approach: Serbia delivered Slobodan Milosevic to the ICTY only because the West made it a condition for a loan of $100 million. To this checkbook diplomacy was added EU demands that cooperation with the ICTY be a prerequisite for opening negotiations for the membership of Serbia and Croatia. This pressure explains why virtually all of the accused were arrested, with the notable exception of Mladic. This strategic bargaining obliges reluctant states to set up procedures at their very core to satisfy Western lending agencies. In the final stage, these institutions internalize these exterior constraints into their own culture. As the process of constraint wanes, pressure comes from the inside, promoting, at least in theory, the development of democracy.

The Centrality of Crimes Against Humanity

If the judicial process developed at this point, it was primarily because it filled an ideological function that was increasingly important. In the context of the wars in the former Yugoslavia and other internal conflicts, crimes against humanity were the expression of a new frontier, the line separating barbarity from civilization, the marker *par excellence* of the new era. Crimes against humanity were the symptom of the challenges represented by neoliberal globalization, challenges that Stanley Hoffmann calls the "shock of globalizations," which were, at the same time, economic, cultural, and political, each rapidly generating its own tensions and leading to the rise of ultranationalism and "ethnism."[56] In such times, the judicial discourse obeying a binary logic of guilty-innocent reassured public opinion. Against cynicism and disenchantment, it raised hope. The combination of Desmond Tutu's discourse on pardon and reconciliation, the Pinochet effect (showing that even retired dictators have no guarantee of impunity), and the creation of the ICC supported by hundreds of NGOs throughout the world, testified to the elaboration of a new normative horizon. The NGOs defending human rights presented these successive developments as an inescapable evolution, bringing with them the disappearance of a post-Westphalian order governed by cynicism and *raison d'état* alone.

In this context, "crimes against humanity," a term that spent the greater part of the Cold War in a "swoon" and reappeared in France (in particular, during the Klaus Barbie trial, where the term remained at the time associated with Nazi persecution), obtained not only legal status but also a central position on the international scene. In the 1990s, the term "crimes against humanity" was applied to ethnic cleansing and, from then on, it played a precise ideological role: If all humanity is hurt by the immensity of a crime, then humanity as a whole is made responsible for judging the criminal. The term, then, legitimized a judicial diplomacy without borders, at the same time that it constructed the image of the enemy as barbarian.

[handwritten margin note: how get justice w/ such imbalance and no impartial?]

During the Cold War, the enemy was perceived to be rational, predictable, and disciplined. Washington and Moscow had established a procedure to avoid the risk of misinterpretation of the adversary's behavior—that is, the "Hot Line," and so on. The world was dangerous and cynical but at least it was predictable. The metaphor of the "Cold War chess game" reflected this clash between two adversaries who had worked out common rules of engagement. But since the Cold War, in the context of ethnic conflicts, the enemy has been perceived as irrational, unpredictable, undisciplined—an economic predator or a fanatic blinded by hate.

"The civilized world" is now set against the "barbarian." The bloodthirsty head of a militia; the nationalist leader who fans the flames of ethnic passions; the suicide bomber willing to kill himself or herself in order to kill many others; the terrorist; the rogue state—all these figures are part of the enemy as criminal with whom negotiations are impossible. The term "crimes against humanity" and the terms "war crimes" and "genocide," which were redefined by a series of arrests by the UN criminal tribunals and then anchored in the Statute of the ICC in 1988, capture judicially these policies of ethnic cleansing, forced displacement of populations, extortion, destruction of religious sites, and plunder of possessions which will from now on be considered threats to international security and regional stability.

In this new configuration, the development of international criminal law has played a strategic role: to eliminate these new outlaws from the political field. Criminalization has concrete effects: the law has become a judicial straitjacket for imprisoning those who put themselves, literally, outside civilization. It is a penal, if not police, vision of the world that has triumphed—not surprising in that the West, and in particular the United States, has never been so powerful, going so far as to consider itself the "policeman of the world."

The judicialization of international relations has legitimized the shrinking of state sovereignty. Humanitarian concerns paved the judicial road: in 1991, in the name of "extreme urgency," the UN Security Council's Resolution 688 authorized the intervention of several Western countries to protect the Kurd-ish people. For the authors of the concept of the right of interference, law professor Mario Bettati and a Doctors Without Borders co-founder, Bernard Kouchner, it is no longer tenable to bow to legal formalism which is tanta-mount to accepting that it could be "permissible, albeit discreditable, to mas-sacre one's own people."[57] A few years later, this legal formality was removed. Chapter VII of the UN Charter, the sole authorization of the use of armed force in the name of peace and international security, which was invoked for the adoption of Resolution 688, was also invoked in the establishment of the UN's ad hoc tribunals. The shrinking of sovereignty was synchronous with the neoliberal globalization process that had removed barriers and deregu-lated markets. The idea of absolute state sovereignty was then judged archaic and obsolete in the name of human rights and economic efficiency. Political and economic liberalism were mutually supportive.

Under pressure from the United States, which gave the initial push to limit state sovereignty, then under pressure from other Western countries and fed by the energy of human rights NGOs, a new idea came to light. It affirmed that state sovereignty was from now on conditional, that it must—at least, theoretically—respect the basic rights of peoples. This new concept of in-ternational relations brought the rise in power not only of the rhetoric of human rights, but also of administrative and legal science. With the multipli-cation of international and semi-international criminal tribunals and the de-velopment of the principle of universal jurisdiction, the perpetrator of mass crimes became the object of management by a bureaucratic and legal appara-tus. Implicitly, this vision of the world marked by moral puritanism carried the message that politics, by nature, is corrupt and morally dangerous. In this spirit, the United Nations recognized "the right to truth about gross human rights violations and serious violations of human rights law in an inalienable and autonomous right. . . . From the conceptual viewpoint, this right there-fore occupies a central and fundamental position in action to combat impu-nity and in the quest for justice."[58] The reign of reason, incarnated in interna-tional law, seeks to master warlike nationalism. This is its ambition. As Agnès Lejbowicz has pointed out, the essence of utopia is to invent another base for social contract.[59] Transitional justice—in particular, international justice—is no exception. Through the search for a world where war criminals will be punished, it offers the glimpse of a world that will from now on be peaceful through the domestication of violence by law, by the establishment of a just

amazon.com

Billing Address
Samantha Lee
29 Bow Road
Belmont,MA 02478
United States

Shipping Address
Samantha Lee
634 Mayfield Ave
Stanford,CA 94305
United States

Returns Are Easy!
Visit http://www.amazon.com/returns to return any item - including gifts - in unopened or original condi
within 30 days for a full refund (other restrictions apply). Please have your order ID ready.

Your order of October 22, 2010 (Order ID 102-4799613-3200214)

Qty.	Item	Item Price
1	**Darfur: A 21st Century Genocide, Third Edition (Crises in World Politics)** Prunier, Gerard --- Paperback (** P-1-A6F100 **) 0801475031	$12.21
	Subtotal	
	Order Total	
	Paid via Mastercard	
	Balance due	

This shipment completes your order.

Have feedback on how we packaged your order? Tell us at
www.amazon.com/packaging.

4/DR5mXXR0R/-1 of 1/-/1SS/second/5325911/1024-04:00/1023-04:04

JM2

peace where the wounds of history can, at last, be healed. It allows the hope for an end of history. It is a policy of purity, if not innocence, that echoes the policies of ethnic cleansing.

Restorative and Criminal Justice:
From Clash to the Package Approach

Transitional justice, as seen above, was built up in successive historical strata. Since the creation of the truth commission in Argentina, each period has modified, enriched, transformed, and invented new procedures and new institutions in function of the challenges posed. Transitional justice—and this is its specificity—was formed around two opposite poles, each reflecting the imperatives of the moment: extraordinary optimism linked to the accelerated democratic transition after 1989, then the multiplication of internal conflicts and the policies of ethnic cleansing marked by the genocide in Rwanda and the massacres of Srebrenica. But a determining point connects them: the hope for universal values.

Carried by the optimism generated by the fall of the Berlin Wall and a sense of moral progress, the political theorist Elazar Barkan notes that never in history have nations "expressed [such] a willingness to embrace their own guilt." He sees in this the emergence of a new international morality. He detects the birth of a "we" that is, according to him, the expression of the triumph of political liberalism:

> Our histories shape our identities. This truism is particularly applicable in the postmodern and post-Cold War world, where an increasing number of groups and nations recognize the malleable nature of history and, on the basis of perceived historical rights, negotiate their own political space. Both realism and tentativeness of historical identity become part of the growing liberal political space that includes no longer merely Western countries, but [has become] attractive to numerous diverse groups and nations globally. For this reason I deliberately use the term "we." "We" refers to a universe that shares vague liberal political and moral commitments to individual rights as well as to group human rights. This universe is studded with abundant contradictions but increasingly subscribes to a shared political culture, which pays greater attention to history as a formative political force.[60]

The "we" Barkan describes is that of a humanity that reaches into the heart of the groups that compose it to found an economy of responsibility. Through the recognition of historical wrongs and injustice, there can be effective reparation. We will pass from rancor, hate, and the desire for vengeance to the recognition of the other. This mutual recognition will be the pledge for a transformation of identity, because "history changes who we were, not only who we are." The expression of commemoration politics participates in this reconstruction of identity, with the goal of pacifying society. But from which viewpoint can this metahistory be written?

Antonio Cassese, the first president of the ICTY, is himself emblematic of this era of internal conflicts. In his first report to the UN Security Council in 1994, he affirmed that international criminal justice is indispensable for achieving peace:

> Some apprehensions were expressed lest the establishment of the Tribunal might jeopardize the peace process. In fact, the Tribunal will contribute to the peace process by creating conditions rendering a return to normality less difficult. How could one hope to restore the rule of law and the development of stable, constructive and healthy relations among ethnic groups, within or between independent States, if the culprits are allowed to go unpunished? Those who have suffered, directly or indirectly, from their crimes are unlikely to forgive or set aside their deep resentment. How could a woman who had been raped by servicemen from a different ethnic group or a civilian whose parents or children had been killed in cold blood quell their desire for vengeance if they knew that the authors of these crimes were left unpunished and allowed to move around freely, possibly in the same town where their appalling actions had been perpetrated? The only civilized alternative to this desire for revenge is to render justice: to conduct a fair trial by a truly independent and impartial tribunal and to punish those found guilty. If no fair trial is held, feelings of hatred and resentment seething below the surface will, sooner or later, erupt and lead to renewed violence.[61]

As discussed above, there had been fierce debate, particularly in the mid-1990s, between the supporters of policies of pardon and those of policies of punishment—to the point that the members of the South African TRC judged the judicial path to be counterproductive and that the ICTY was hostile to the creation of a truth commission for the former Yugoslavia. Supporters of pardon felt that criminal justice was neither possible nor even desirable, that the priority should be given to the restoration of victims. They also denounced the international criminal court's abstraction, its disembodied quality of "the dream of justice rendered by angels in a world of men."[62] They argued that international justice, intoxicated with lawyers' thirst for purity, had lost its reason for being: to engage society in a process of social reconstruction. On the other hand, the supporters of punishment judged that, unless justice worthy of the name was rendered, the cycle of violence would only continue. They also thought that the truth commissions' close relationship with politics undermined the ethical foundation on which they were built. In an article pointedly titled "Justice: The First Casualty of Truth?" the advocacy director of Human Rights Watch, Reed Brody, argues that the reconciliation so highly praised by the promoters of the truth commissions is all too often revealed to be but a "cruel joke" for victims confronted with their unpunished torturers and that these commissions are also "increasingly seen by abusive governments as a soft option for avoiding justice."[63] Argentine journalist Horacio Verbitsky, who spearheaded the campaign to overturn Argentina's amnesty law, says that "to try to impose reconciliation between the families of the victims and their executioners would be sadistic from an individual point of view and irrelevant for society. The only solid base on which to build the future is for all citizens to accept the law and its procedures."[64]

In the end, the limits of both truth commissions and penal pursuit rendered the terms of the debate null. The supporters of restorative justice recognized that it was necessary to punish the perpetrators of crimes against humanity. Supporters of tribunals were also obliged to accept the evidence: the tribunals had proven to be too expensive, too slow, totally incapable of handling the number of accused, and too cut off from the society they were supposed to address.[65] According to Eric Stover and Harvey Weinstein, more than 70 percent of Serbs were hostile to the ICTY and 87 percent of Rwandans had practically no knowledge of the actions of the ICTR.[66]

For this reason, a global approach was called for and, with it, the idea of a toolbox of transitional justice. But the debate was also weakened by realities in the field that showed that the tools of transitional justice were not exclusive. Argentina began with trials, then created a truth commission, and years later returned to a legal approach in annulling the amnesty laws. Chile passed from restorative justice to a criminal approach. Sierra Leone had both a semi-international criminal tribunal and a truth commission. What was truly important was the birth of one or several external and independent authorities that permitted the refounding of society.

The Eclipse of Hope

A new period opened with the attacks on 11 September 2001 and the Bush Administration's "War on Terror." The security paradigm imposed itself and brought with it an erosion of the norms of international humanitarian law: the hope that criminal justice could curb violence died. Under the influence of the superpower United States, "soft power,"[67] the capacity of a state to influence political actors through cultural or ideological means, now found itself confronted with "hard military power." The ICC was the stakes in this ideological confrontation between the United States and Europe, which carried over into legal and political relations.

In July 2002, less than one year after 11 September 2001, the ICC was established after the necessary sixty ratifications were met. The Bush Administration spared no political means to destroy it, creating strong tension with the countries of the EU. The most common argument for justifying Washington's intense hostility was the fear that the Court would press charges against U.S. soldiers for political reasons. Without dismissing this reason, however, the fundamental reason for its opposition appears to be ideological.

As in every profound crisis, the attacks on September 11 brought out a society's essential values, and the American experience was no exception. The ideological divide between Americans and Europeans appeared. This divide was evidenced all the more forcefully as Clintonian multilateralism was replaced by the Bush Administration's unilateralism. The controversy concerning the ICC opposed two different views on the relation between law and politics. The ICC represented the subordination of politics to the universal reign of reason. It was a view that corresponded to the historical experience of European construction. The EU had been constructed in relation to wars that ravaged the Old Continent over centuries. The ICC only validated and universalized the European experience in a specific field, that of criminal law.

From the United States' perspective, this subordination of law to politics was contrary to American culture, which did not separate the two. As Paul Kahn remarks:

> American political culture does not accept the cosmopolitan view of an op-
> position between law and politics, with law cast at the expression of reason

and politics as self-interest. In the American constitutional frame, popular sovereignty and the rule of law are a single phenomenon constitutive of the national political identity.[68] It follows that the law whether it comes from natural law, from norms of *jus cogens* or from common law is not seen as an external or political hindrance. On the contrary, through the Constitution, the law expresses the will of "we the People."[69]

This, Kahn notes, was America's "national myth," and this myth had been put in question by the existence of the ICC. The Court participated in the construction of a transnational world which, at the level of principles, submitted politics to the law. By its very existence, the ICC implied, on a symbolic level, the end of the American dream, the dusk of American exceptionalism. At the end of his fine analysis, Paul Kahn emphasizes that

> behind the formal dispute over the Rome Statute is a deeper dispute over the character of law, and behind that is an even deeper dispute over the place of sovereignty in the contemporary moment. The United States has responded to the 9/11 attack in the pattern of the powerful, modern nation-state that it is, while our European allies have, for the most part, . . . appealed to the mechanisms of international law enforcement.[70]

The ICC, supported by the Europeans, had embodied adhesion to the idea that "soft power" can temper international tensions. This idea was a pipedream in the eyes of the neoconservatives of the Bush Administration. In an article with a neoconservative tone that is deliberately provocative, Robert Kagan pokes fun at the cowardly Europeans, who, in contrast to the Americans, had deserted the battlefield. Kagan crystallizes the dialectic between "soft" and "hard power" with a scathing metaphor: Europeans were from Venus, while Americans were from Mars. (Kagan is referring to a best seller then current, *Men Are from Mars, Women Are from Venus.*) The first were characterized by lascivious abandon; the second, by warrior courage to defend civilization against barbarity. This Hobbesian vision of the world was translated into a policy of emancipation from rules and norms judged obsolete, justified in the name of an unprecedented war—"unlike any other we have seen"[71]—against terrorism.

It was in the name of defending these values that on 6 May 2002 the United States revoked its signing of the ICC Statute. It launched a diplomatic and political offensive that Human Rights Watch wryly termed an "ideological jihad."[72] The United States threatened sanctions against any country—with the exception of NATO members and Japan—that ratified the Statute of the ICC. It also brought political and economic pressure so that states engaging in bilateral treaties agreed not to transfer American nationals to the ICC. With a certain success: some one hundred countries are thought to have accepted, some in secret, bilateral accords. The U.S. Congress passed the American Servicemembers' Protection Act on May 2002, which stipulates that the United States will participate in peacekeeping forces only if U.S. soldiers are placed out of the jurisdiction of the Court. This same law authorizes the use of force to deliver Americans imprisoned by the ICC. This clause becomes known ironically in Europe as the "Hague invasion clause."

To this anti-ICC campaign was added, in the name of the "War on Terror," a policy to erode the norms of international humanitarian law. Thus, the Bush Administration obtained from Congress the "authority to interpret the meaning and application of the Geneva Conventions."[73] In his article "The Institutionalization of Torture Under the Bush Administration," Cherif Bassiouni, the first president of the committee to draft the ICC Statute at the Rome Conference, writes that "the institutionalization of torture became a reality when President Bush authorized the establishment of Camp Delta in Guantanamo Bay, Cuba, concluded that Geneva Conventions did not apply to combatants seized in Afghanistan (Taliban and Al Qaeda), approved the use of 'enhanced interrogation techniques,' issued an Executive Order that bypassed Congress, and unilaterally established a new parallel system of justice to deal with 'terrorists' through Military Commissions."[74]

Julien Cantegreil, a lawyer specializing in terrorism, points out that Bush proposed a double reading of the Geneva Conventions, by which the United States authorized the use of torture in secret detention sites outside its own territory and allowed, notably, the practices of subjecting prisoners to stress, extreme temperatures, sleep deprivation, and, eventually, "waterboarding." No explicit prohibition was made against the use of evidence thus obtained. Rape and sexual abuse were defined in contradiction with international law.[75] Crimes of sexual violence were defined in such a limited way that some of the scandalous practices at Abu Ghraib, such as forced nudity, were not punishable. Paul van Zyl, then director of the International Center for Transitional Justice, notes: "There is ample evidence that U.S. leaders created the legal, institutional and political conditions that made torture inevitable, and rewarded the results of torture when it happened."[76]

This policy to erode the norms of international humanitarian law had its effect on international criminal justice. The second half of the 1990s saw the rise in force of a collective security system made of international tribunals, a system that Antonio Cassese describes with a certain optimism:

> The International Criminal Court is intended to enhance and bring to fruition the modern, Kantian model of international community. It serves both as a practical and symbolic articulation of that scheme, and as a powerful push to its full realization. The Court is intended to sanction the idea that the use of force must be curtailed as much as possible, both in international and internal relations, and that whenever individuals resort to violence that is contrary to some fundamental legal standards of the world community, they must be held to account.[77]

But this model, which created rules limiting the margin of action for states,[78] never managed to really impose itself. After all, the international tribunals depended for their functioning on the political, financial, and military support of states. After September 11, under the Bush Administration's impulse, the neo-Hobbesian model resurged with force. The United States challenged international justice's ambition to universalize, but it was not hostile to its occasional use. This strategic legality, which seized international justice for the reasons of political opportunism, was not new in itself. The impunity enjoyed by Serbian president Slobodan Milosevic for years, and his indictment in the middle of NATO's military campaign, was one example. What was new in the 1990s was the aura of utopia that international justice carried. It was this utopia of a world governed by law that died after September 11, even if its legal instruments lingered: the risk was that the norms elaborated over the preceding decade become toothless options from which to choose. The question remains as to what the Obama Administration will keep as a legacy of this period of mistrust vis-à-vis international law and international justice.

The twentieth century has already witnessed this dialectic between law and politics. At the beginning of the 1900s, cosmopolitan lawyers attempted to impose international law to curb the use of force. The Hague Conventions, the Society of Nations, the Briand-Kellogg Pact, and the International Court of Justice are some of the best-known results. After World War II and before the Cold War totally froze East-West relations, and then the fall of the Berlin Wall, it was this neo-Kantian wind that carried the process of judicialization of international relations. After September 11, it came up against the resurgence of a neo-Hobbesian vision of the world. Two different and competing systems of international relations were, from then on, in tension. One, traditional, based on the nation-state and eroding under pressure of neoliberal globalization, found new vigor after the attacks on the United States on September 11. The other, which aspired to a technocratic management of international relations, depended, nevertheless, on the support of the most powerful states. The UN Conference Against Racism in Durban would see the confrontation between these two representations of the world.

Chapter 3

The Durban Conference

An Attempt at Universalism

T HE UN'S THIRD world conference against racism opened in the South African city of Durban on 31 August 2001. It was intended to be an event for working out "the standards, the structures, the remedies—in essence, the culture—to ensure full recognition of the dignity and equality of all, and full respect for their human rights."[1] With ethnic conflicts multiplying throughout the world, this impressive standard-setting conference was directly inspired by the instruments of restorative justice that the United Nations wanted to launch. The purpose behind it was that the recognition of crimes, the public expression of repentance, voluntary programs of reparation, and elaboration of a common narrative of the crimes of history, on a global scale, would participate in "a dialogue of civilizations" and the pacification of the international community's mores. The ambition of this diplomatic conference was to expose racism, point out barbarous crimes committed in the name of this ideology, and propose solutions.

Instead, the conference degenerated into a serious crisis in international politics. This crisis would have been even more dire if the attacks on 11 September 2001, which occurred only seventy-two hours after the conference ended, had not almost immediately obscured it. But Durban's political effects, added to those of September 11, would be felt.

This chapter will discuss the failure of the Durban Conference to produce antiracist norms. This failure was inevitable; the United Nations' attempt to universalize the South African example led the organization into an impasse. The international community is not a political community, but an aggregate of states that are supposed to agree on a minimum of common rules. By raising the expectation that it would be possible to elaborate a universal account of history's mass crimes and by calling together some 192 states to do so, the United Nations unintentionally created the conditions for a generalized conflict. The United Nations asked states—by definition, motivated by individual national interests and self-image—to put themselves into a post-Westphalian order. This contradiction would prove insurmountable. The fact that the United Nations had invited thousands of NGOs to a preparatory conference could only feed the competition for victimhood, at the risk of perverting the mechanisms of transitional justice. The virtuous circle that the United Nations meant to create was, thus, transformed into a dangerous taking of sides. The Durban debate threw a harsh light on the manner in which, in recent years, the shock of commemoration and collective representation between the Arab, African, and Western worlds on the question of defining crimes against humanity had been structured.

With this meeting, the United Nations hoped to symbolically recast the international community. The objective of the Durban Conference was, in effect, to "repair" the crimes of history and, in the medical-social vocabulary of the time, to "heal" the wounds of slavery and colonialism while clearing out the miasma of racist ideologies, which were the "source of numerous conflicts."[2] In the direct line of the South African normative approach, it was about transforming the history of massacres and human slavery into an inclusive history that brings societies together. The United Nations approached the question of mass crimes as a process of prescriptive and therapeutic management at the global level, as explained by former president of Ireland Mary Robinson, who was at the time the UN High Commissioner for Human Rights and as such the secretary-general of the Durban Conference: "The conference must constitute a healing process for the past. It is essential that the international community, together, confront the painful episodes of the past, in particular, the question of slavery and the slave trade."[3]

The intention behind the conference was to carry victims' voices and their need for reparation from the haves to the have-nots. This was urgent, the United Nations insisted, because the crimes of yesterday had structured an unequal system that prevailed and that would lead to new ethnic clashes, if nothing was done to defuse them. As Mary Robinson analyzed it in an interview at the time: "The inequalities of our world are not at all coincidental, nor accidental, but are born of colonialism and exploitation."[4]

In the same tone, UN Secretary-General Kofi Annan warned the West of the potential for rage on the part of humiliated peoples, that the debt of blood demanded justice: "The dead, through their descendants, cry out for justice," he insisted, adding that "the pain and anger are still there."[5] Annan urged "the international community to respond to the expectations of the whole world" to ward off ethnic demons through symbolic, even financial, reparation.[6] If not, warned the president of the Congo, Denis Sassou Nguesso, despair and violence would win: "We must not forget that people without memory are people without hope."[7] The genocide of 800,000 Tutsis in Rwanda and the policies of ethnic cleansing in the former Yugoslavia a few years before had crudely shown the destructive power of ethnic and ultranationalist ideologies. In the face of these dangers, the United Nations hoped that this conference would be an immense collective ritual of atonement and social purification.

It was in this perspective of preventing new crises that the United Nations resorted to the instruments of restorative justice. The establishment of historic "truth" public recognition of crimes perpetrated, the awarding of compensation, the writing of a common history—together, these instruments should lead to the formulation of a global antiracist culture. To set the goals of the meeting, Mary Robinson and Nelson Mandela wrote "Tolerance and Diversity," a short text signed by seventy-five heads of state.[8] In the name of urgency to "confront" the horrors of racism, "from slavery to the holocaust, to apartheid, to ethnic cleansing," the United Nations wanted to spread the values, norms, and practices of restorative justice around the planet.

This social engineering sought to defuse the resentment of Africans but supposed that the international community and, in particular, the West would claim "the duty to remember" the crimes committed by slavers and the ex-colonial powers. Africans and the descendants of slaves had been left out of the process of commemorative rehabilitation that accelerated with the emergence of transitional justice from the 1990s, so Africans needed to catch up with the globalized history of cruelty being written. The Jews, the Armenians (with the notable exception of Turkey), the Tutsis, the Amerindians, the indigenous people of Australia and New Zealand, the Japanese Americans held in camps in California during World War II, and the Roms (at least in some countries) had all obtained recognition for their suffering and, sometimes, reparation. The planners of the Durban program exhibited an almost Promethean will to "fix" history. The roots of hatred would be dried up by this metahistory of human cruelty, Mary Robinson affirmed: "This is the first time that there is a common will to write the history of difficult subjects. For some countries, colonialism represents their greatest moments of glory; for others, it is synonymous with devastation. Durban can only be the starting point for unifying these visions."[9]

Unlikely Cement for the International Community

The United Nations did not escape the general passion for restorative justice incarnated in the South African model at its high point. The peaceful transition from a racist and authoritarian regime to a multi-ethnic democracy represented a rare glimmer of hope in the 1990s. It is for this reason that the UN conference was held on South African soil. The new "rainbow nation" was the symbol of two great challenges the planet must take up: racism and profound social inequalities.[10]

The work of the Truth and Reconciliation Commission presided over by Archbishop Desmond Tutu struck the imagination of the entire world: in particular, the twenty thousand victims and the hundreds of executioners who testified in public hearings, their dramatic face-off, and the absence of punishment justified in the name of "pardon." The conference would be carried by this wave of reparative and reconciliatory ideology, with Nelson Mandela as host, godfather, and model. The United Nations aspired to create a supranational moral authority. Instead, it created the conditions for a head-on collision between two worldviews: a Westphalian one based on the defense of national interests and a post-Westphalian one that sought to be universal. This contradiction was the root of the failure in Durban.

The United Nations' miscalculation was to accentuate the South African experience of restorative justice, as if it were possible to replicate on an international scale what had occurred within a particular political community. But restorative justice cannot be the cement for fragmented humanity; the different viewpoints of world events, the responsibilities attributed for the crimes of the past, and the dramatic inequalities of the present are simply incompatible.

The United Nations was in an extremely fragile position, lacking any capacity to influence international power struggles. It was because of this weakness that the United Nations promoted transitional justice as a solution; it believed that it was unthreatening to states. The United Nations had only moral persuasion, but in 2001 even this capital was depleted, although the responsibility should be attributed to the Permanent Members of the Security

Council rather than to the organization's Secretariat. Three decades of struggle against racism directed by the United Nations (1973–2003) had culminated in the genocide in Rwanda, the massacres in Srebrenica, and the United Nations' nonintervention in both cases. A shocking metaphor of contemporary reality was the lawsuit filed in 1997 against the South African government by thirty-nine of the largest pharmaceutical companies. By blocking an affordable treatment for HIV/AIDS in the name of protecting intellectual property, this legal action confirmed de facto subhumanity on Africans.[11] The World Health Organization's slogan launched fifteen years earlier—"Health for all in 2000"—now seemed comic, if it were not tragic. In addition, the very idea of "development"—at the heart of UN rhetoric for decades (1950–1980)—had collapsed, as well as two important belief systems, that of the moral and technical "progress" of mankind and that of socialism and *tiers-mondisme*.

The West had never been more powerful and Asia was developing, but Africa, drained by conflicts and AIDS, was marginalized, with the exception of South Africa and a few pockets of relative prosperity. The multilateral system inherited from World War II was in tatters. In many places on the planet, a state was no longer capable of assuming its most essential tasks, if it had not collapsed outright, as Somalia had. At the same time, inequalities continued to grow. Encouraged by the UN secretary-general, in September 2000 the UN General Assembly adopted "The Millennium Development Goals," the primary objective of which was to cut in half the number of people living below poverty level (one billion living on less than $1 per day) by 2015. This goal alone was evidence of the sad state of mankind.

In these hopeless conditions, restorative justice as represented by the South African model appeared to be the best hope for bringing together the "family of man." No doubt, the United Nations seized on the South African model because of the charismatic personality of Nelson Mandela, for he had the rare advantage of representing one of the only possible meeting points between the ideologies and interests of states as different as those of Fidel Castro and George W. Bush. But those two heads of state lived in different worlds: the first saw the South African experience as the victory of a national liberation movement; the second applauded a peaceful transition that would not disturb the interests of American companies in South Africa.

All of these factors ensured that the use of the moral vocabulary of transitional justice—the keywords of *truth, justice, pardon,* and *reconciliation*—would become mere incantatory rhetoric, a far cry from the United Nations' hope to pacify and even recompose the "human family."[12]

The Limits of Restorative Justice

The Contradictions of the International Community

The 2000 Brahimi Report on the failure of UN peacekeeping operations doesn't beat about the bush: member states had given the United Nations mandates that were often ambiguous, without giving them the means to act—thereby all but dooming these missions to failure.[13] What was true for peacekeeping was also true for human rights. The first two UN Conferences Against Racism, in 1977 and 1983, degenerated into East-West confrontation, crystallizing passions around the nature of Zionism and the condemnation of the apartheid regime. The Durban Conference would have the same outcome. It would bring into play what was least tangible and most difficult to negotiate—national identity, collective memory, self-perception, ethnicity, values, and one's vision of the world—while underestimating their weight in the formulation of foreign policy.

From the very beginning, the standard-setting mechanism that the United Nations wanted to set up broke down. The causes were many: the deterioration of the international climate, the irreconcilable nature of collective memory, an organizational dynamic that turned out to be counterproductive. Mary Robinson adopted a format whereby an NGO forum would open the intergovernmental conference. Robinson mistrusted national interests; but she trusted in the militant virtues of the NGOs to put pressure on governments and to establish new norms, build an antiracist culture, and draft a new universalism in an era of neoliberal globalization. Because of her convictions, Robinson misunderstood the interests of the majority of NGOs, as well as of the governments. She wished to give voice to the voiceless, thinking, no doubt, to create a democracy between victims, but the conference would become a theater for the expression of myriad wounded memories, the multilateralism of frustrations and ethnic claims.

Circumstantial Reasons for Failure

A little more than three years separated the UN General Assembly's adoption on 12 December 1997 of the principle of a Conference Against Racism (Resolution 52/111) and the event itself. During those three years, the political environment deteriorated profoundly. Two factors weighed most heavily. First, with the beginning of the Second Intifada on 28 September 2000, the Israeli-Palestinian peace process that was under way in 1997 had collapsed and the conflict moved into a new phase of confrontation. Second, in January 2000 the Bush Administration had replaced the Clinton Administration in the White House. President Clinton had been a natural partner of the United Nations: his support for multilateralism was repeated domestically in his fight against racism, as in his personal launch of the National Initiative on Race. In contrast, the new U.S. president did not hide his hostility toward the United Nations and had neither the interest nor the personal investment of his predecessor in fighting racism. In addition, given the lack of results of President Clinton's personal efforts in the Middle East, Bush did not give this area priority, causing profound frustration (even among the United States' Arab allies) that would be felt strongly in Durban. (To the astonishment of American diplomats, one of the most radical countries in the Arab world, Egypt, had for decades received $2 billion in aid annually from Washington, making it the second-largest recipient of U.S. aid.) The renewal of violence in the Middle East, the hostility of the Bush Administration toward the United Nations, the frustration of the Arab and Islamic world as a whole, as well as, to a lesser degree, that of the European Union countries, together created an environment that was not auspicious for working out a compromise.

Irreconcilable Collective Memory

As mentioned earlier, the United Nations took inspiration from the South African model of transitional justice for a number of reasons, notably because it was one of the few points on which Africans and Westerners agreed. But even this consensus was superficial, for their interpretations of the South African model fundamentally differed. The African governments and "radical" states like Cuba saw the ANC government as a triumph of a people against racist exploitation. The Western governments, however, focused on the peaceful transition that had questioned neither the division of wealth nor the capitalist system that generated such inequality (reinforced, it must be said, by apartheid's laws of racial discrimination). The Western governments saw in the spirit of restorative justice a reassuring vision for reforming society. The conference opened on this initial ambiguity.

Into this environment, two visions of the history of slavery and how to commemorate it collided: that of the majority of NGOs and African states vs. that of the Western governments. National identities and collective memories had been built around each of these incompatible visions. Most Africans accepted the view of "white savagery" forcefully expressed by Rosa Amelia Plumelle-Uribe, a writer of African-Colombian heritage who was indignant at the good conscience shown by white people toward the Blacks they had banned from humanity for centuries:

> Black people, separated forever from their children, their wives and husbands, their brothers and sisters and parents, pushed down to the sub-human level, dehumanized, treated as merchandise, have experienced suffering and helplessness every bit as heartbreaking and pathetic as the victims of Auschwitz experienced upon arrival in the camp—in both cases, of people being torn apart before being sent to their death. If this comparison shocks Europeans, it is simply because Auschwitz belongs to their memory, while the martyrdom, the suffering and the death of millions of men, women and children who have paid for white supremacy with their lives have never entered into the Western memory. . . . The nations of Europe responsible for this disaster have never asked forgiveness from their victims. They procrastinate and assume a right that defeated Germany itself never dared claim, that of defining their crimes, and, in the place of their victims, to decide what historic weight to give or not give to these events.[14]

For a number of participants at Durban, the West had set up the hierarchy of race and had legally and methodically created the exploitation of tens of millions of human beings to whom humanity has been denied, without, even today, condescending to recognize the extent of this crime. Already in 1948 Aimé Césaire wrote in his introduction to *Esclavage et colonisation* by Victor Schoelcher that the West was guilty not only for the past, but also for its way of looking at the past. The West, he said, recognized the Jewish tragedy and Auschwitz because whites were the victims, but not the black tragedy and Gorée, because they concerned Africans: "Nazi Germany only applied on a small scale, in Europe, what Western Europeans had applied for centuries to whatever races had the audacity or clumsiness to get in their way."[15]

For most of the African representatives at Durban, "white savagery"[16] constituted one of the founding aspects of Western modernity. According to this perspective, the link with the Jewish tragedy was imperative because the extermination of the Jews by the Nazis was interpreted as the ultimate expression of the dehumanizing process that was applied previously to non-whites. For Aimé Césaire and many others, this link was clear in the similarity of the creation of subhumans, although the West refused to recognize the relation between these two crimes. In its 10 Point Declaration of 1960, the Black Panthers, among other Africans and African Americans, emphasized this denial of recognition: "Forty acres and a mule, that's what was promised us 100 years ago as compensation for slave-work and the genocide of our people. We'll take payment in cash. The Germans are helping the Jews in Israel because of the genocide of the Jewish people. The Germans murdered six million Jews. The racist Americans participated in the massacre of more than 50 million Blacks. That's why we consider our demands to be modest."[17]

The law professor Robert Roth is right to insist that, contrary to the classical judicial organization, "the roles of Prosecutor and victims merge here: it is the victims—or, more often, their descendants—who play the role of Prosecutor."[18] Put on the defensive, Western governments recognized that slavery was, of course, an abomination. But they considered that it was neither a characteristic of Western modernity nor one of its essential components. They affirmed that if the West had a clear share of the guilt, the Arab world that organized the trans-Saharan and East African slave trade was just as guilty, as well as a part of Africa itself that actively collaborated with slavery. They pointed out that these practices continue even today in some African countries. They emphasized the fact that slavery had been practiced in all societies, including ancient Rome, and that it was the West that abolished it. Without saying so explicitly, they accused the Africans of not having thought out their own responsibility and of having dumped it on the West. This perception was fed by the analysis of historians who showed that many different slave trades existed and that it was, according to them, an oversimplification to concentrate on only one of them: "17 million Africans were sold as slaves on the Indian Ocean coast to the Middle East; from North Africa, 12 million Africans were taken to the Americas; 5 million Africans were taken in slavery across the Sahara and East Africa to other regions of the world."[19]

U.S. congressman Tom Lantos, himself a survivor of Auschwitz and the spearhead of the U.S. delegation in Durban, was behind a resolution adopted by Congress (408 votes to 3, with 3 abstentions) on the last day of the preparatory session for the Durban Conference that recognized "the pain, suffering and extreme humiliation imposed on millions of Africans."[20] The resolution showed that the United States was not insensitive to the crime of slavery, but its formulation, a succinct recognition of the facts, was light-years away from the strong gesture expected by the Africans.

NGOs: The Victimization Package

The Escalation of Battered Memory

Mary Robinson, the UN High Commissioner for Human Rights, committed two errors that would add to the confrontation of commemoration. First, she fixed the preparatory meetings (held between September 2000 and February 2001) by region and in the order of increasing difficulty—Strasbourg (France), Santiago (Chile), Dakar (Senegal), and Teheran (Iran)—although it was foreseeable that the final two, Dakar and Teheran, would be the least consensual and that it would take time and difficult negotiations to find common ground. In the Final Declaration of the Dakar preparatory meeting, the African states demanded compensation for slavery and colonization. The Teheran meeting gave a taste of what was to come in Durban: the delegates of Jewish NGOs as well as the Israeli, New Zealand, and Australian representatives were denied access to the conference (the three countries had no diplomatic relations with Iran). The Arab-Islamic world wanted to resuscitate the UN General Assembly's Resolution of 10 November 1975 that assimilated Zionism and racism before it was abrogated in 1991 under U.S. pressure.[21] In other words, the pre-Durban dynamic already showed that the goal to produce antiracist standards had been replaced by a political confrontation between the three principal groups—the West, the Africans, and the Arab-Islamic states—on the subject of Zionism and compensation. The confrontation was so predictable that the United Nations organized an emergency session in Geneva a few weeks before Durban, without result.[22]

The United Nations' second error was to misunderstand the power plays and interests within the NGOs. The United Nations wanted to use the NGOs' energy and their capacity to stigmatize and to generate ideas to recreate the international system. The United Nations was convinced that it could channel to its own profit these "entrepreneurs of norms." Theoretically, the process of creating norms could be broken down into a few operations: first, the NGOs would denounce states that violated human rights; then, they would mobilize public opinion; finally, they would present propositions, which would be taken up by governments who would modify them to make them palatable to the majority of the international community. When a critical mass of states and institutions accepts a norm, it becomes effective. It was this process that the

United Nations sought to put in place in Durban and it is for this reason that the United Nations organized the conference in two steps: from 28 August to 2 September 2001, the NGO meeting would precede and then overlap the intergovernmental meeting to be held from 31 August to 8 September—all the better to "tally with" the work of the diplomats.

But the immense majority of the three thousand NGOs at the conference shared neither the values nor the global interests of the large Western NGOs like Amnesty International, Human Rights Watch, and the International Human Rights Federation. In part financed by the European Union and various Western governments, these big NGOs understood the norm production process and had developed a real expertise in the matter: as noted in Chapter 2, they were the post–Cold War era's missionaries of universalism. But at Durban, the big NGOs found themselves in a minority, with the vast majority of NGOs engaged in the immediacy of political battle, focused on particular conflicts. Their interest was not so much to participate in the elaboration of new norms as it was to use Durban as a resonance chamber for making their own claims heard. Their goal was to impose their account of suffering in the international public domain—and Durban offered the perfect occasion, with thousands of representatives from NGOs, diplomats from the world over, and hundreds of journalists on hand. Anyone dominating that space could transform an emotion into power, set oneself up as "just," and stigmatize one's adversary. Unintentionally, the United Nations removed a censor by creating an arena where, through the confrontation of memory, the frustrations and political struggles of the time could clash. The NGO conference resulted in a confrontation between the Western vision of the world and the revival of a *tiers-mondiste* vision and contributed to the crystallization of positions at the intergovernmental conference.

In the cauldron of their individual claims, the African and Arab-Islamic NGOs combined a Third World approach with the legal vocabulary of the 1990s centered on crimes against humanity. In rhetoric inspired by Frantz Fanon, the most radical of the NGOs justified "good" violence—that of the weak, the dominated, the exploited, violence that is legitimate, just, and necessary—while condemning "bad" violence, that of the colonizer, the neo-imperialist who has all the means of domination at his disposal. Durban was, no doubt, one of the rare places where those who considered themselves the new "wretched of the earth" could take their revenge and use legal terms like a weapon. Because the West had, for centuries, even into the first half of the twentieth century, legitimized white supremacy through law (Louis XIV's "Black Code," for example), they could turn around the legal categories of the abominable: the notion of "crimes against humanity" created during the massacres of the Armenians by the Turks, the charge of genocide established after the Holocaust, became the key words in the confrontation with the West. Why should Armenians and Jews be recognized as victims of genocide and not, among others, the Hereros of South-West Africa (Namibia) who were exterminated by the Germans at the beginning of the twentieth century? Not only did the West refuse to admit that it was genocidal, but, in its arrogance, it never stopped giving moral lessons to the rest of the world about good and evil, whether the matter at hand was sexual equality, the banning of excision, freedom of expression, or the banning of child labor. Profound anger stirred many of the NGOs at Durban, all the more so because they saw in the functioning of the economic system the perpetuation of the deadly exploitation of the past. In assimilating the slave trade and colonialism as international crimes, the African NGOs sought to obtain recognition from the West of its criminal responsibility. In using the categories of imprescriptible crimes, they sought to open a field of financial claims by tying together memory, demands for repentance, and reparations. Alioune Tine, one of the most eloquent speakers among the African NGOs, readily acknowledged this thirst for both revenge and justice: "We demand that slavery and colonialism be recognized as a double holocaust and as crimes against humanity and we demand compensation from the West for the pillage of resources, the forced displacement of people, inhumane treatment and the current poverty of Africa, the fruit of this history of crime and despoilment."[23] Using Marxist terms, Egyptian political analyst Samir Amin explained that "racism and discrimination are generated, produced and reproduced by the logic and expansion of capitalism in its so-called liberal form. . . . And that it can only produce apartheid at the global scale."[24]

The radical asymmetry of international power causes talk to be generally muffled in real decision making. Here, it was for once solicited in a purely symbolic and political space. Even if the NGOs fell back on a *tiers-mondiste* discourse, their political vision was not far from that of Hans Morgenthau, one of the founding fathers of the realist approach to international relations. Like Morgenthau, the NGOs did not believe in the virtues of the United Nations' technocratic and normative approach. For them, this approach was merely a strategy to de-politicize social actors, and de-politicization is merely the politics of the powerful to conserve their advantage: by throwing a few scraps to some, they weaken solidarity among the oppressed. How can we create harmony within the "family of man" if we leave out the two to three billion people living on less than $1 a day? As for the great ideals proposed by the states, they were surely not far removed from how Morgenthau, in bitter irony, describes the moralizing foreign policy of Presidents Wilson and Theodore Roosevelt: "What the moral law demanded was by a felicitous coincidence always identical with what the national interest seemed to."[25] As for the language used by the United Nations in calling for humanity, it was yet another ruse of the powerful who sought to camouflage the reality of power struggles. In the words of Carl Schmitt: "To confiscate the word *humanity*, to invoke and monopolize such a term probably has certain incalculable effects, such as denying the enemy the quality of being human and declaring him to be an outlaw of humanity; and war can thereby be driven to the most extreme inhumanity."[26]

The images of Israeli repression of the Intifada became, for the Arab-Islamic and African NGOs at Durban, the unbearable embodiment of North-South domination. The technocratic vision of the United Nations' handling of the crimes of the past was jostled, even smashed, by the claims of the thousands of NGOs present from the opening of the meeting on 28 August, themselves warmed up by the protests of tens of thousands of antiglobalization protestors and Palestinian sympathizers in the streets of Durban.

To the NGOs' *tiers-mondiste* vision can be added the particular dynamics of the meeting. These thousands of NGOs found themselves subjugated by a merciless law of the market that is still true today: To achieve the public recognition at the international level that they seek, they must come out on top of a neo-Darwinian selection process. The NGOs are, in effect, subject to a media logic based on the principle of intense competition. In this system of symbolic supply and demand, the media can absorb only a limited amount of information. Only the NGOs with the strongest communication strategy or those who have solid political support can make themselves heard. The media functions as a sorting station, spotlighting the claims of some NGOs, while leaving hundreds, if not thousands, of others in the dark. They participate in the organization of the hierarchy of victimhood in the public domain. As a result, the NGOs' "law of din," which seeks to "create an event," gets out of hand. Which victims' group will be able to impose its version of events on the global scene? To achieve visibility, the NGOs drag each other into a sordid escalation of victimhood. The word *genocide* is thrown about by innumerable groups, like an "open sesame" that will unlock the door to public recognition of their sad history.

Supported and inspired by African American organizations, the African contingent wanted to obtain recognition of slavery as "the greatest crime against humanity ever committed." The Arab-Islamic world put forward the "Palestinian Holocaust" perpetrated by the Zionists. Beside these two main claims, countless groups also sought recognition of their suffering. Indian Dalits denounced the "Daliticide" of which they were victims; the Kurds recalled the chemical gas attack on the people of Halabja and their repression by the regime of Saddam Hussein; Tibetans called for the end of Chinese occupation; the Roms denounced xenophobia in Central and Eastern Europe; Brazil's landless denounced the *latifundiaires*; gay and lesbian groups denounced the discrimination against them; the Papuans, Sahrawis, Puerto Ricans, and Martinicans, and the Uighurs of China, claimed independence in the name of a people's right to self-determination. Only a few voices rose to the top; the rest were lost in the competition for victimhood.

Was Durban the rebellion of the wretched of the earth? After the violent protests in Seattle, Nice, Göteborg, and Genoa, Samir Amin and others believed so, detecting at Durban the beginning of a vast movement of rebellion by the peoples of the South against "imperialist domination." "The wind of Bandung (1955)—a seminal moment in the Non-Aligned Movement—is stirring again," they prophesied. To this dynamic vision of people striving for their own dignity, as drawn by Samir Amin, can be added a more disturbing analysis of isolation along ethnic lines. The NGOs had put forward a discourse built around their martyrdom and the denunciation of social inequalities to advance their cause, not one built around a collective ideology of social and political transformation of the world. Neither socialism nor *tiers-mondisme* nor any other unifying ideology emerged from Durban as an alternative to neoliberal globalization. It is as if, faced with the American hyperpower, all that could be done was to invoke past suffering and to reclaim a bit of justice and a bit less of the current misery.

It was this victimization dynamic that the United Nations—in spite of itself—launched with the Durban Conference and was incapable of handling. The United Nations intended to play fireman by putting out ethnic identity fires; unwittingly, it stoked them. The premise of transitional justice, based on the recognition of the other's suffering, turned into the celebration of one's own suffering and the negation of the suffering of one's fellow man. The hope of bringing together "the family of man" led to an even worse rupture between its members. The "tyranny of memory" ended up in a process of dehumanization of those considered to be the enemy.

The Holocaust vs. the holocausts

The Holocaust was at the center of the semantic and ideological war that was played out in Durban. As discussed in Chapter 1, since the 1990s the Holocaust had become the symbol in the West of suffering; it was the metaphor of the twentieth century and Auschwitz was the symbol of the annihilation of humanity. The rivalry for power between North America and Europe included the rivalry in the ranking of victimhood. Ideologically, to the Arab contingent and a number of African countries versus a Jewish world assimilated to the West, it represented imposing the slave trade and colonialism as Number One in martyrdom for which Europe and the United States bore the greatest responsibility. A convergence of interests appeared between the Arab-Islamic/African countries and NGOs against Israel. This alliance implied that the Africans and African Americans denounced the trans-Atlantic slave trade rather than that organized by the Arab traders in Central and East Africa and assimilated Zionism to apartheid. Among others, this was the weapon of choice of the Free Palestine Campaign and Islamicforum, NGOs whose rhetoric illustrated this will to "Nazify" the Jewish state:

> Apartheid lives on in the land of Zionism. The facts speak for themselves. The Palestinian children are armed with slingshots and stones. The Israeli soldiers are armed with guns and tanks. . . . This is not an anti-terrorist struggle. Neither is it a war. This is a genocide. The children of the victims of the Holocaust are now perpetrating that same heinous crime on another people. The world can no longer stand aside. The World Stopped Nazism! The World stopped Apartheid! The World must stop Zionism![27]

A complex dynamic was set up. In the 1990s the commemoration that for a half-century had been linked to the liberation of the Nazi death camps, the process of commemoration begun in many countries, the public apologies for the abandonment of European Jewry, and the demands for reparation opened by American Jewish organizations reopened the symbolic wounds of other communities that considered themselves victims as well and who felt excluded from the new hierarchy of victimization—in particular, the crime of the trans-Atlantic slave trade that had remained without voice or reparation on a scale worthy of this abomination.

As the Senegalese professor Dialo Diop pointed out, for the representatives of a number of African and African American NGOs, Durban was key to the recognition of this crime. In their opinion, "the Holocaust in Europe" was only one expression of "white savagery" among "other holocausts such as the slave trade, slavery and colonialism in Africa," which were of a much larger scale, "both in time, space and the number of victims."[28] The legal argument of non-retroactivity invoked by Western governments was merely a decoy, because the tribunals of Nuremberg and Tokyo applied judicial concepts retroactively and Israel benefited from reparations for acts that were committed even before its existence.[29] These demands for compensation were reactivated by the "Swiss precedent"; in 1998, after intense controversy, the major Swiss banks signed an agreement with the most important American Jewish organizations to turn over $1.25 billion in Swiss bank accounts that were opened by Jews before their assassination by the Nazis and whose assets had never been returned to their heirs.[30]

The debate took place against the background of the Intifada, and the scenes of Israeli repression in the Palestinian territories appeared to the eyes of many NGOs as the modern embodiment of the injustice of North-South relations. To aim at Israel, then, was also to hit by ricochet the all-powerful United States, which provided Israel military and diplomatic support through its Security Council right to veto. In addition, at a political level, Zionism was perceived by many Africans—in particular, South Africans—as a form of apartheid. This reading goes back to the former ties between the ANC and the Palestinian Liberation Organization (PLO). Due to this heritage of the ANC's years of struggle, the South African government, as host country of the conference, could not play the role of broker in this crisis, for it shared the views of a majority of the NGOs and Arab and African States.

The NGOs of the Arab-Islamic world thus used the meeting in Durban to denounce the Zionist enemy. They put on an equal footing the "Jewish holocaust" and the "Palestinian holocaust perpetrated by the Zionists"[31] and used the vocabulary of the Jewish organizations against Israel, evoking, for example, the "anti-Semitism perpetrated by the Zionists." How better to discredit the justifying discourse of the Jewish state than by comparing the Nazi genocide of the Jews with the suffering of the Palestinians under the Israelis? Hence, the Arab-Islamic NGOs and delegations were determined to write "holocausts" with a small "h" and in plural form in the Final Declaration of Durban. This banalization spilled over into the revisionist current that sought to chase the Jew from the pantheon of suffering and to depict him as a perpetrator of genocide.

Against this portrayal of the Israeli as a usurping colonial on Palestinian land, the marginalized Jewish NGOs attempted to counteract by portraying the Jews as victims of history and Zionism as an appropriate response to the Nazis' attempted annihilation of them. This confrontation had an ideological stake, as noted by Pascal Bruckner: "Making a claim for crimes against humanity is a way of saying: 'Don't judge me!' It is taking up residence in the most impregnable spot, that of the wretched of the earth."[32] In the Nakbah versus Shoah dispute, the partisans of the former overwhelmed by sheer numbers. The condemnation of Israel also focused attention elsewhere rather than on issues that might have been embarrassing for a number of Arab governments—for example, the massive violation of human rights in their territories, including the continuation of slavery, as well as their religious discrimination against minorities.

In their final declaration of 2 September, the NGOs accused Israel of being "a racist state guilty of perpetrating acts of genocide, war crimes and practices of ethnic cleansing" and called for "the establishment of a war crimes tribunal." The Final Declaration of the Forum of NGOs affirmed that Zionism was "a racist doctrine that seeks to promote the racial domination of one group by another" and demanded the isolation of the Jewish state.[33] Thus, the Final Declaration emphasized in Article 159: "We declare and call for an immediate end to the Israeli systematic perpetration of racist crimes including war crimes, acts of genocide and ethnic cleansing."[34] The NGO Action Plan is equally radical: Article 119 called for "the establishment of a war crimes tribunal to investigate and bring to justice those who may be guilty of war crimes, acts of genocide and ethnic cleansing and the crime of Apartheid which amount to crimes against humanity that have been or continue to be perpetrated in Israel and the Occupied Palestinian Territories."[35]

In exchange for their support of the Palestinian cause, the African and

African American NGOs obtained recognition that the trans-Atlantic slave trade—but not the Arab-conducted East African trade—was "a unique tragedy in the history of humanity" that justified compensation on an appropriate scale, as affirmed by Article 64 of the Final Declaration and Articles 59 and 63 of the NGO Action Plan:

> We affirm that the Trans-Atlantic Slave Trade and the enslavement of Africans and African Descendants was a crime against humanity and a unique tragedy in the history of humanity, and that its roots and bases were economic, institutional, systemic and transnational in dimension.
>
> Monetary compensation [for] the victims, including Africa, Africans and African descendants, by closing the economic gap created by these crimes [should encompass] debt cancellation, programs for creation and enhancement of participation in production enterprises, full accessibility and affirmative inclusion in all levels of employment opportunity, [and] grants of cash payments based on assessment of losses resulting from the violations of human rights and crimes against humanity.[36]

The major international NGOs and those of Eastern Europe distanced themselves from the declaration and were maligned for this by the African and Arab organizations. Before the Final Declaration had even been drafted, there were serious excesses. Anti-Semitic caricatures circulated at the NGO forum, and there were attempts to intimidate the Jewish NGOs. As a result of the Declaration, the division between the Western European NGOs over the question of Zionism was such that it fractured the NGOs' relationships in the worst imaginable manner—along racial lines. Some members decided to break off and create a European Black Caucus, accusing "white professionals of being in the pay of their bosses—in particular, the European Union—and not linked to the interests of black and African victims."[37] Besides being pathetic, this tearing apart of the European NGOs revealed the powerful stakes involved in commemoration which were at play in Durban. It also shows that the United Nations' goal to write a global history of cruelty so as to recompose "the family of man" was an illusion. The conflicts of the present were also structured by identities and exclusive memories, as the intergovernmental conference would confirm.

The Intergovernmental Conference: The Escalation

Denunciation of the Jewish State

The United Nations was correct in thinking that the NGO conference would serve as an inspiration for the intergovernmental conference, but not in the way it had imagined. Following the NGO declaration, the rhetoric against Israel caught fire. The radical condemnation of Israel in the NGOs' Final Declaration gave additional legitimacy to the efforts of Arab-Islamic governments—from the Iraq of Saddam Hussein to the Egypt of Hosni Mubarak—to harden their positions. Symptomatic of this hardening was the Arab governments' abandonment of their promise to Mary Robinson not to assimilate Zionism to racism. For the Arab-Islamic governments, the antiracist conference was from then on but a tribunal.

Abdelouahed Belkeziz, the secretary-general of the Organization of the Islamic Conference (OCI), protested from the height of the tribune, "the racist policies of Israeli politicians that are based on cynicism, pretended racial superiority and the idea of the Chosen People."[38] The Lebanese representative denounced "the holocaust whose victims are the Palestinians since the year 2000." Among other speakers, Yasser Arafat saw in the policies of the Jewish state a "colonial conspiracy":

> This is a colonial conspiracy of aggression, forced eviction, usurpation of land and violation of sacred Christian and Muslim sites in Jerusalem, El-Shareif, Bethlehem. . . . This brutality and arrogance stems from the mentality of superiority practiced in racial discrimination and based on the principle of ethnic cleansing and deportation and offers its protection to daily aggression of colonials against our people. . . . The condemnation of Israeli occupation, of its racist practices and laws based on racism and superiority are today the imperative demand of our people.[39]

The outrageousness of the attacks against Israel paradoxically served the purposes of the Sharon and Bush governments. The ranting rhetoric, the excesses, and the anti-Semitic caricatures that circulated in the NGO forum under the impetus of certain Arab organizations discredited their authors and encouraged the hostility of the Israeli authorities and Bush Administration toward the United Nations. After having consulted with their respective capitals, the representatives of the United States and Israel left the conference on 3 September. Before leaving Durban, Israeli ambassador Mordechai Yeid denounced the hidden anti-Semitism of the conference and the "hatred of the Jew that, under cover of anti-Zionism, has emerged out of this conference." He accentuated the Israeli position on the Jewish martyrdom and the uniqueness of the Shoah.[40] Paradoxically, the confrontation around Israel brought the two camps to the same argument: the double standards applied to Israel. From the Arab point of view, the Zionist enemy was guaranteed impunity, protected from any condemnation by the American Security Council veto. From the Israeli perspective, the Jewish state was the only country in the world to be stigmatized: "It is regrettable that a conference against discrimination itself should fall into the trap of discriminating against one State alone, Israel, while all other situations are ignored. . . . Neither the Talibans who discriminate against Hindus, nor the Sudanese in whose country slavery still exists, neither Chinese repression of the Tibetans, nor the Saudis whose women have an inferior statute, have been mentioned even once," said Tom Lantos.[41]

The American withdrawal from the conference on the question of Zionism allowed the Bush Administration to avoid addressing the issue of compensation for slavery.[42] Given the size of the black community in the United States, its electoral weight, and the importance of the Black Caucus in South Africa, the issue was very delicate. It had been calculated that if every African American was compensated $50,000 as reparations for slavery, the total amount of compensation would amount to $500 billion. A demand of $300 billion had already been filed and rejected by the Bush Administration. Michael Southwick, a high official of the U.S. delegation, acknowledged that "the question of compensation is a non-starter," explaining that "his country" had lost more than six hundred thousand men during the Civil War to put an end to slavery, more than all the Americans killed in all the wars that followed.[43] In other words, the United States had paid in blood and had, in addition, put in place policies of "affirmative action," that is, positive discrimination. Here as well, the shock of memory, including that of the representatives of the Black Caucus and the Bush Administration, yielded no compromise. No doubt, the U.S. government that had sent Secretary of State Colin Powell, a descendant of slaves, to Durban as a symbol of the vitality of the American democracy was relieved to avoid the confrontation on the issue of compensation that would have set it against not only the African nations but also a part of its own (voting) public opinion.

Slavery and Colonialism: Demands for Compensation

The radicalization of positions on the Middle East during the NGO meeting led to a hardening at the intergovernmental conference, which, in turn, brought stalemate on the issue of compensation. From a political point of view, the two issues profoundly overlapped; the organization of the ranking of victimization was at heart.

The African countries were not unanimous in their positions. A majority led by Zambia and Namibia took the hard line, in part to satisfy the anger of their people toward the West but also due to more political reasons. It was an opportunity to shift the blame for the failure of development policies after independence onto the rich nations.[44] Zimbabwe's President Mugabe, who indulged in anti-white and anti-Semitic declarations during the conference, was particularly intransigent, attempting to provide a diversion to a society whose standard of living had plunged abysmally over the past few years. The conference's focus on the issue of slavery and Zionism allowed him to silence internal problems, including those of contemporary forms of slavery and discriminatory practices, notably toward women in Muslim societies. Thus, with remarkable aplomb, the Sudanese minister of justice, Ali Mohamed Osman Yasin, demanded compensation for slavery, although his country was one of the few places in the world where the slave trade was ongoing: "We must learn from the past and, notably, from the slave trade which constituted the denial of human dignity and which allowed the rich world to develop. Today, this phenomenon continues in the phenomenon of globalization, unjust and unequal. We consider that those responsible for the slave trade and colonialism must assume their responsibility by paying compensation."[45]

In the background, the radical African countries advanced three arguments to support the demand for compensation. First, they called for equal treatment with other victims of crimes against humanity and, in particular, Jewish victims.[46] Second, they insisted that Africa's misery was the result of the exploitation of its people and resources.[47] Finally, in a *tiers-mondiste* vein, they interpreted slavery as a metaphor of lingering injustice in North-South relations. This argument was presented forcefully by the Ivory Coast's minister of justice and public liberty, Oulai Siene:

> If you think that slavery has disappeared, think again. How else can one understand the fact that the price of a product made during long months of hard

labour, in sun and rain, by millions of peasants, is determined by someone sitting on a chair behind a computer in a cold office, without taking into account their suffering. Only methods have changed. They have become more 'humane.' The blacks are no longer loaded onto boats for the Antilles and America, they must stay at home to till the soil, to sweat blood and water to see the price of their labour fixed in London, Paris, or New York. The slavers did not die, they became speculators.[48]

Several African leaders disagreed with this line of thinking. They felt that nothing could be won through political confrontation with the West, with whom it would be better to deal after the conference. They also pointed out African responsibility for slavery and noted the risk that financial compensation—if, hypothetically, it should come—would poison relations between Africans of the continent and the descendants of slaves. Thus, the president of Senegal, Abdoulaye Wade, pointed out that he himself came from a family that owned slaves and declared: "We continue to suffer today the effects of slavery and the effects of colonialism and we cannot evaluate these effects in monetary terms. I find it not only absurd but also insulting to demand material compensation for the death of millions of people."[49]

Ugandan president Yoweri Kaguta Museveni emphasized the role divisions and collusion among Africans themselves played in the slave trade: "While we are condemning White and Arab greed and cruelty, we must also condemn the greed and myopia of African chiefs who used to wage war on one another, capturing persons from this rival tribe and selling them to the Whites or the Arabs."[50]

President Obasanjo of Nigeria feared that financial compensation would deteriorate relations between Africans and the descendants of slaves: "The issue of compensation is not a rational option for it risks worsening relations between the Africans of the continent and those of the diaspora who have suffered slavery."[51] The president of Nigeria might have added that the tensions between certain African tribes went back to the time of collaboration with the slavers. Historian Nadja Vuckovic notes that the "Yoruba have never forgiven the kings of the Fon ethnic group for their complicity in slavery. So, who should be compensated, when the practice of slavery continues today in some African countries?"[52] As a way out of this potentially burning debate, the presidents of Senegal, Cape Verde, Nigeria, and Uganda pronounced themselves in favor of a development plan for Africa that President Abdoulaye Wade called "the new African initiative."[53]

But this proposition was swept aside by a majority of the African governments who positioned themselves as victims of a wicked international order. At the bottom of the dispute was the nature of the relations between the West and Africa: in the moralistic and Manichean vocabulary of the 1990s, of which Durban was the ultimate expression, who was civilized and who was the savage? A few years later, in 2005, discussion about the provocative French commemorative law "on the positive aspects of colonialism" would revive the banked coals of this polemic. In that discussion, in which historians and anthropologists were totally missing and politicians and NGOs alone occupied the field, the African governments accused the West of having built its wealth on a policy of concentration camps and economic exploitation of tens of millions of men, women, and children. They considered slavery and colonialism to be not peripheral phenomena to Western culture but, on the contrary, essential components.[54] Thus, Francisco Proaño Arandi, the representative from Ecuador, passed on African criticism and invited "from today, the West to seize the opportunity of re-humanizing itself. The West must recognize its responsibility for slavery, colonialism, the pillage of resources" and make "just compensation."[55] For Western governments, who were triumphant from the end of the Cold War, to be invited to "re-humanize themselves" by governments often far from democratic—the majority of whom had failing institutions and who found themselves, in addition, on the edge of bankruptcy—the proposition was absurd.

In his opening speech on 1 September, UN Secretary-General Kofi Annan anticipated the African-Western clash and attempted to promote the idea of voluntary reparations, noting that "the further those events recede into the past, the harder it becomes to trace lines of accountability" for "the exploitation and extermination of indigenous peoples by colonial Powers, or the treatment of millions of human beings as mere merchandise." Annan reminded Africans that "tracing a connection with past crimes may not always be the most constructive way to redress present inequalities, in material terms." He also reminded the ex-colonial and slave-trading powers that "the effects remain; the pain and anger are still felt; the dead, through their descendants, cry out for justice" and that "man does not live by bread alone."[56] But in this conflict concerning memory, identity, and politics, the UN secretary-general went unheard.

The representative from Zambia, who presided over the African Union, refused Annan's proposal as unacceptable charity. In the name of the African contingent, he demanded that there be set up "an international mechanism to compensate the victims of the slave trade and a compensation fund for development that will provide additional resources destined to the development of countries affected by colonialism."[57]

Against financial claims judged by a European diplomat as "unreasonable, bordering on psychotic,"[58] the EU countries took a common position. They considered Africa's current poverty to be the result of a number of causes, including ill-adapted development policies put in place since independence and the effects of corruption. They would be willing, within strict limits, to make a symbolic gesture of repentance for the crimes of slavery and colonialism, but they refused to put themselves on trial. Their primary objective was to deadbolt any formula that could open the door to future legal actions seeking compensation for crimes committed during the colonial era, which was why they resisted the idea of recognizing slavery as a crime against humanity.

The fifteen nations of the EU established three lines of defense. The most important was purely juridical: the slave trade and colonialism were perfectly legal at the time they were practiced. Hence, there was no reason that these policies should be subject to compensation, because the retroactive use of juridical concepts was (and still is) not legal.[59] They were reticent to "apologize" for the slave trade and, even more so, for colonialism. This strict legalism was London's main argument and was supported by the Netherlands, Spain, and Portugal. Only France took a separate, if incoherent, position: in May 2000 the French parliament recognized the trans-Atlantic slave trade as well as the Indian Ocean trade, carried out from the fifteenth century against African, Amerindian, Madagascan, and Indian peoples, as a "crime against humanity" and, thus, imprescriptible, but, nevertheless, excluded the idea of "compensation." As for colonialism, in contrast to slavery, the European countries stood well back from criminalizing its nature. Thus, French minister Charles Josselin, delegate to the International Organization of la Francophonie, insisted that "it is not a question of reducing colonialism to its excesses and to systematic harm on human dignity, but of having the courage to accept certain evidence. Yes, colonialism had lasting effects on the political and economic structure of countries concerned."[60]

The second line of defense, as Charles Josselin notes, was "to remember that the practice of slavery has existed from time immemorial . . . , used by all civilizations." Why, then, were the European countries singled out for a practice that was universal?

The third line of defense concerned the break in the temporal link with the victims of the slave trade. This break emerged from a series of interrogations: how, for example, to sort out responsibility for the desperate condition of the Republic of the Congo between the legacy of slavery, colonialism, and the responsibility of dictators Mobutu and Laurent-Désiré Kabila? Who were the heirs for crimes committed more than a century ago? Could states that had so little respect for human rights be the representatives of the martyrs of African slaves? How far back in time should a demand for compensation be allowed? To the Inquisition? The Crusades? Antiquity? And if colonialized peoples were to be compensated, why not the descendants of the children of Manchester, Liverpool, and elsewhere, who were the factory slaves of the Industrial Revolution?

Faced with the certain failure of the conference, the EU countries, in the minority on the issues of Zionism and compensation and unwilling to be put on the defensive, also threatened to leave the conference before its end.[61] Mary Robinson's goal to set standards was forgotten in the clash between collective memories and identities. The departure of the Europeans (which, no doubt, would be imitated by such countries as Canada, Switzerland, Australia, and so on) on the heels of the Americans would transform this international conference into a simple meeting of southern countries. This setback would cost South Africa politically at a time when it was trying to emerge as an African power and a player on the international scene. Driven by these objectives, the South Africans proposed a compromise text at the last minute. All "anti-Zionist" references were erased and slavery was held to be a "crime against humanity which should have always been recognized as such." This convoluted formula satisfied the Africans and the EU. The first group wished to believe that it opened the door to compensation before the courts; the second was convinced that it closed any such door completely. To ensure that the latter interpretation prevailed, Canada demanded to include a reservation underlining that "a crime against humanity cannot be punished if it was not considered as such at the time it was committed" (and was met by loud disapproval from the crowd). The Europeans neither presented "apologies" nor offered "compensation." They limited themselves to recognizing that "mistakes" were committed in the time of "slavery and colonization, promising economic aid to Africa—while keeping well away from any hard figures."

The great global antiracist charter to which Mary Robinson aspired did not come about, nor did new standards emerge. The United Nations had hoped that managing crimes of the past through the mechanisms of transitional justice would be possible, but the base for a minimal political compromise was not there: irreconcilable collective memories were awakened. The Western countries judged that they would win nothing by entering the apology process. With power in their favor, they would be the artisans of the juridical status quo.

The conference showed the impossibility of finding an authoritative voice able to create a common culture among some two hundred states present and thousands of NGOs. The failure showed that the weight of the world's ethnic identities, values, and representations was such that it prevented any elaboration of a universal account of a mass crime. As the extermination of the Jews shaped the West's relationship to evil, slavery and colonialism played this role in Africa and the colonization of the Arab world.

To this different relationship with evil in history was added the radical criticism of the West formulated by the Arab-African world and taken up by the African group, a criticism of the West spoken in the West's own language and used against it—in particular, the semantic confrontation of "Holocaust" vs. "holocausts." It was also the recognition of crimes against humanity. There was an understandable but painful irony for the Jewish state and the United States, but also for the rest of the Western world, that their own moral and legal vocabulary had now become a weapon pointed against them.

This conference was testimony to the fact that transitional justice, as the United Nations intended, could not be removed from politics—at least, to combat racism. On the contrary, Durban showed that there was no "outside," no objective place from which to look down, that would allow the foundation of a culture common to humanity. It was with radically different perceptions and profound divisions that this "inside history" was expressed.

The conference brought about an unusual political evolution: beginning with the ambition to elaborate a universal project, in the end it fed the idea of the clash of civilizations. In the view shared by many African states and

NGOs, Pierre Sané, under-secretary-general of UNESCO, saw in the Durban Conference the lingering blindness of the West toward its own crimes:

> To the demand for justice, they oppose the limits of contemporary law; to the demand for recognition of the gravity of the acts perpetrated and dignity insulted, they oppose the arrogance of conditional apology and circumstantial remorse. To the demand for recognition of the unique character of the crime, to the fact of its duration (four centuries), to its immensity (tens of millions of human beings deported) and to its effects (structural racism, exclusion), they oppose an attempt to banalize the crime as an unfortunate incident of history. To the demand for compensation to relieve the consequences of this tragedy, they oppose the contempt of money logic.[62]

This radically different reading of the conference in Europe and the United States placed the accent on the politicization of the meeting, which led to weakening of the United Nations, an aggravation of the conflict in the Middle East, and—ironically—to the use of antiracism for racist ends. Thus, according to Richard Holbrooke, who as assistant secretary of state was formerly responsible for U.S. foreign policy, the conference was an operation of political recovery by the non-aligned nations that destroyed the credibility of the United Nations at the risk of provoking new violence in the Middle East: "The non-aligned have taken control of Durban and transformed it into travesty. This is a tragedy, for it will push back the prospects for peace in the Middle East and it will be damaging to the United Nations."[63]

The French historian Pierre-André Taguieff denounces the conference's perversion of the antiracist fight to attain racist ends: "In Durban, a symbolic pogrom was achieved; in Durban, the Jews were put metaphorically to death in the name of antiracism and tolerance."[64]

However, the Durban Conference did have a certain merit: by its radical nature, it brought into the international public domain the issue of compensation for slavery and colonialism. It formalized soon-to-arise debates in several countries on the treatment of past crimes. In particular in France, debate arose around the law on the positive aspects of colonialism, adopted on 23 February 2005, which was then abrogated due to the turmoil it provoked. This liberation of the victimization discourse, in the context of multicultural societies and in a world where compensation was seen as one's due, could not be, without risk, muzzled. No doubt, lawyer Louis Salas-Molins is right in saying that the erasure of the debt toward nations historically victimized resolves little without a veritable social debate. He calls on the effort of partisans and opponents of compensation to make their cases, by articulating, on one side, "not the inestimable value of interrupted lives, but the hours and days and years, the decades and centuries of slavery, all quantifiable," and on the other side, "the reasons for opposing compensation" (for example, African collaboration, inter-African slavery, the trans-Saharan slave trade operated by the Arab world, and so on).[65] Perhaps, in a time of international tribunals and the multiplication of compensation lawsuits, this debate will lead to a way out of the clash of exclusive memories of which Durban was the expression.

Durban revealed a profound clash of memories. How, indeed, would countries allay the fears that, in the name of antiracism, people would close themselves off along ethnic or community lines, at the risk of fragmenting even more the idea of a common humanity? How would the world escape the worry at this drift that transformed a legitimate demand for truth about the crimes of the past into a tribunal of history where one could be only victim or executioner? Having been kicked out the door, the idea of collective guilt had come furtively back through the window.

The United Nations hoped to turn the page of a bloody century by hosting a conference where each country would begin to examine its own conscience. Instead, it raised the curtain on an era heavy with challenges, marked by global inequality, societies increasingly dismantled, and the clash of collective memories. Durban does not signify rebellion, however, but desperation. The significance of the meeting continues to resonate with the profound frustration with the West, which has been held responsible for the injustice in the world order and the impossibility of founding a common culture for humanity.

In the perspective of restorative justice, the legacy of the Durban Conference is, to say the least, complex. Coming just before the attacks on September 11, the memory of it now merges with a date that itself signifies a break in international relations. The violence of the clash of collective memory, added to the attacks on September 11, mark the end of global enthusiasm for transitional justice interpreted as a hope for the international community's ethical progress and a "dialogue of civilizations." It was the end of what anthropologist Véronique Nahoum-Grappe calls "the poignant dream of justice that drills into the collective imagination."[66] Begun in 1989, this dream of justice lasted 12 years before September 11 and the Bush Administration's "War on Terror" shifted the priority to national security to the detriment of international justice, law, and multilateralism.

If the hope carried by transitional justice disappeared, at least temporarily, as an ideology to transform the world, its institutions, norms, and practices continued to develop in different countries. More than ever, they would become part of a quasi-automatic response of states and even the international community to attempt to put right specific situations.

Chapter 4

Morocco

The Globalization of Truth and Reconciliation Commissions

THE CREATION IN Morocco in January 2004 of the Arab-Islamic world's first and, to this day, only Truth and Reconciliation Commission (TRC) marked the success of its globalization. It now seemed clear that transitional justice, if it was to be used at all, would be exported, transformed, and manipulated by local actors, according to the local political and historic equation and priorities. The Equity and Reconciliation Commission (ERC)—as the Moroccan TRC was known—demonstrated this appropriation process, in particular, through the features that distinguished it from the thirty other TRCs created earlier in Latin America, Africa, and Asia:

- Unlike almost all other TRCs, the ERC came into being not during a period of political and institutional change, but in the institutional and political continuity of monarchic power.
- The ERC's creation was not the outcome of a political process, as in almost all other cases, but a decision by the king, by virtue of prerogatives given to him under the Moroccan Constitution. The ERC was based on an alliance between the king and certain personalities from the NGO world.
- The ERC functioned in the context of the rise in power of political Islam in Morocco and the so-called War on Terror launched by the Bush Administration in reaction to the attacks on September 11. Morocco became one of the battlefields of the War on Terror after the attacks on 16 May 2003 in Casablanca (45 dead) and Madrid in March 2004 (200 dead, 1,000 wounded) that were carried out by Moroccan nationals.

- The ERC presented itself as an example of "reconciliation and rehabilitation of the victims of human rights violations for other Arab-Muslim and African societies."[1]

These four features have added new problems to the political, strategic, and symbolic stakes in TRCs by raising three challenges:

1. How should a society of Arab-Muslim culture approach the issue of forgiveness in the framework of restorative justice? Until now, Christian and/or African societies alone had experimented with truth commissions, legitimizing the absence of penal punishment in the name of religion (that is, Christian forgiveness) and/or culture (that is, *ubuntu*). What, then, was the cultural dimension in setting up a TRC? And, if this was significant, did the Moroccan model apply to other societies with a strong Muslim component? (For example, Afghanistan, Bosnia-Herzegovina, and Lebanon had all envisioned or were still considering creating TRCs.)
2. How did a truth commission fit into the context of an anti-terrorist war? Some high Moroccan officials believed that the ERC would participate in the battle by rallying hearts and minds of the people, that it would be part of the "soft war" arsenal in the confrontation with radical Islamists. To what degree did this "soft war" really prove effective?
3. Can a truth commission do its work effectively when no institutional or political break has been made? The given objective of the Palace and commissioners of the ERC was to "consolidate the democratization process" by shining light on the "errors of the past." To what degree did the ERC contribute to refounding Moroccan identity and act as an effective catalyst for democratization? Or, did it instead serve as a political marketing tool to legitimize the new king, co-opt a segment of civil society by sterilizing the political field, and seduce the West with talk of human rights?

Context: The Progressive Process of Liberalization

After forty-four years as a French protectorate, Morocco achieved independence in 1956 under the reign of King Mohammed V. In 1961, Hassan II succeeded to the throne and directed the kingdom with an iron fist until his death in 1999. Hassan is considered the father of modern Morocco. His reign covered two distinct periods: "the years of lead," from the beginning of the 1960s to the end of the Cold War in 1989, and then a period encompassing the slow process of liberalization. The term "years of lead" is a cautious reference to the often harsh repression (the ERC puts the number of torture victims at ten thousand and the dead in the hundreds) of opponents and all those considered to be enemies. After decades of repression, under strong international pressure,[2] in early the 1990s, Hassan II launched the slow process of democratic transition. The new international climate explained this: the Cold War was over, the Soviet Union was in the process of being dismantled, and the far left Moroccan movement, flattened by repression and out of ideological steam, was no longer considered to be a threat to the regime. The majority of its members had long since given up on armed struggle to overthrow the monarchy; many of those who had been hard-core members in the 1960s and 1970s had moved to the center left.

Elements of the liberalization process included the creation of the Consultative Committee of Human Rights (CCDH) in 1990; the ratification of the UN Convention Against Torture and Other Cruel, Inhuman or Degrading Treatment or Punishment in 1993; a succession of amnesties, including in 1994 the amnesty of prisoners who had "disappeared" nineteen years earlier into the secret prisons; the setting up of the government led by socialist Abderrahmane Youssoufi in 1998; and the approval given one month before the king's death in 1999 to the creation of an arbitration commission to award compensation to some five thousand ex–political prisoners.

After his father's death in July 1999, Mohammed VI took the throne. He accelerated the political liberalization process. During his speech on 20 August, the new king recognized state responsibility for the "disappearance" of opponents carried out by the Moroccan Secret Service, something his father had never done. He immediately pushed aside the powerful minister of the interior, Driss Basri, the personification of political repression under Hassan II. In 2002 the king allowed the organization of legislative elections, the freest that the country had ever known. The new king authorized the return of political exiles, liberalized the media, reformed the penal code in 2003, and firmly committed in 2004 to the adoption of a personal code (the *moudawana*) guaranteeing the equality of men and women. However, this process of reform was accomplished without any institutional or political break with the Hassanian reign: Morocco remained an executive monarchy where power was concentrated in the sovereign's hands. It was in the context of this carefully managed liberalization that King Mohammed VI launched the ERC.

The reforms, of which the ERC was a strong component, were a strategic decision. They represented the Palace's much-vaunted ambition to create a new social pact between Moroccans and their institutions, opening files linked to decades of repression, bringing the nation together again behind the image of a youthful and modern monarchy, and projecting the image abroad of a dynamic and democratic Morocco. In taking this strategy, the Palace was trying to undercut the rising power of Islamic movements and respond to a triple challenge: the failure of ideologies of progress and development; a profound social and economic crisis; and a regional and international environment that was increasingly unstable.

The Islamists are a diverse group, but they do have one thing in common: they represent today the only alternative social project in Morocco to the current system. As such, they are able to capitalize on the frustrations of the population hit by a severe social crisis: long-term unemployment for young people, including university graduates; absolute poverty for more than 20 percent of the population who survive on less than a dollar a day; a record level of illiteracy (57 percent), and so on. The Islamists' ability to mobilize increased as the Israeli-Palestinian conflict and the United States' "War on Terror" and intervention in Iraq fed anti-West resentment. In the elections of 2002, the Islamists of the Justice and Democracy Party (PJD) became the country's third political group. If the PJD had not limited the number of its candidates, fearing an "Algeria scenario,"[3] its win would have been still more significant. The PJD was itself in competition with the Justice and Charity Movement (which was not recognized as a political party), led by Sheik Yassine, who did not hide his criticism of the monarchy. In 2000, Yassine published an open letter in which he called on the new king to "redeem your father from torment by restoring to the people the goods they are entitled to"—in other words, give the royal fortune (which, according to Yassine, was equivalent to the kingdom's foreign debt) back to the people.[4] Meanwhile, the radical Salafist networks carried out attacks in Casablanca on 16 May 2003 (forty-five dead, including twelve of the perpetrators). Cells composed of Moroccans close to Al-Qaeda hit in Madrid on 11 March 2004 (two hundred dead, a thousand wounded). According to Saudi authorities, most Al-Qaeda suicide attacks had been committed by Moroccan nationals, an allegation that worried both the monarchy and Western governments.[5]

The Mandate of the Truth Commission

The ERC was created in a particular context that would structure and influence its entire work and give it an ambiguous character from which it would never be free. Political parties played no significant role in setting up the ERC in Morocco. The ERC was an alliance between the throne and elements of civil society. Its momentum came from former political prisoners who placed their bets on a Moroccan *glasnost*. They believed in reform from the inside of the system and, to achieve this, wished to use a truth commission as a lever for democratic change.

On 7 January 2004, King Mohammed VI announced the creation of the ERC.[6] Its creation raised real hope within Moroccan society: within a few months, more than twenty thousand victims opened files to obtain information on the "disappeared" and to obtain compensation for torture endured over decades of repression. Moroccan authorities presented the truth commission as proof of their commitment to the process of liberalization. They also presented it as a model of democratization and reform in a region where impunity and autocratic regimes had been the norm.

The king gave a triple mandate to the ERC: "shed light on all cases of forced disappearance and arbitrary detention" and "compensate" and "seek to redress all damages suffered by the victims." In addition, the ERC was mandated to "establish a report . . . analyzing the violations of human rights . . . as well as recommendations and propositions to preserve memory, guarantee the definitive break with practices of the past and resolve the consequences of suffering caused to victims, to reestablish and reinforce confidence in a State of law and respect for human rights."[7] The ERC's mandate covered the longest period ever investigated by a truth commission: forty-three years, beginning with the country's independence in 1956 and ending in 1999, with the death of King Hassan II and the creation of the commission for independent arbitrage to compensate the victims of "disappearance" and torture.[8]

The Dynamics of Civil Society: The Historic Deal

The idea of a truth commission for Morocco took hold in the Truth and Justice Forum launched in 1999 by the country's first president, Driss Benzekri. This platform brought together people of different ideology and political stripe who shared one thing: they had all been victims of the policy of repression under Hassan II. The dynamic set in motion by the Forum gave birth to the ERC. Influenced by the Chilean, Argentine, and South African precedents, the Forum called for truth and justice "in the name of the struggle against impunity." In June 2000, Driss Benzekri called for the establishment of a commission of inquiry with wide powers of injunction to clarify the past and to obtain, toward this end, the necessary documents and testimony. In the same breath the Forum recommended the idea of a truth commission, accompanied by the return of the bodies of the "disappeared"; compensation; and free access to health care for the victims of torture, as well as the dismantling of the special police (the DST, Defense and Surveillance of the Territory, and the DGED, General Direction of Studies and Documentation), or, at least, that these bodies be placed under parliamentary control.

The king's counselors entered into negotiations on the formation of a truth commission. At the end of these discreet discussions in 2002, the movement of Driss Benzekri joined the state organization CCDH, of which Benzekri became president. In the framework of a future truth commission, this group of former prisoners agreed to give up the idea of criminal prosecution on one condition: that the king firmly commit himself to democratization. It was a "historic bargain" proposed by former prisoners, as one of them, Salah El-Ouadie, notes:

> The historic bargain that we were proposing was that the State must recognize its wrongs, commit itself to a profound process of reform with constitutional guarantees to avoid any risk of repetition, and promote a real culture of human rights by setting up a democracy worthy of the name. In exchange, we would renounce prosecution. It was a strategic pardon, in effect. I do not believe in *lex talionis* because, as Desmond Tutu says, with an eye for an eye and a tooth for a tooth, everybody ends up blind and toothless.[9]

The idea to renounce any judicial prosecution had already been raised. El-Ouadie, one of the founders of the Forum, wrote "like an outcry"[10] the "Open Letter to My Torturer," which was published on 16 April 1999 in two Moroccan newspapers, the French-language *Libération* and the Arabic *Al Ittihad Al Ichtiraki*. In his open letter, El-Ouadie wrote that he was ready to take the hand of his torturer if he recognized his crimes: "I ask you yourself, your superiors, your protectors and partners and those who have covered for you, to demand public forgiveness of your victims, to resign the positions that you have used to trample the law and despise human dignity. When you have done that, you will find me at your door ready to give you my hand . . . to help you to regain your humanity."[11]

But contrary to the proposition contained in Salah El-Ouadie's open letter, the torturers would not be called to "recognize their crimes." The authorities imposed their own demands on these militants for human rights:

the ERC could not mention either the names of those responsible for violations of human rights or the names of those who carried out their instructions. Salah would not take the hand of his torturer, for he would never even see him. The torturers and the givers of orders were to be sheltered, not only from criminal prosecution, but also from public opinion. With Palace-bestowed impunity, they were and remained at the heart of Moroccan society but untouchable.

By putting the internal security system off-limits, the authorities meant to ensure continued support and to ward off any unpleasant questions about the reign of Hassan II and, indirectly, the monarchy. Driss Basri, ex-strongman of the chérifien kingdom during the years of repression, had already warned that "to judge me is to judge Hassan II."[12] The narrow limits of the ERC's mandate limited the establishment of historical truth. The commission had no power of subpoena; the agents of the security service were able to set the degree to which they would cooperate with the ERC.[13] The symbol of this carefully controlled historical truth was the word *equity* in the commission's title: it reflected the idea of reparation, replacing the usual word, *truth*.

On 10 April 2004, the CCDH recommended the creation of the ERC. The final paragraph of the document determined quite clearly the limits of action to be enjoyed by the future commission: "The Commission's action is within the current framework of extra-judiciary regulations concerning the regulation of the files on past human rights violations. The Commission may not, in any case, after having made the necessary inquiry, invoke individual responsibilities whatsoever. It must abstain from taking any initiative of a nature to provoke disunion or rancor or to disseminate discord."[14]

A few days later in Agadir, the king gave the speech constituting the ERC. He emphasized the commission's compensatory dimension for victims but omitted any reference to establishing blame, even symbolic, on the part of those who had violated human rights: "We remain committed to the definitive closure of this affair (compensation of the victims of human rights violations) by supporting equitable non-judicial regulation and by ensuring that the damages of the past be compensated and the wounds healed. We will adopt, to this end, a global approach, bold and enlightened, based on equity, rehabilitation and reintegration, in addition to the will to draw the lessons imposed and to establish the facts."[15]

The mandate's limits are clear: the Moroccan commission would be nothing like the ERCs of Peru or South Africa. In Peru, the truth commission had transmitted some of its files to the examining judges, allowing them to charge dozens of perpetrators of crimes. In South Africa, hundreds of human rights violators had testified. In Morocco, there would be no face-to-face meetings between victims and torturers, nor, *a fortiori*, the slightest criminal prosecution. Only the institutions responsible would be made evident.

Divisions at the Heart of the Human Rights Movement

The principle of a truth commission was applauded by the human rights movement as a whole; in fact, it was one of the recommendations of the Truth and Justice Forum. However, the limits placed on the ERC's mandate were strongly criticized. The Moroccan Association of Human Rights (AMDH), composed of some of the former victims and human rights militants, and the Islamists, as well as an important part of the militants for Western Saharan independence denounced what they considered to be unacceptable impunity for the torturers and their bosses. They argued that, under the cover of transitional justice, the torturers and other cogs within the machine of repression would be, if not whitewashed, at least spared any sanction, with the benediction of hundreds of their former victims. For them, the road that led to the establishment of the democratic state could not economize with justice for crimes committed in the past. AMDH had published a "not-exhaustive list of 45 presumed torturers in Morocco," or "the names of some of those responsible for whom AMDH has presumption of their implication in the crimes of kidnapping, murder, arbitrary arrest and torture."[16] Some of these people, such as General Ben Slimane, head of the police and one of the former strongmen of the regime for decades, and General Hamidou Laanigri, general director of national security, kept their jobs even after the end of the ERC work.

The second criticism that some human rights militants raised against the ERC was the fact that violations were still occurring against, in particular, some three thousand Islamists arrested after the attacks in Casablanca; these arrests had been made under an anti-terrorist law adopted in the urgency and emotion in the aftermath of those attacks. The report by the American NGO Human Rights Watch emphasizes: "Many were held for days or weeks in secret detention, where the police subjected them to various forms of ill-treatment and in some cases to torture in order to extract confessions. The courts denied them their right to a fair hearing. They routinely refused defense motions to call witnesses, and refused to order medical examinations for those who claimed to have been tortured."[17]

These criticisms of the ERC made it obvious that, in spite of surface reforms, the system had not intrinsically changed. The institutions had evolved little; in addition, it was often the same men, in the same posts, who were carrying out the repression, and the forces of order continued to commit abuses. It was not enough for an enlightened monarch to have replaced an autocratic sovereign. According to these critics, Benzekri's group had fallen into the Palace's traditional trap: they were themselves becoming co-opted into the *makhzen*, the governing elite centered around the king. This would have a serious consequence: it would weaken one of the rare non-Islamist voices in the country, thereby contributing to the sterilization of the political field.

Of course, Benzekri's partisans disagreed completely. They pointed out the necessity of "strategic pardon," justifying it with two arguments: the first was the profound crisis in which Morocco, like the rest of the Arab world, found itself; the other emphasized the historic opportunity of having a modern sovereign for interlocutor.

On this first point, Driss el Yazami, one of the leaders of the ERC, recalled the dark assessment of the Arab world in the report by the United Nations Development Programme (UNDP): "The Arab States are among those who have least developed in the past 50 years. There are fewer subscribers to the Internet in the entire Arab world than in Israel alone. More than 20% of the Moroccan population is undernourished. More than half of Moroccans are illiterate."[18]

According to UNDP's analysis, the concentration of power in the hands of the executive—whether it is monarchic, military, dictatorship, or the result of one-candidate presidential elections—had created a "sort of 'black hole' at the heart of political life" and "reduced its social environment to a stasis where nothing moves." To improve this situation, "political and legal reforms are needed that are strong and immediate, respecting fundamental freedoms of opinion, expression, association, guaranteeing the independence of justice and abolishing this state of emergency . . . that has become permanent even in the absence of dangers that justify it."

Driss Benzekri and Driss el Yazami, who would, in effect, direct the ERC, shared the UNDP's analysis. They believed that Moroccan society had the potential to pick up the development challenge. Strategically, this implied a pragmatic alliance with the young guard around Mohammed VI. These human rights militants had closely followed the experience of Solidarity in Poland and Gorbachev's will to reform the Soviet Union. They dreamed of a

Solidarity that faced not General Jaruzelski, but Gorbachev. Their gamble was to reform the Moroccan system from within by leaning on the modern elite around the king. In their view, clarifying the crimes of the past, the democratization process, and the establishment of a true state of law were the prerequisites for socioeconomic development. And their new monarch, by the considerable power given him by the constitution and by his will to change his country, was the indispensable partner. There was a price to pay: the absence of punishment. But these were realistic men: they knew the state of Moroccan justice and how vulnerable it was to pressure. The price was all the more easy for them to accept in that the "conditions for an equitable trial of torturers and their bosses are not in hand."[19] They also thought that without an alliance with the Palace, Morocco's political situation left little hope for democratization.

For the members of the ERC, then, the political function of the Moroccan truth commission was different from that of previous ones: it was not so much to incarnate political change, as in South Africa, as it is was to use the commission as a lever of democratization to accelerate the process of change. In other words, the ERC did not come in after the break with the past had been consummated by the emergence of a new power. It was created to send a strong signal of mobilization to civil society as well as to give momentum to the reforms led by the king. The ERC commissioners always had in mind that the symbolic work accomplished by the ERC was to "rewrite" the national story. Through the victims' public testimonies of the torture they endured, the commissioners wanted to draw a new boundary between acceptable and unacceptable, individual rights and their violation. Such were, for the most dynamic commissioners, the political stakes of the ERC and their gamble.

The King's Motivation

According to the country's constitution promulgated under Hassan II, the king of Morocco has almost unlimited powers. Article 23 of the constitution states that "the King is inviolable and sacred." He holds executive power, naming and revoking the prime minister. He can suspend the constitution and dissolve Parliament; he is the commander in chief of the armed forces. And, as *Amir-al-Mu'minin*, commander of the faithful (Hassan II gave himself this title in 1962, formalizing it in Article 19 of the constitution), the king holds spiritual power over Moroccan Muslims. This addition of spiritual to temporal power allows the king to monopolize legitimacy of the political-religious field, according to a so-called two-floor constitution: The top floor expresses caliphate law, awarding political-religious power to the Caliph-King and, at the same time, establishing his relationship with subjects who make up a community of believers. The lower floor sets constitutional law— properly speaking, that is, the body of juridical standards that make the parliamentary game possible and which, applying only at the level of Parliament and the government, enjoy only relative influence.[20] The combination of Articles 19 and 23 set the king above any criticism (Article 38 of the *dahir* of 15 November 1958, modified by Article 41 of the *dahir* of 10 April 1973); the sovereign's sacredness extends to royal acts and initiatives and the king's messages to Parliament and the nation "can be the object of no debate" (Article 28).

In addition, the monarchy is the first economic agent of the kingdom, holding large areas of land and a number of companies, including the ONA, the jewel of the Moroccan economy, which alone makes up more than half the Casablanca stock market. The monarchy has a personal fortune estimated, according to *Forbes*, to be worth several billion dollars: this fortune was built under the reign of Hassan II; Hassan's father, King Mohammed V, had no fortune.

Given this environment of power, the king's support of the formation of the ERC can be explained by a number of factors. The king had expressed his will to modernize Morocco and state institutions. This depended on creating confidence between citizens and state services, so that energy could be turned to the challenges of economic and social development. The monarchy would lean on elements of civil society and on a discourse of human rights, of which the ERC was the strongest institutional symbol. This positioning established the political legitimacy of the new king and gave him an identity distinct from his father's. These functions emphasized the appropriation of the Truth and Reconciliation Commission, as much by the Moroccan sovereign as by the representatives of NGOs according to purely local stakes. By forging such an alliance through the ERC with the representatives of NGOs, the majority of whom were tortured under the Hassan regime, Mohammed VI presented himself as a reformist sovereign, democratic and dynamic, asking forgiveness for the reign of his father but without breaking institutionally with the regime of which he is the heir and upholder.

Politically, this alliance with personalities of the Left, however weakened, had several goals. The majority of political parties were perceived by public opinion as having been co-opted by the government; with the exception of the Islamist organizations, they appeared as empty shells. Bringing in former prisoners who had dearly paid for their opposition to the Hassan regime gave credibility to the king's will to reform: these ex-prisoners were, at least provisionally, above suspicion of being pawns of the Palace. The alliance was also a counterweight for the most conservative members of the *makhzen*,[21] who checked the process of economic and political liberalization to maintain their own interests. It benefited the modernizing elite that would profit from the privatization process and from a better functioning of institutions. In addition, this balancing act allowed the creation of a firebreak to the rising power of the Islamists. It incarnated the Moroccan way against the theocratic alternative of the Islamists. It also constituted one of the dimensions of the soft war in the clash with radical Salafist networks.

By its mandate, the ERC allowed the administrative and political closure of files of victims of state repression. In 1999 the example of the Arbitrage commission, made up of high officials of the regime, showed its limits. Out of fear of displeasing the monarch, the commission did not complete its work, recognizing only part of the cases of "disappearance." Not surprisingly, the criticism of local and international NGOs continued. This time, by choosing people from the NGO world who had paid for their political commitment through long years in prison, the king hoped to put an end to this matter and to disarm, partially, their arguments about the excesses of the "War on Terror."

Internationally, the establishment of a truth commission reinforced the image of Morocco as a state of human rights, a model modern state in the Arab-Islamic world. In other words, the use of the institutions and practices of transitional justice produced benefits for the image that were far from negligible: the country was seen to represent a model of democracy in the Arab world, and U.S. president George W. Bush, attempting to justify military action in Iraq, never missed the opportunity to cite Morocco as an example of what could be achieved in Iraq.[22] This international respectability, in addition, made for easier political and economic *rapprochement* with the EU countries and the United States, leading notably to the adoption of free-trade agreements. It was an additional asset in terms of tourism, Morocco's second source of foreign exchange.

Two Founding Ambiguities

The ERC contained two fundamental ambiguities that would weigh heavily on the work of the commission and on the will to proceed with reforms it recommended. The first concerned the king's relationship with the Hassanian heritage. The second concerned the political end results of the ERC.

Mohammed VI maintained an ambiguous position between fidelity proclaimed to his father—in particular to the post-1990 Hassan II—and distancing himself from his father's regime. This ambiguity was at the heart of the ERC's action, and the ERC never managed to lose it. The ERC's mandate covered the reign of both Mohammed V and Hassan II, grandfather and father of Mohammed VI. This period delineated a "before" and "after" that could not have been more different: the ERC mandate could have ended with the beginning of liberalization in 1990 or with the amnesty of 1994. But it stopped, officially, in 1999, with the establishment of the commission of compensation but also the year of Hassan's death. Symbolically, the ERC marked the beginning of a new era: that of Mohammed VI. However, the new king justified the creation of the ERC by placing it not as a break, but as the prolongation of his father's acts:

> Materializing our firm royal will to advance in the promotion of human rights, both in practice and as part of our culture, we are today proceeding to the installation of the Equity and Reconciliation Commission, and, thus, setting the final milestone on the journey leading to the definitive closure of a thorny case, at the end of a process begun at the beginning of the 1990s. . . . We bow, with humility and deference, before the memory of the initiator of this process, our august father, His Majesty the King Hassan II—may God have mercy on him.[23]

This ambiguity with the Hassanian heritage was apparent in the new king's speech. At no moment did Mohammed VI name those responsible for the "years of lead." Even the term "years of lead," used on many occasions in official texts, was deliberately vague and subject to conflicting interpretations. This euphemism permitted a moral distancing from the reality—hundreds of dead, thousands tortured, society muzzled—that Hassan II maintained through fear of denunciation and arrest. Mohammed VI questioned neither the repressive regime of his father nor the core of the radical Left that, at the time, promoted armed struggle against the monarchy. Instead, he put the emphasis on the necessity "for Morocco, to reconcile with one another and the past," calling on his citizens not to "remain prisoners of the negative aspects of the past."[24] The symptoms of repression were denounced publicly—torture, "disappearance" by agents of the state, arbitrary detention—but concerning the decades of repression, the state was silent. Abdelhay Moudden, commissioner of the ERC and political scientist at the University of Rabat, notes that "the official story does not exist in Morocco. There are long periods of silence because the State does not express itself about the past."[25]

The sovereign's ambiguity about his father's repressive regime made for two possible interpretations of the ERC: that it was a refounding of society, through the king's demand for "collective pardon" by which the victims were to "empty their hearts" through the autobiographical account of their sufferings; or, as described by Mauro Bottaro, that it was "a reconciliation with the Hassanian past, that is to say, with a truth that is manipulated and ideologically centered on the statute of Commander of the Faithful in the name of which Hassan II proceeded to monopolize the political-religious field at the price of abominable violence."[26]

During the seven public hearings organized by the ERC, the portraits of Hassan II were sometimes present, sometimes absent, and, when they were present, they were of the same size or smaller than those of his son. The ambiguity about his legacy was never completely lifted. Was Hassan II the architect of modern Morocco or the one most responsible for the decades of repression? And, if he were both, how were these two aspects to be sorted out? The current duty to inventory was still forbidden, as the report of the ERC would show. The weight of the Old Guard at the heart of the security service and the army perhaps explains this prudence.

This first ambiguity on the legacy of Hassan II led to the second: What was the outcome of the ERC? Was it about refounding Morocco, at least partially as a political community? And if so, on what terms? What was the end point of the process of democratization? On this point, the commissioners, at least the leaders of the ERC,[27] and the monarchy differed.

Driss Benzekri's gamble through the ERC was to set off a dynamic of institutional reforms to create a constitutional monarchy in the short term. His ambition, then, was to refound the monarchy. King Mohammed VI, however, was never explicit about his political objective: he said that he wished to "bring to completion the democracy and State of law" and "to build a modern democratic society where all citizens may exercise their rights and fulfill their duties, in liberty, with responsibility and dedication."[28] But what is the political horizon toward which Morocco is heading? Does the king accept Benzekri's idea to set up a constitutional monarchy in the near future? Or is the action of the ERC merely a circus "with the ideological goal of perpetual repetition of the order established by the Alaouite monarchy"?[29] Here, too, there is uncertainty at the top. Is this uncertainty due to tactical prudence given the reticence of the Old Guard and the army? Or is it due to other reasons? In an interview with *El País*, the king refuted the idea that Morocco was becoming a constitutional monarchy with himself as a new Juan Carlos: "One must not transpose the model of European monarchies. We have our own particularities and obligations that trace the way that we must go." The question remains open; as noted by political scientist Malika Zeghal, "the reign of Mohammed VI gives off a feeling of hesitation and uncertainty."[30]

The Functioning of the ERC

Selection of Members

Half of the seventeen commissioners of the ERC were members of the CCDH and the other were from "civil society," heads of NGOs, a political scientist, and a doctor. Six ERC commissioners were ex–political prisoners, ex-militants of the extreme Left,[31] of whom two were forced into exile. One of these, Mbarek Bouderka, had been condemned to death *in absentia*. For decades, they had abandoned revolutionary ideology to work for human rights. The four people with the greatest media visibility and who had invested the most in the work of the ERC were all former Marxist-Leninist militants, beginning with the president, Driss Benzekri, imprisoned for seventeen years (1974–1991); Salah El-Ouadie, condemned for twenty years (he served ten); Driss el Yazami, who was forced into exile; and Latifa Jbabdi, the only female commissioner, who went to prison for the first time at the age of fifteen.

There was not one religious leader among the seventeen commissioners. Nor were there any Islamists, although they represented the most important political force in the country. The reasons for this absence are multiple. Historically, the main repression between 1960 and 1990 was, by far, directed against the militants of the Left and Far Left rather than the Islamist groups. Some of these former Marxist militants launched the idea of the ERC and were willing to partner with the Palace in setting it up. Third, the ERC was set up in 2004, a time when the Islamists were held in suspicion, after the terrorist attacks in Casablanca and Madrid, and the government wanted to avoid giving legitimacy to the mistrusted.

The Public Hearings

Ever since the founding of the South African TRC, before which victims and their torturers faced off, the world of transitional justice has been conscious of the importance of staging. In setting the scene of a piece of history, the new national account and values are presented to society as a whole. This theater of cruelty is, thus, full of meaning, all the more effective in that the victims' stories are emotional. Such dramaturgy implies strategic choices: Who are the recipients of the victim's story? What is the precise content of the message to be transmitted? What is the role of each actor on stage?

On the first point, the commissioners would equivocate for three months before reaching agreement. The majority of the commissioners wanted to connect with Moroccan society as a whole, to set off a social dynamic. They knew that, in a country where the majority of the population was illiterate, television and radio were the most effective means of communication. The daily newspapers, altogether, had a circulation of only 300,000–400,000. The minority of the commissioners, however, feared that the public hearings would generate acts of revenge and tension within society. They finally allowed themselves to be convinced, insofar as the royal advisors were not hostile to television broadcasts. The Palace believed that the precautions put in place in the elaboration of the ERC's mandate were solid enough to prevent excesses and were convinced that the king had everything to gain from broadcasting the public hearings. It was true that the risks were limited: the leaders and underlings of decades of repression were, literally, out of reach, the beneficiaries of impunity, when they were not still in service. Public television broadcast the first two hearings live in a slot that was not prime time (6:30 p.m.); the subsequent hearings, edited to ninety minutes, were pre-recorded. This demonstration should have been relayed to the large national and international media, in the presence of leaders of local and international NGOs. Not only Moroccan society, but the entire world, should have seen that Morocco was firmly engaged on the road to democracy.

Given the strict limitations on its mandate, the ERC's message was relatively complex. The commissioners were to signify publicly and emotionally the new era, that of the democratic opening envisioned by Mohammed VI. But, at the same time, the break with the past had to be cautiously formulated, because it had still not been accomplished. Hassan II, under whose reign virtually all of the violations of human rights occurred, could not be criticized. With his portrait hanging on the wall of some of the hearings, he could even be interpreted as one of the guardians of the commission. Because the names of torturers, commanders, and leaders that had made up the repressive system had been banned, the fabrication of the new institutional truth of Morocco's post-colonial past was based less on historical "truth" than on the "truth" of the individual memories of the victims, that is, on subjective truth through the stories of suffering.

This strategy to avoid individual and monarchist responsibility meant that the dramatic intensity of the public hearings depended on the victims alone. It was they who had to occupy the space, who had a monopoly of speech. The victims could mention the places of their suffering (Tazmamart, Agdez, Derb Moulay Chérif, and so on) and the institutions (the army, police, gendarmerie, security service) that mistreated them. To make the hearing more propitious, the commissioners had decided not to interrupt the victims and, contrary to other TRCs, to ask no questions. The plan was to create an atmosphere of contemplation and compassion for the suffering that these men and women had endured. They could speak in the language they chose (classical Arabic, Arabic dialect, Berbère, French),[32] for their diversity signified the unity of Morocco recovered in the new era. The victims, especially among the less politicized,[33] fulfilled a sacrificial function: to exhibit publicly their suffering, to put aside their shame, and, thus, to offer their unhappiness up to the nation so as to bandage its symbolic wounds. The effectiveness of their testimony was all the greater when the victim was both emotionally overwhelmed by the telling of his or her suffering, the rapes and the torture, and was a political innocent. Before the spectacle of suffering inflicted on an absolute victim, without any justifiable motive except his or her blood ties with an opponent of the regime, the nation could come together in consensus. The key question, however, was whether the gift of their testimony opened perspectives for an identity and cultural refounding of the Moroccan nation—or if their words had been used to give the appearance of change that remained merely cosmetic.

The audience reached by the television and radio broadcasts of the first public hearings was never statistically quantified. But, for the first time, the heretofore abstract work of the ERC touched the heart of Moroccan society. It produced several effects, depending on the segment of the public. The emotions raised by the freedom of speech in the very first hearings initially increased expectations for change in Moroccan society before plummeting again. Fearing a trivialization effect, the ERC, which had planned some twenty public hearings, reduced the number to seven (two in Rabat and one each in Errachidia, Figuig, Khénifra, El-Houcéma, and Marrakech).

Without ever lifting the ambiguity concerning the legacy of Hassan II, Khadija el Melki, a victim tortured under the reign of Hassan II, attempted to rationalize the conditions of his testimony: "When I spoke of my suffering before hundreds of people, the portrait on my left, that of King Mohammed VI helped me to struggle against the one on my right, that of his father, Hassan II."[34] This contradiction between gagging historical truth and allowing the expression of individual memories reached fever pitch in the public hearing of 3 May 2005 in Al-Hoceima. A dozen victims were to testify about the harsh repression that occurred in the Rif region when a group of protestors began to chant in Berber, interrupting the meeting: "The Rif refuses the public hearings. The Rifain people want the truth. All the truth, total and complete. The Equity and Reconciliation Commission must leave this region."[35] Later that night, the meeting resumed behind closed doors.

The Moroccan Association of Human Rights (known by its French acronyn, AMDH) organized parallel public hearings—unprecedented in the history of transitional justice—practically in the same towns where the ERC held its own meetings (Rabat, Khénifra, El-Hocéma, Marrakech, and Paris), under the evocative title "Freely Given Testimony for Truth."[36] In these alternative hearings, the names of the torturers were mentioned publicly, and the abuse of human rights committed after the end of the ERC's mandate (1999) were denounced. The ERC, then, had permitted the clearing of space for expression beyond the limits imposed in the official truth commission mandate. This advance was significant without being revolutionary. Since the beginning of the process of liberalization, silence on the identity of the torturers had been broken by the NGOs, the press, and many works and testimony of ex-prisoners, militants, and writers.[37]

The Cancellation of the Public Hearing
in Layoune (Western Sahara)

Of all the files with which the ERC was charged, the most explosive was that of Western Sahara. This territory is still disputed between Morocco, who has controlled it since the Green March (1975), and the militants of the Polisario Front independence movement (Frente Popular de Liberación de Saguía el

Hamra y Rio de Oro) supported by Algeria. Moroccan authorities consider this region to be an integral part of the kingdom, while the Sahrawis claim their right to self-determination. In 1975 the International Court of Justice recommended a referendum, which never took place. The last peace plan, presented by former secretary of state James Baker, was rejected by Morocco. Today, no international solution is in view. In November 2005 a public hearing in the U.S. Congress opposed partisans of "the right to self-determination for the last colony in Africa" to those who consider it "absurd" to create a state on such an enormous territory inhabited by only three hundred thousand people, a territory that could constitute a base for terrorist networks.

The Western Sahara, then, was the test *par excellence* of the commission: Could the ERC help defuse tensions, given that the violations of human rights committed there were part of the ongoing political conflict? Was the device of transitional justice mature for this region, which had been the object of a particular dynamic, breaking with the rest of the chérifien kingdom? The ERC did not succeed in meeting this challenge: a commission named by the king of Morocco could with difficulty present itself as a neutral arbitrator in a still-contested region. No doubt the task was above its capability: how could a device of transitional justice be set up when consensus had not been found within the population on the key question of sovereignty? It was regrettable that the truth commission's summary report said not a word about this region, no doubt the one most harshly hit by repression. No one contested that the Moroccan services carried out "disappearances" of Sahrawis and inflicted collective punishment, even if the numbers of disappeared remain controversial.

From the beginning, the commission advanced across a minefield. It was trapped between the "hard-core" members of both camps: on one side, the local authorities who functioned according to security concerns; on the other, the sympathizers of Polisario, who used human rights violations to justify "an Intifada against the Moroccan occupier." In this context of tension, the ERC's public hearing, planned first in Tan-Tan, then in Layoune, forced everyone to choose sides. The truth commission was an indicator of the strategies, fears, and ambitions of all, provoking sometimes unexpected convergence of interests among adversaries: for example, the Moroccan "security forces" of Western Sahara did not want public hearings, for they feared that hearings might be the pretext for new trouble, and they wanted to avoid being accused of the bloody repression that they had carried out in the past. They were joined in their opposition to the ERC by their adversaries: the most radical independence fringe was hostile to any collaboration with an institution created "according to the pleasure of the King of Morocco," which, in their eyes only served to justify "an illegal occupation." They, too, wanted the ERC to fail, for if the ERC succeeded, it would signify a loss of control over part of their population. On the contrary, the moderate independence fighters and a part of the Sahrawis who considered themselves Moroccan saw the ERC as a rare platform for denouncing the violations of human rights and for defusing even to a small degree the current tensions. As human rights militant in Western Sahara, Lahcen Moutik, explains, "For once, a public hearing allowed us to tell the Moroccan society the reality that it doesn't know. What's more, by collaborating with the ERC, we could honor the memory of the disappeared and obtain individual and collective reparations."[38] The latter arguments carried the most weight with the Sahrawi victims: they hoped to gain information on the circumstances of the deaths of their loved ones and, above all, places of burial. Destitute, they also hoped to obtain compensation for the torture they had suffered. This double reason explains why 4,000–5,000 Sahrawis, almost one-fourth the total number of victims who testified at the ERC, come from this region.[39] In addition, proportionately more Sahrawis were tortured.

But there was little trust between the victims and the ERC. Only one of the seventeen commissioners was Sahrawi, and even he was identified with an old local family allied to Moroccan power. The commission carried out secret negotiations with the Sahrawis to identify victims who would talk during the public hearing in Layoune. But riots denouncing "30 years of Moroccan occupation" broke out in the spring of 2005, and the Moroccan flag was burned. Polisario sympathizers were determined to stop the hearings, for they did not want, under any circumstances, a Moroccan institution to achieve credibility.[40] Iguilid Hammoud, president of the (banned) section of the Layoune, AMDH, did not hide his willingness to torpedo the ERC: "We were determined to disturb the public hearing of the ERC. We wanted to judge the torturers who continue to go about here with their heads high and in full liberty. They are still in the forces of repression."[41]

These activists believed that the question of arbitrary arrests, the disappearances, or show trials would only be resolved with "the end of Moroccan occupation." Independence was, for them, the indispensable prerequisite to improving human rights. Djmi el Ghali was one of the victims who testified at a "parallel" hearing organized by AMDH in Rabat. As vice president of the

Association of Sahrawi Victims of Grave Violations of Human Rights (a banned association), she was herself the daughter of a "disappeared" and spent four years in prison. Initially, she filed her testimony with the ERC but "realized that the commission prefers to compensate us rather than tell us how our loved ones died, for the powers that be would have to admit guilt for their crimes." El Ghali is one of thirty-two Sahrawi victims to have signed the memorandum to the ERC. She was hostile to the ERC's hearings: "One cannot talk about repression in this region without talking about political causes. We have been persecuted, simply because we are partisans for self-determination for Western Sahara. What good is it for me to stand, if I cannot explain why I was imprisoned for four years and name those responsible? When I testified in Rabat, I could talk about the political causes behind my kidnapping and name the names of those who tortured me."[42]

Given the radicalization of the independence movement and the bad will of the local authorities to ensure the hearing's security, the ERC postponed the hearing until the summer and then canceled it on various pretexts.[43] The unnatural alliance between the security forces and the radical militants for Sahrawi independence had accomplished its goal.[44]

Collective Pardon on Islamic Soil

Moroccan authorities congratulated themselves on many occasions that the creation of a truth commission in the Arab-Islamic world and in a society that was almost exclusively Muslim was unprecedented. Indeed, the thirty earlier commissions had all been in countries with a Christian and/or African culture, even if they sometimes contained important Muslim minorities.[45] The absence of a TRC in Islamic countries raised a number of questions: Were truth commissions truly universal? Was there an Islamic exception concerning pardon that Morocco had succeeded in breaking?

Such questions stemmed from a cultural interpretation of truth commissions, and the strategic stakes of this interpretation were important. The cultural interpretation of truth commissions was largely inspired by the comments of the president of the South African TRC, Archbishop Desmond Tutu. Archbishop Tutu often explained that pardon and reconciliation in South Africa was the product not only of Christian forgiveness but, even more so, of African culture. Repeatedly, he insisted on the strength of the concept of *ubuntu*,[46] which, he said, made pardon possible for Africans. To push Desmond Tutu's reasoning to its furthest (something he himself did not do): the cultural capacity for reconciliation would be best satisfied, first, in African societies, then Christian, and finally Islamic, because neither *ubuntu* nor Christian forgiveness is part of the third culture.

However, it is clear that granting amnesty to criminals, in South Africa (or elsewhere), is a political choice. In South Africa's case, the principle of a TRC based on forgiveness in exchange for truth was a compromise worked out by de Klerk and Mandela. The religious and cultural dimension was introduced afterward with a strategic objective: make a "deal"—one that would guarantee amnesty for torturers *and* be acceptable to Africans. How? By metamorphosing amnesty into a pardon charged with a spiritual dimension. Cultural symbolic systems (Christian and African) were mobilized for a praiseworthy goal: to ensure that the country avoided a bloodbath by choosing the path of stability. The overrepresentation of top religious leaders in the South African TRC reflected this will. By their participation in this exercise, their blessing to this amnesty became "pardon." There was a subsidiary effect on personal truth at the individual level: by putting the emphasis on the spiritual dimension, the victims and torturers who felt a call to their conscience could more easily give or ask for true forgiveness.

For society, the transformation of amnesty into pardon aims to clear the debate on the validity of this choice. The political dimension is erased in favor of a spiritual interpretation of pardon. At once, this amnesty-pardon becomes more acceptable to people than if negotiation had been based on a power struggle. In this lies the strategic and political background to the cultural interpretation of truth commissions. Of course, there are many Africans as well as non-Africans who did not accept the approach popularized by Desmond Tutu.

The Moroccan case was, from this point of view, equally a product of the political stakes linked to the justification of amnesty-pardon, even if it was played out on a radically different cultural register. In Morocco, two different strategies collided, that of the monarchy and that of the ERC. King Mohammed VI promoted a position based simultaneously on religion and politics, to call for "reconciliation" and to justify impunity.

From his strength as "Commander of the Faithful," the king first invoked God to legitimize the absence of punishment in his speech on 6 January 2006: "I am certain that the work of sincere reconciliation that we have accomplished . . . is, in fact, a response to the divine injunction 'Absolve with a beautiful absolution.' This is a gracious gesture of collective pardon."[47] The gesture was even more gracious in that, contrary to the South African example, the torturers and their bosses remained protected in the shadows—when they were not still actively at work.

The king's second argument was political. Absolution was conditioned by the political preamble for reconciliation "between Moroccans and their past" in the name of building a new Morocco. In this view, legal and political disagreements had to be brought to an end by recognizing "errors committed" to better free up energies: "The goal is to reconcile Morocco with its past. . . . Some say that this initiative in insufficient, because the witnesses may not reveal the names of their torturers. Obviously, I must insist that I do not agree. This initiative is not, as some pretend, to divide Morocco in two. There are no judges nor judged. We are not in front of a tribunal. We must examine without complex nor shame this page of our history. From there, we can advance towards better conditions."[48]

The third argument of a cultural order was presented by the media close to the throne. They affirmed that "revenge is not Moroccan." The idea of criminal sanction was purely and simply assimilated to an act of vengeance. Language was manipulated to remove any positive value in punishment.

However, the ERC commissioners rebelled against this cultural argument, seeing in it a symbolic manipulation of religion. For them, the absolution called for by the king was acceptable in the name of political realism.[49] They justified their consent by an ethic of responsibility, believing that the political and social benefits of participating in the creation of a state of law had to transcend the question of the repression of crimes committed in the past, well aware that justice was not yet independent. Thus, the charges filed by the USFP on the 1965 disappearance in Paris of Mehdi Ben Barka, a leader of the Moroccan Left (murdered by the Moroccan services) led nowhere, although witnesses to the crime were still alive.[50]

For the ERC commissioners, the demand for absolution was interpreted as a purely political act and it was vital that it be understood as such. Abdelhay Moudden was hostile to any cultural justification for, he insisted, "the commission has been thought, conceived and defined in function of a political objective: democratization."[51] To "culturalize" absolution boiled down to making it into folklore, with the obvious danger of making the truth commission lose its potential for social mobilization. Realistically, the commissioners had no choice but to accept that the monarchy could justify its call for collective pardon by a cultural whitewash, but they hoped that this wash would be as translucent as possible. For the ERC, what was important was to throw light on "the responsibility of the State and its institutions."[52]

The ultimate factor that worked in favor of strategic absolution was the fact that this absolution could only be temporary. A number of commissioners had understood the lessons of Chile and Argentina. During informal exchanges, they pointed out that laws of *punto final*, intended to offer definitive amnesty to torturers, had been reopened with time. They knew that a truth commission left the door open to a new balance of power within society that could lead to revoking amnesty laws and open trials again in five, ten, or twenty years.

The Truth Commission and the "Anti-Terrorist War"

The ERC's action cannot be interpreted independently of the political and security context in which it was created and functioned. At each decisive step of the commission, the "anti-terrorist war" played a major role. It colored the process of its creation, its functioning, its conclusions, its perception by public opinion, and its impact. The impact and credibility of the truth commission never stops being affected by the context at once national and international of the "anti-terrorist war."

The king created the ERC in January 2004, only a few months after the terrorist attacks in Casablanca on 16 May 2003—in other words, at a moment when Morocco had become one of the principal conflict spots in the "War on Terror" launched by the Bush Administration six months earlier. This confrontation crossed a new threshold with the attacks in Madrid on 11 March 2004 perpetrated by Moroccan nationals (two hundred dead and a thousand wounded). According to U.S. major general Jonathan S. Gration, director of strategy, policy, and assessments for the U.S. European Command (EUCOM), Morocco and all of North Africa "is a strategic region in the war against terrorism. We consider it to be a regional threat whose shock waves can affect the stability of Europe and Africa."[53] This, then, is the context in which the ERC worked. Some top Moroccan officials in the Interior Ministry even offered a "security interpretation" of the truth commission. As one of them put it, "The ERC is an arm in the fight against terrorism. We are waging this war on two fronts. On one side, the 'hard war,' the repressive dismantling of cells, and on the other, the 'soft war,' which consists of bringing the population over to our side. The ERC is one of the elements of this 'soft war.'" In this perspective, the ERC was part of a larger operation to win the trust of the people, thereby shrinking the core of sympathizers of the "terrorists."[54] In practice, however, the use of the ERC in the anti-terrorist "soft war" led to considerable difficulties, if not the contradiction between the security rationale and the democratic agenda. Thus, quite possibly, in a less tense context, the commission would have been given wider powers of investigation. As it was, the government preferred to reassure the agents of repression engaged in dismantling Salafist networks. The monarchy guaranteed them not only impunity, but also the possibility to refuse to collaborate with the ERC: a prerogative that they employed widely. For the Palace, the commission's objective of "truth" must not destabilize the security apparatus in such a "sensitive" period. The limitations imposed on the ERC's mandate weakened the commission's[55] effectiveness and, ultimately, the credibility of its work.

There is no doubt, either, that the "War on Terror" being waged globally weakened the ERC: the defense of human rights was no longer a priority in the post–September 11 international plan. The major NGOs, like Amnesty International, the International Federation of Human Rights (FIDH), and Human Rights Watch, which supported the democratization process and put pressure on governments, were now on the defensive. The Bush Administration's restrictive reinterpretation of the Geneva Convention, the internal debate in the United States on whether or not torture was legitimate, the detention without trial of presumed "terrorists" at Guantánamo, the supposed existence of secret prisons maintained by the CIA in Europe and the Arab world, including Morocco, had all weakened international humanitarian law and created— including in the countries that had proclaimed themselves the defenders of freedom—an acceptance of lower standards. What was Western credibility worth after the images taken in Abu Ghraib? Did the CIA have secret prisons, including a "Moroccan Guantánamo" as the Moroccan media reported, where prisoners were being tortured?[56]

The ERC's limited room for action, added to a new national and international climate, increased skepticism in Moroccan public opinion about the truth commission. To what degree could a society stick to a process of shedding light on the "years of lead" if high state officials refused to cooperate with a commission set up by the king himself? How could such a society subscribe to a democratization process, of which the ERC was the symbol, if, in the name of the "War on Terror," the security forces carried out mass arrests (more than three thousand Islamists arrested after the attacks on Casablanca) marked by abuse and sometimes serious blunders? Abdelhay Moudden notes:

"People tell us: how can you investigate the past when, even if they are not comparable to the past, human rights abuses continue and are even encouraged by our American allies?"[57] From a theoretical point of view, the ERC could be considered an asset in the anti-terrorist war, but the security rationale was in practice incompatible with a concern for transparency and accountability for earlier human rights violations.

The ERC's Report: Truth Under Wraps

The final report was one of the key points of a truth commission. It represented the new national narrative, interpreted periods marked by mass human rights violations in the light of present-day values, and recommended institutional and political reforms to prevent the repetition of such wrongs. After twenty-three months of work, the ERC delivered its conclusions in a report of some seven hundred pages,[58] divided into three parts: a historical section, a second devoted to reparations, and a third proposing institutional reforms, all accompanied by a thirty-page summary.[59]

Amputated Historical Truth

In writing the "historical clarification" section of the report, the commissioners were under contradictory pressures. A number of victims, human rights militants, and the major international NGOs wanted the ERC to go as far as possible in shedding light on the violations committed and in revealing the institutional responsibilities (because accusing individuals was prohibited by the ERC's mandate). On the other hand, the Palace and political parties—let alone the security agencies—were deeply reluctant for the ERC to write a new account about past human rights violations. These latter pressures, partially, won out.

To establish the facts, the ERC affirmed that it had been able to find out about 742 cases of forced disappearance. It was unable to reveal what happened in 66 other cases and recommended that the state pursue the investigation. The commission criticized the obstacles, both voluntary and involuntary, from agencies and agents of the state that had handicapped its work, citing "the deplorable state of the archives when they even exist, the uneven cooperation from the security forces, the imprecision of testimony of former officials and the refusal of others to contribute to the effort of establishing the truth." According to some Moroccan papers, the army had flatly refused to cooperate with the ERC.[60]

The report documented the practice of arbitrary detention and described the "systematic use of physical and moral torture" inflicted on prisoners, which "have sometimes led to psychological repercussions and permanent infirmity, even death." The report notes that moral and psychological torture consisted "in threats of death or rape, insults and other attacks on dignity . . . , torture or the threat to torture a family member or someone close to the prisoner." The report also noted that "women endured in addition specific forms of abuse, living in terror of rape, which was sometimes committed." The report also documented the "excessive and disproportional use of public force" to repress demonstrations, leading to casualties that had nothing to do with the events. It established that the security services, on a number of occasions, had fired real bullets and not used other means to disperse protestors that would have saved lives. It was clear from medical logs and testimony that many deaths had been caused by bullets shot at the head, chest, and abdomen levels. The commission had been able "to certify that a large number of children, of whom some were under 10 years of age, were among the dead." The report acknowledged, however, that, given the lack of cooperation from the state, some events remain obscure. And it recommended a follow-up mechanism so that light could be shed on these events within the following six months.

The final report's most striking omission concerned Western Sahara. It was in this region that human rights violations and repression, including collective punishment, were most severe. According to an expert who testified to the U.S. Congress, Moroccan forces have been responsible for the death of five hundred opponents (or those considered to be such) since 1975.[61] The ERC report was equally silent on the organization of the repression. It stated discreetly: "The analysis of the data and information collected from diverse sources, as well as investigations, have allowed us to establish that, in the majority of cases, the responsibility belongs to the different security agencies. . . . Moreover, the commission was able to establish in many cases the existence of shared responsibility, even solidarity, between several security agencies."[62]

But who gave the orders? What was the chain of command? Repression was never the product of isolated acts committed by state agents acting on their own initiative; it was a hierarchical system, strictly controlled, which went to the top of the Hassan regime over two decades. This historical truth was not mentioned in the report. However, in a separate letter to King Mohammed VI, the president of the commission did transmit the names of a certain number of top military and civil officials who were directly responsible for setting up the repression. The use of this information and the possible dismissal of these people will depend on royal will alone.

The last stage of historical clarification is traditionally the most delicate and the most important. It is what gives a society an interpretation of the political and ideological causes of the violation of human rights. From the creation of the ERC, the establishment of this interpretative level had raised intense debate, not only among the commissioners, but also within society itself. In the end, the final report gives neither context nor historical interpretation. What are the reasons for this repression? The weight of ideology? The respective roles of King Hassan II and the armed groups seeking to overthrow the monarchy? Here again, nothing is said. This omission satisfies both the monarchy and the political parties, which themselves were not always blameless.

The ERC hesitated before choosing the most prudent line possible. While the commission was halfway into its work, Abdelhay Moudden listed several possible historical approaches:

> We were faced with several theses. The two most radical were these: one emphasized the repressive character of the State; the other emphasized the responsibility of the armed groups in the escalation of violence. For us at the ERC, our concern was neither to legitimize the repression by State agencies, nor to ignore the responsibilities of the revolutionary groups supported by Algeria, Libya and Syria. We were also able to share out the responsibility between the monarchy and these armed movements. Finally, due to the lack of sufficient documentation, we left to historians the duty of dividing up the responsibility of each for the escalation of violence and repression.[63]

All told, the combined hostility of the king and the Left limited the commissioners' ambitions. Each feared that the ERC would be turned into a "tribunal of history." The monarchy did not want the reign of Hassan II to be accused of wrongdoing. The Socialist Union of Populist Forces (USFP) did not want the Left, which had justified armed struggle but whose capacity for action had been extremely limited, to be given equal responsibility with Hassan II for the crimes committed. To this end, there was a stark convergence in viewpoints between Mohammed VI and Mohamed Elyazghi, first secretary of the USFP. During his speech at the official end of the ERC's work, on 6 January 2006, the king declared: "It is not our intention to judge History, or to mix together the active and the passive. Only historians are able to evaluate the march of history with the impartiality and objectivity required, and to be above any short-term political consideration."[64]

The Left showed the same reluctance for any attempt by the ERC to interpret history. Mohamed Elyazghi, himself a former political prisoner, warned the ERC:

> The ERC does not have to write the political history of Morocco or that of the political differences between the parties and the Palace. That is for historians to write. And it is up to the political parties to analyze and evaluate their own actions. Morocco has lived through dark moments in its history. What has happened in terms of human rights violations must be said. One must not say of someone who has disappeared or tortured that, after all, he was wrong to say something or to have chosen such and such political line. Is the Equity and Reconciliation Commission trying to justify the mistakes by trying to evaluate the political choices of this or that one during those terrible years? In doing so, it is not in its right role. Its mission is very clear. The charter is very clear and the speech the Sovereign gave at the Commission's opening is especially clear.[65]

The report's caution in not naming those responsible leaves open all historical interpretations. The absence of any code of interpretation by the ERC damages, in part, the credibility of its work, lacking any analysis of responsibility for the "years of lead." No national narrative was offered to take the place of partisan memory, neither of the Left, which never undertook a critical analysis of its story, nor of the Old Guard, which continued to evoke Hassan II's "legitimate defense" against an anti-monarchical Left. The ERC's silence came from the deliberately ambiguous formulas of King Mohammed VI concerning "certain discrepancies of the past,"[66] referring to a state policy that resulted in the murder of hundreds of people, "the disappearance" and torture of thousands of others, and a climate of intimidation and fear for thirty years. How could Moroccan society "reconcile with itself and with its past," according to the official formula of the ERC's objectives, if the documentation concerning the "years of lead" did not lead to an interpretation of responsibility?

Reparations: Finishing the Job

The objective of restorative justice concerns the victims and, beyond them, society as a whole. Traditionally, financial compensation to victims of repression, at least where it exists, follows the work of a truth commission. The Moroccan case is particular. The Commission of Arbitrage created in 1999 by Mohammed VI compensated thirty-seven hundred victims for "disappearance" and torture, distributing around one billion dirhams (the equivalent of $100 million) on 10 July 2003. But, too close to political power, the Commission of Arbitrage could not go to the end of its mandate.[67]

After receiving the mandate to complete the work of the Arbitrage commission, the ERC granted financial compensation to around ten thousand victims, for a total amount of some $70 million.[68] The decisions concerned the victims of forced disappearance, of arbitrary detention with or without trial, or of capital punishment, death, wounds, arbitrary detention during the urban riots, forced exile, and sexual violence. Six criteria were retained by the ERC: loss of freedom; specificity of forced disappearance; conditions of detention or confinement; torture and all other inhumane, degrading, or cruel treatment; physical and psychological repercussions; and the loss of opportunities and livelihood. Financial compensation would be completed for some victims by measures of reintegration in the public function, by their administrative or professional regularization, and so on. In its recommendations, the ERC recognized the extension of obligatory medical coverage to all victims identified by the ERC and their heirs and the creation of a permanent mechanism of orientation and medical assistance for victims of violence and mistreatment.

The truth commission also recommended, in the name of community reparation, the adoption of socioeconomic and cultural development programs for several regions and groups of victims, notably the women of several cities (Casablanca) and regions such as Rif, Figuig, Tazmamart, and Middle-Atlas, which were affected by political violence, marginalized, and excluded. Driss el Yazami emphasized that about $15 million, half paid by the state of Morocco and half by the EU, was part of these reparations given to specific communities.[69] The Moroccan TRC was among the first to broaden the scope of reparations beyond victims of political rights violations, a development welcomed by the UN high human rights commissioner, Louise Arbour: "The approach taken by the Moroccan Commission is a welcome expansion of the scope of reparations programs. Often in situations of political transformation, both law and policy are caught between different imperatives, such as between the past and the future, between the individual and the collective that I believe deserves further reflections when thinking about the mechanisms of transformation. . . . Transitional justice mechanisms thus have a crucial role to play in recommending the adoption of such measures as part of the necessary reparation for victims and as part of a comprehensive strategy of national reconciliation and peace."[70]

Institutional Reforms

From the beginning, the stakes for the human rights militants who became the leaders of the truth commission gave momentum to the democratic dynamism begun years earlier. This was the meaning of the "historic bargain" concluded with the monarchy by Driss Benzekri and his friends: no judicial suits in exchange for continuing the democratization process. At the end of the ERC's work, Benzekri spoke in favor of the establishment of a "form of constitutional monarchy in Morocco, which will see the day in a relatively short period of time." The recommendations contained in the ERC's final report were inspired by this vision and showed the road that remains to be traveled to get there.

The ERC recommended consolidating constitutional guarantees of human rights, notably by inscribing principles of the primacy of human rights into internal law, the presumption of innocence, and the right to a fair trial. The ERC proposed making explicit in the constitution fundamental liberties and rights, relative to rights of circulation, expression, assembly, association, and strikes, as well as such principles as privacy of mail, the inviolability of one's home, and respect for privacy. The report also recommended reinforcing the principle of separation of powers and the independence of judicial and legislative bodies, the adoption of an integrated national strategy against impunity, and better control of the security agencies.[71] Finally, the report asked the prime minister (not the king) to assume responsibility in the name of the Moroccan state for human rights violations committed in the past and to present formal excuses to the nation.

Society's Reactions

As an extrajudicial institution, the ERC relied largely on resonance within the monarchy, the political class, and Moroccan society. Its work was followed attentively by the media. On several occasions the commission generated great interest within Moroccan public opinion; of greatest interest was its creation with personalities who were considered to be credible (given their known commitment to human rights and their long prison terms) and the testimonies of the victims during the first public hearings. For the first time, victims were able to express themselves in the public domain, including on national television and radio. The work of the ERC gave visibility and legitimacy to a part of the country's history that had been obscured by official history, without, however, ever lifting the ERC's contradictions.

Indeed, the ambiguity of the ERC's objectives culminated with the king's speech on 6 January 2006 to mark its closure. Mohammed VI decided to speak before an audience composed partly of victims. But he qualified this act of recognition with a reference to the "immaculate soul" of the late King Hassan II, speaking to families who had lost one or more members of their own families: "[I hope to see] this fortunate and comforting news [the closing of the files regarding the "years of lead"] by mediation of the angels of the Merciful, to the immaculate soul of my venerated father and to the heart of all the victims, persons having endured harm and grieving families that we most certainly encircle with our sympathy and our solicitude."[72]

Should these words be taken as proof that the ERC was the beginning of a rehabilitation of the Hassan regime? Or were they merely the expression of a "dynastic reflex"? Was the speech a "makhzenien intellectual lock"? A debt paid to those of "the old guard still on the job"? The Moroccan press wondered.[73] More critically, Mauro Bottaro felt that "against all the prophets of democratic transition in Morocco, the Truth and Reconciliation Commission is in the wake of pure Hassanian Machiavellianism of which Mohammed VI is the ideological heir thanks to the title of Commander of the Faithful in the name of which Hassan II carried out a remorseless job of symbolic manipulation of Islam and its principles to preserve the primacy of the Alaouite dynasty on the post-Colonial political scene of Morocco."[74]

For their part, the families of the disappeared interpreted the work of the ERC in different ways. Some were touched by the sovereign's recognition of their suffering and by the ERC's work. Khadija Rouissi belonged to one of several emblematic families of the disappeared. Rouissi believed that she would never have recovered the body of her brother, Abdelhaq, without the Truth and Reconciliation Commission. The body of this twenty-five-year-old, arrested in 1964, was found near Rabat more than forty years after his murder. "For a long time, I fought alone, like so many others," said Rouissi in an interview. "Benzekri brought us together and gave us a strategy."[75]

In contrast, a large number of the families of disappeared Sahrawis had a very critical view of the commission. They had profound doubts that the grave sites of the loved ones indicated by the ERC corresponded to reality. They demanded scientific expertise in determining the identities of the remains. Other families never received any information on their missing loved ones from the ERC, which appeared incapable of revealing the conditions of those disappearances; these families denounced the commission's cowardice. One such family was that of *tiers-mondiste* leader and great figure of the Moroccan Left Mehdi Ben Barka, who was kidnapped in 1965 in Paris with the complicity of the French, and, in all likelihood, murdered by the Moroccan secret service. His son, Bachir Ben Barka, has lambasted "the summary, incomplete and tendentious presentation of the facts which have led to the deformation of the historic reality."[76]

If the ERC received contradictory reactions within Moroccan society, its work was, on the other hand, praised unanimously by the chancelleries and Western NGOs, happy to find a counterexample, in this time of tension between the Arab-Islamic world and the West.[77] Indisputably, in the international arena, King Mohammed VI benefited from the work of the truth commission. With a certain mordancy, *Journal-Hebdo*, one of the most critical voices in the Moroccan media, observed: "What could be better than a former political prisoner, who spent 17 years in the monarchy's prisons, singing your praises to live down the tortured of Témara?"[78]

Without historical distance, the political impact of the commission in Morocco, however, remains difficult to evaluate. The commission was never able to depend on the support of a vast popular movement, due to factors that are as much sociological as political.

The majority of human rights violations were committed between 1965 and 1985—that is, some twenty years before the creation of the ERC. In a country where more than half the population is under twenty years old, many Moroccans have no direct memory of the "years of lead." It is, thus, difficult to mobilize people on issues of memory that seem far in the past. To this generational fracture can be added the weight of social issues. An important part of the population lives below poverty level. Young people—including university graduates—are concerned with unemployment and other life issues that are more immediate than a reinterpretation of the past.

Finally, the political environment has played an important role in the reception of the commission's message. Created by Mohammed VI and financed by the royal treasury, the commission paid the price of its particular birth. Placed outside the political field by the monarch, it was often perceived as an operation piloted by the Palace. The commissioners were accused of having been co-opted, the traditional strategy of the chérifienne monarchy. Thus, Abdallah El Harif, a former cell mate of Driss Benzekri, affirms that the ERC is "a makhzénienne den" and that its president "supports the status quo" rather than working for real change, judging the attitude of Benzekri to be "dangerous because the system that permitted the crimes of the past is still in place."[79]

The (Islamic) Justice and Democracy Party (PJD) denounced the commission as a "political operation," with the Palace and the Left working together to "whitewash" their respective crimes, but keeping quiet about the ongoing abuse of Islamists. Thus, Lahcen Daoudi, member of the General Secretariat of the PJD, accuses:

> Our party has become the party to destroy. It is for this that the monarchy has made an alliance with the left. They have agreed to rewrite history. The real responsibilities are obscured: on one side, the left poses as a victim, although it believed in armed struggle. On the other, the monarchy was at the time a dictatorship. They were two devils fighting each other. Today, they are writing a truncated truth and the ERC does not investigate the torture and violations that have been committed after the attacks in Casablanca.[80]

On their side, the AMDH and the unrecognized Sahrawi human rights associations, as well as a certain number of victims, criticized the ERC commissioners' choice of accepting "a policy of impunity" regarding those who for decades were the agents of repression. Abdelhamid Amine, president of the AMDH and also a former cell mate of Driss Benzekri, affirms: "The abuse continues in Morocco and impunity persists."[81]

The beginning of this chapter raised three initial questions:

First, how does the "cultural dimension" apply in Islam countries, especially regarding pardon? The evidence shows that the cultural dimension is marginal in the choice of whether or not to punish the perpetrators of mass human rights violations. The cultural factor intervenes only to legitimize a policy of amnesty. The Moroccan case is particularly significant on this point, for it underlined the political stakes linked to the process of justifying impunity. The monarchy put this decision into a religious context, while the commissioners maintained it in a strict political one, hoping thus to maintain social pressure on the state to undertake fundamental reforms. According to its political objectives, each state draws on its cultural and religious rationale to mobilize symbolism that legitimizes the strategies of amnesty, if there is one.

Second, how did the "War on Terror" affect the work of the commission? The answer is clear that at every stage, the context of the "War on Terror" made the commission's work and its perception within Moroccan public opinion more problematic. With the attacks on New York, Casablanca, Madrid, and London, the imperative of a security rationale took precedent over the defense of human rights. The effects were also felt in Morocco. In practice, a truth commission cannot be effectively used in a "soft war" against "terrorism." The tension is too strong between the will of the agencies of repression to have as much room as possible to maneuver and the demands of a commission determined to reveal the repression conducted by those same agencies. *E contrario*, one can hope—although it is difficult to deny or confirm—that the will of the ERC to shine light on past crimes may have limited certain excesses by the forces of order.

The third question is the most far-reaching: Did the ERC constitute an effective lever for democratization and refounding the monarchy? Were the commissioners right to bet on the "historical bargain" that the monarchy proposed against the desire for historical truth and justice for ambitious recommendations? Indeed, this is the decisive point. It supposes a substantial refounding of the nature of Moroccan power, as remarked Prince Moulay Icham, who is Number Four in line for the throne and who is known for his unorthodox remarks: "Democracy and the sacredness of the king are incompatible concepts—that is the entire problem of the Moroccan system. It is a question that affects all of us. . . . The issue now is to dissociate the monarchy from the caliphate system, or to make the latter evolve. Reforming the monarchy is the only way to ensure that it will continue."[82]

The current sovereign's lingering ambiguity about the Hassanian legacy was demonstrated once again with the limits put on the ERC's writing of the historical truth. Oscillating between political recovery and will to reform, the government indicated uncertainty about Morocco's political development.

Despite its unquestionable limits, the ERC gave legitimacy to the word of victims. It proposed reforms that, if put in place, would have transformed Morocco into a constitutional monarchy. The ERC was a breach in that it proposed a possible map toward a true state of law. No one knows how the security forces will react to the commission's proposition of democratization while engaged in the "anti-terrorist war." And what about the economic forces, who have had a direct interest in maintaining their acquired privileges? How will the king maneuver, given the contradictory pressures of Moroccan society?

Indeed, no one knows what use the monarchy and the political class will make of these recommendations. Will they adopt them? If so, Morocco will have demonstrated that the mechanisms of transitional justice are effective for freeing new political space and rebuilding trust between the state and society and will constitute a stimulating precedent in the Arab-Islamic world. Or, rather, will the truth commission have been an exercise with no tomorrow? If the commissioners fail to renovate the Moroccan system, they will face the sentiment of frustration within a society that feels that it has been duped. The ERC will then have laid the groundwork for the Islamist extremists, who believe that violence alone can lead to real change.

The ERC's Moroccan experience underlines the globalization of transitional justice. It makes evident the process of reappropriation by local actors of this commission, according to local political and cultural realities. Steeped in politics—that is, in deliberation and negotiation—a Truth and Reconciliation Commission, by unlocking the past, potentially created a new temporality, a new relationship to oneself and, thus, to national identity.

Chapter 5

Uganda

*Traditional Justice vs.
the International Criminal Court*

T HE DURBAN CONFERENCE marked the failure of transitional justice to
serve as a foundation for a common international culture. Morocco's
Truth and Reconciliation Commission, however, does allow a glimpse
of the potential, if not for internationalization, then for the globalization of
norms of transitional justice—that is, the possibility that a political community can restructure itself by importing a model of the institution and then
adapting it to the local context.

This final chapter examines the intervention of an international authority,
the International Criminal Court (ICC), in a national space, Uganda. It analyzes the charges filed in 2005 by the ICC prosecutor against the five principal
leaders of the Lord's Resistance Army (LRA) for crimes against humanity and
war crimes. These were the first indictments ever made by the ICC, investing
them with an additional political and symbolic charge. More specifically, this
chapter looks at the liberal argument, which claims that there cannot be any
real peace without justice, and at the realist approach, which states that peace is
achieved with leaders in power, independently of the crimes they might have
committed. The peace versus justice debate took an acute form in Uganda.
The indictments of the LRA leaders ignited fierce debate about the ICC's nature and action. The ICC has been called the product of Western judicial neo-
imperialism against "African values." In addition to that, the new court was criticized for being counterproductive: by prohibiting amnesty for crimes against
humanity, it has prolonged war. I intend to refute this cultural argument by showing that the choice between policies of punishment or pardon in Uganda was the
result, above all, of a rational calculation by local actors.

The Ugandan Context: Crimes, Amnesty, and Justice

From its very first case, the ICC has confronted the delicate question of rendering justice in a time of war. The ICC's investigation of crimes committed by the Lord's Resistance Army in northern Uganda already constitutes a powerful indication of the difficulties involved in applying this new judicial diplomacy.

Since 1986, the Ugandan government has attempted—in vain—to put down the LRA militarily. Even if responsibility for the crimes is still to be established in court, no one disputes the reality or even the extent of the abuse committed. Under the leadership of a charismatic chief, Joseph Kony, who claims to have supernatural powers, the LRA has committed horrific crimes. Over two decades, Kony's men have mutilated and murdered thousands of civilians and kidnapped between twenty thousand and thirty thousand children (who were, on average, between ten and fifteen years old) to serve as cannon fodder and sex slaves for the commanders. Under these dehumanizing conditions, the children have too often become criminals themselves. Between 85 and 90 percent of the LRA's soldiers are kidnapped children, many of whom were forced to kill their own parents or people of their communities. The abuse committed by the LRA has forced almost 2 million people—mainly Acholis—to leave northern Uganda and seek refuge in camps administered by the Ugandan authorities; the sordid conditions in these camps have been noted by all observers.

In March 2002, government forces launched Operation Iron Fist, which led to the release of seven thousand prisoners held by the LRA, but also, in June of that year, to the kidnapping by the LRA of more than ten thousand other children.[1] The conflict between the LRA and the government is a continuation of old tensions between northern and southern Uganda, which goes back at least to English occupation of the country in 1894. President Museveni comes from the southern part of the country; Joseph Kony is a member of the Acholi group, which lives in northern Uganda, as are the great majority of his victims. Kony says that he wants to overthrow the government, put the Acholis in power, and govern according to the Ten Commandments.

In this war, which has caused at least a hundred thousand deaths, it is not only the LRA but also government forces, the majority of whom are from the south, who are responsible for violence against the Acholis. The Ugandan Army has been accused of committing atrocities on civilians—notably, executions, torture, rape, arbitrary detention, forced displacement of population, and the recruitment of child soldiers.[2] In his article "The Secret Genocide," Olara Otunnu, the UN under-secretary-general and special representative for children and armed conflict, writes:

> Under the cover of the war against these outlaws, an entire society, the Acholi people, has been moved to concentration camps and is being systematically destroyed physically, culturally, and economically . . . the LRA is frightening, but Northern Uganda's people have more to fear from their own government. It's time that the world understood that. . . . . For more than a decade, governmental forces have kept a population of almost two million (from the Acholi, Lango and Teso regions) in some 200 concentration camps, where they face squalor, disease, starvation, and death.[3]

In 1994 the Ugandan government opened peace talks with the LRA and asked Betty Bigombe to lead the negotiations that, off and on, have continued to this day. In 2000 the Ugandan Parliament promulgated an amnesty law, which benefited some five hundred members of the LRA, including around twenty commanders. Following September 11, the American authorities drew up a list of terrorist organizations, which included the Lord's Resistance Army. In December 2003, Ugandan president Yoweri Museveni officially requested that the ICC prosecutor assess the situation in the north of his country. At the end of July 2004, the ICC formally opened an inquiry. On 13 October 2005, the ICC prosecutor indicted Joseph Kony and four of his commanders with thirty-three charges for war crimes and crimes against humanity. Citing Article 53 of the Statute, which refers to "Iron Fist" and "the interest of justice," the prosecutor put off publishing the charges for two months so as not to disturb the negotiations being led by Betty Bigombe; the negotiator considered this period of time "ridiculously short." In mid-May 2006, President Museveni announced that he would offer total amnesty to Joseph Kony and his commanders if they agreed to put down their arms. As of this writing, the ICC still considers the case open and affirms that it cannot take back the charges because of pressure from the belligerents. To support the peace process, UN undersecretary for humanitarian affairs Jan Egeland met with Joseph Kony on 12 November 2006, at the risk of discrediting the ICC, but the meeting did not bring any breakthrough. Since that time, the LRA has moved to the Democratic Republic of Congo, where it has committed new atrocities and seems to be mostly based.

The intervention of the ICC, President Museveni's flip-flop, and the positions taken by NGOs, the victims, various clergy, and elder councils have unleashed intense debate. In substance, opponents of the ICC accuse it of compromising the possibility of ending one of the most terrible and ignored conflicts that have ravaged Africa,[4] to the point of accusing the Hague Court of being a modern form of Western colonialism, an illegitimate and counterproductive authority. To properly analyze this accusation, it is necessary to look at the general framework of the debate to determine whether or not intervention of international criminal justice in a time of war is valid. The norm of international justice has developed progressively; its successive adjustments indicate the perilous balance involved in the search—simultaneously—for peace and justice.

Defining the Norms: Justice in a Time of War

Since the UN Security Council's creation of the International Criminal Tribunal for the former Yugoslavia (ICTY) in 1993, international criminal justice has intervened during wartime. This has been a break with the classic timing of international relations; traditionally, war has been followed by peace and, sometimes, an attempt at justice. With the advent of the ICC in July 2002, the judicialization of international relations has considerably broadened. The extension of law even into the heart of war poses a fundamental question: is the intrusion of international criminal justice beneficial or is it counterproductive for the populations that it purports to assist? Does it hasten or disrupt the search for peace? The charges brought by the ICC against the leaders of the LRA embody this tension between the search for justice and peace and constitute a precedent heavy with meaning.

Let me first state my agreement with Edward Hallett Carr that the tension between liberal idealism and realism remains impassable: "The theory of divorce between the spheres of politics and morality is superficially attractive, if only because it offers an escape from the insoluble problem of finding moral justification for the use of force. But this theory is, in the end, unsatisfying. . . . For we can neither moralize power nor even less expel power from politics and, so, we are confronted with a dilemma that can never be completely resolved."[5] Carr continues by citing, justly so, theologian Reinhold Niebuhr: "Politics will remain, until the end of history, the place where power and conscience meet, where ethics and the power struggle feed and develop their difficult compromise."[6]

The foundation of the liberal approach is the conviction—realists would call it dangerously utopian—that legal standards can curb barbarity and that, by punishing the perpetrator of abominable crimes, criminal justice has a dissuasive effect on future crimes and lays the groundwork for peace. This approach assumes that there are universal values that transcend the definition of national interest and from which states cannot, theoretically, derogate. It follows that states are accountable for their acts before the new judicial institutions. In the 1990s this new approach disturbed the traditional logic of international humanitarian law built on the Westphalian model. It was no longer only a question of limiting war's abuses, as the Geneva Conventions have done since the middle of the twentieth century, but of punishing their perpetrators while the fighting is still taking place. This approach postulates the idea of an overhanging justice that succeeds in taming and containing violence. It can be read as one of the strongest expressions of post–Cold War liberalism: through the weapon of law, international justice intends to take action against war criminals, even when they are still in power. It is a new model for the regulation of international relations that emerges and collides with the traditional model, which is based on state sovereignty.

Under the influence of this liberal ideology, in the 1990s the states adopted the rule that restated the relations between justice and war. The idea of international criminal justice had first been launched a century earlier by one of the founders of the Red Cross, Gustave Moynier. On 3 January 1872, at the Geneva headquarters of the International Committee for the Relief of the Wounded,[7] Moynier read his eight-page paper, "Creation of an International Judicial Institution, Capable of Preventing and Punishing Infractions of the Geneva Convention," in which he outlined the need for "international jurisdiction" to save civilization against the process of globalization, a term that was still a long way in the future: "The more that the relations between peoples multiply, the obligation to solve disputes through peaceful means becomes imperative for the civilized nations." That was the guarantee for humanity's survival.[8]

By extending Moynier's thinking, liberals mean to bind states' will to power in the mesh of a system of norms and rules of law, themselves originating in a system of collective security. This hope, which U.S. president Woodrow Wilson made his own after World War I, aimed to muzzle the warmongering of nations. After World War II, the believers in the liberal paradigm insisted that those who commit war crimes are the enemies of the human race and, as such, must be individually punished. These criminals not only offend humanity—worse, they constitute a danger to international peace, as affirmed by the Allied military tribunal in Nuremberg: "Where law exists a court will rise. . . . It would be an admission of incapacity, in contradiction of every self-evident reality, that mankind . . . should be unable to maintain a tribunal holding inviolable the law of humanity, and, by doing so, preserve the human race itself."[9]

The realist point of view is radically different. Drawing its lessons from World War II, realists accuse liberals of being responsible for an angelic vision of international relations that leads to "successive capitulations when confronting a State, ideology or man that respects force alone."[10] Realists believe that "security comes in the taming of violence by the threat of counter-violence. They intend to master force by dividing force against itself," as Jean Barrea puts it.[11] Hans Morgenthau's pessimism about political action is clear in his great postwar book, *Politics Among Nations: The Struggle for Power and Peace* (1948). His comment on ethics in international relations is masterfully enlightening on the realistic paradigm:

> Neville Chamberlain's politics of appeasement were, as far as we can judge, inspired by good motives. . . . Yet, his policies helped to make the Second World War inevitable, and to bring untold miseries to millions of men. Sir Winston Churchill's motives, on the other hand, were much less universal in scope and much more narrowly directed for personal and national power, yet the foreign policies that sprang from these inferior motives were certainly superior in moral and political quality to those pursued by his predecessor. . . . It follows that while ethics in the abstract judges the moral qualities of motives, political theory must judge the political qualities of intellect, will and action.[12]

If liberals believe that bloody despots are a threat to peace and must be judged, realists oppose the intrusion of justice that, under the cover of morality, would be profoundly immoral. They emphasize the dangers of justice that destroys opportunities for a peace accord. The second approach won during the Cold War. Notably, it was for this reason that the UN Convention on the Prevention and Punishment of the Crime of Genocide (1948) did not lead to the establishment of a permanent criminal tribunal, as planned.[13]

The argument between realists and liberals took a new turn only at the end of the Cold War. Two new institutions changed the terms of the debate—respectively, the ICTY and the ICC.

With the creation of the ICTY in 1993, as noted above, international justice intervened during, not after, wartime. This intrusion of international
criminal law makes the international (or semi-international) criminal prosecutor one of the protagonists of the conflict. He could open charges against
military or political leaders if he judged them to be responsible for international crimes, even if it meant wrecking a peace process. The prosecutors of
the new courts believe that only a just peace (that is, by their definition, one
not signed by a presumed war criminal) is worthwhile. Thus, David Crane, prosecutor for the Special Court for Sierra Leone, publicized the charges against
Liberian Charles Taylor on the same day that, after four years of efforts by the
United Nations, Taylor decided to go to Ghana to participate in peace talks.
Crane knowingly torpedoed these talks and claimed so:

> I wanted to show to the West Africans that none is above the Law, that the rule
> of law is stronger than the rule of a gun, that by a stroke of a pen, a warlord
> could be de-legitimized in front of his peers. I was ready to take on custody,
> but I didn't intend to have Charles Taylor arrested. I wanted to take him out of
> the peace process. I knew that new arms shipments were on their way to Mon-
> rovia. Taylor had signed 14 cease fires, and eight peace accords, he respected
> none of them, I wanted to prevent him [from signing] a ninth peace agree-
> ment, because afterwards, it would become very difficult to indict him.[14]

This judicial diplomacy changed the terms of conflict. Stanley Hoffmann has
quite rightly remarked that justice is no longer symbolized by a blindfolded
statue holding weights on a balance but, from now on, by a soldier armed with
a sword.[15] Mediators, steeped in their own realist vision of international relations, denounce judicial diplomacy that, in the name of morality, leads to the
prolongation of war and suffering. Their mandate obliges them to negotiate
with anyone who holds real political and military power, for they are the only
ones who can stop a conflict.

From their perspective, the existence of an international criminal court
introduces a factor of incertitude that makes a peace accord all the more prob-
lematical. Political and military leaders fear being indicted and, thus, have an
interest in continuing conflicts that keep them in power. According to the mediators, the "human-rightist" vision is dangerously naive, for it delays the signing of a peace accord, and this delay is responsible for prolonging the war and
for civilian suffering. In the "realistic" perspective, the idealism of the judges

as well as the international prosecutors and all those who support them are potentially guilty for the death of hundreds or thousands of civilians and soldiers. This accusation, of course, objects to the tenets of international criminal justice.

In its purest form, this exchange of arguments took place in the journal *Human Rights Quarterly*, opposing an anonymous writer (without betraying his identity, I can say that he is close to the mediators) and then-prosecutor of the ICTY, Richard Goldstone:

> The quest for justice for yesterday's victims of atrocities should not be pursued in such a manner that it makes today's living the dead of tomorrow. That, for the human rights community, is one of the lessons of the former Yugoslavia. Thousand of people are dead who should have been alive—because moralists were in quest of a perfect peace. Unfortunately, a perfect peace can rarely be attained in the aftermath of a bloody conflict. The pursuit of criminals is one thing. Making peace is another.[16]

Goldstone argues that a true peace without justice cannot exist: that, at best, it can only be a truce, because the war criminals who have lied and cheated will only maintain the truce as long as their direct interests constrain them to do so; but, as soon as the situation changes, they will unleash new hostilities:

> A peace accepted by a society with the willingness and ability to heal, with the willingness and capacity to move itself beyond the abuses of the past, is the only really viable peace. Such is the peace that the international community should be seeking to promote. A peace masterminded by and in order to accommodate the concerns of vicious war criminals defiant of all fundamental international law prescriptions or norms is no such effective or enduring peace.[17]

Goldstone considers peace without justice an illusion of peace. Such an illusion, in fact, is not even worth signing. UN high human rights commissioner Louise Arbour agreed in her remarks at the press conference to announce the indictment of Slobodan Milosevic: "I do not think that it is appropriate for politicians—before and after the fact—to reflect on whether they think the indictment came at a good time; whether it is helpful to a peace process. This is a legal, judicial process. The appropriate course of action is for politicians to take the indictment into account. It was not for me to take their efforts into account in deciding whether to bring an indictment, and at what particular time."[18] We are not far from a republic of judges, or more accurately, a republic of prosecutors. As Frédéric Mégret notes, the evolution that saw international criminal justice participate actively "in the management of international affairs" with the birth of *judicial diplomacy*[19] established a technocratic-judicial management of crises and conflicts, the fruit of the liberal point of view.

In 1998, five years after the creation of the ICTY, the states partially changed this perspective and adopted the Statute of the International Criminal Court. The states feared that an all-powerful court, blinded by moral certainties, would sink peace accords, however imperfect. Two articles in the Statute of the ICC were introduced to curb judicial power in the name of the superior interests of peace. Their mode of operation was very different. Article 16 gave jurisdiction to the UN Security Council to ask that "no investigation or prosecution may be commenced or proceeded with under this Statute for a period of 12 months after the Security Council, in a resolution under Chapter VII of the Charter of the United Nations, has requested the Court to that effect, that request may be renewed by the Council under the same conditions."[20] Thus the Great Powers protected their leeway to bring about peaceful resolution while reserving the explicit right to curb the Court. But the use of Article 16 required a unity and determination that was rare within the UN Security Council.

By Article 53 of the ICC statute, the states gave the prosecutor the jurisdiction for suspending an inquiry or delaying trial, if "taking into account the gravity of the crime and the interests of victims, there are nonetheless substantial reasons to believe that an investigation would not serve the interests of justice." This article explicitly recognized the tension inherent in the search for these two objectives (justice and peace) and left a margin of discretion to the prosecutor. It integrated into its penal strategy a political component, which was the content that it intended to give "in the interests of the court." The states abandoned the fiction of a purely legal approach, and the constraints linked to politics reappeared. In reality, they had never disappeared, but international justice operated according to the convention that they never existed. From now on, these constraints were institutionalized, but it was the duty of the prosecutor to integrate them into his judicial strategy. The prosecutor's power was strengthened by this disposition, because, in certain moments, he could weigh the hypothesis of a future peace accord, decide a priori that an accord could not be signed by presumed war criminals, and decide to keep peace negotiations from taking place by issuing an indictment against one or another protagonist.

This approach consecrated the prosecutor's role as practitioner of judicial diplomacy. From then on, he had the tools to arbitrate the match between the search for justice and peace: theoretically, the prosecutor could respond both to the imperative of justice and the imperative of peace, turned toward the future with the objective of finding a political settlement for the conflict.[21] Thanks to his control over the schedule, his expertise, and the information that he receives from many sources, the prosecutor can henceforth—if necessary—delay the delivery of justice. Thus the prosecutor recognizes, articulates, and takes responsibility for the tension between peace and justice. In the prolongation of this approach, UN Secretary-General Kofi Annan wrote in his report of 3 August 2004: "Justice and peace are not conflicting goals; on the contrary, properly set up, they reinforce one another. The question is, then, in no case to know whether they agree to promote justice and establish responsibility, but to decide when and how to do so."[22]

The important question was, from then on, sequential—that is, when should the work of the mediators stop and that of the prosecutor and judges begin? But this technical management of war raises considerable difficulties, as shown in the charges brought by the ICC against the Lord's Resistance Army.

This approach is part of the larger idea that the international community now has of a "toolbox" for intervening in conflicts. With the ICC, the states have established an outside authority to restructure the conflict, for it redistributes political power between different actors. This new authority operates on the principle of triangulation: the national protagonists are temporarily overruled by the international court before they reappropriate the decisions of this authority, contesting them, if necessary. What has happened in Uganda is an example.

The ICC: Judicial Arm of the Ugandan Government?

The ICC cannot totally escape being manipulated. By its statute as authority, it influences a conflict and modifies the behavior of belligerents and other local players who, for their part, attempt to use the Court to their own ends. In Uganda, it was President Museveni who called in the ICC, guided by a purely political objective: to weaken the LRA. Museveni wanted to increase political pressure on Joseph Kony by isolating his movement all the more. In other words, the aim of criminalization of LRA leaders by an international authority was to stop the support of the government of Sudan, which supplied bases for the LRA and, at the same time, to smother the guerillas politically and militarily.

The ICC prosecutor took the case, although the Court's authority was fragile. No one had serious doubts about the reality of the horrific abuses by the LRA—even if those abuses still had to be proven legally. The case was so strong, in fact, that pressing charges against the leaders of the LRA appeared to the brand-new judicial institution as a blessing hard to resist. Here was a movement described by all as bloodthirsty with practically no political program, listed as "terrorist" by the U.S. government, conducted apparently by a madman whose soldiers had kidnapped thousands of children to transform them into robot killers. It was a movement, in addition, that had gained its only support from the regime in Khartoum, itself suspected of crimes against humanity in Darfur! For a court seeking to validate its legitimacy to the world, especially to the U.S. government, it would have been harder to find better candidates for indictment than the leaders of the LRA.

But, even if the Ugandan president and the ICC prosecutor had a political interest, at least temporary, in collaborating, the ICC's authority was open to debate. Indeed, the founding principle of the ICC is that it intervene only by default, after national jurisdiction has first been solicited. In fact, as Article 17 of the ICC Statutes clearly states, the Court is supposed to intervene when the national courts lack the will or capability to render justice. The opponents to the ICC's intervention in Uganda insisted that President Museveni had declared himself "willing" to judge the leaders of the LRA. The issue, then, was defining the capacity to judge: Does this incapacity come from the absence of a state judicial structure worthy of the name? Or does it come from the fact that the state has no means to capture the suspect? Those opposed to ICC intervention in Uganda favored the first, most restrictive, interpretation. They emphasized Article 17.3, which states: "In order to determine inability in a particular case, the Court shall consider whether, due to a total or substantial collapse or unavailability of its national judicial system, the State is unable to obtain the accused or the necessary evidence and testimony or otherwise unable to carry out its proceedings."[23]

The opponents emphasized that, because Museveni had declared himself able to judge the crimes committed by the commanders of his own army and had disposed of an adequate judicial structure, the ICC had no authority. As

Katherine Southwick notes, "With the Ugandan government both willing and able to conduct prosecutions, the ICC's involvement appears to stretch, if not breach, the provisions of Article 17."[24]

The prosecutor, however, had a different interpretation of Article 17. He defined his competence by the seriousness of the LRA's alleged crimes, and by the fact that he could obtain results beyond the Ugandan government's reach: "The arrest warrants issued by the ICC will help galvanize international efforts to apprehend the suspects. The responsibility to execute the arrests is that of the States' Parties and the international community."[25]

The purely judicial argument on which the prosecutor based the tribunal's competence was, to say the least, debatable. As for the more political argument of "stimulating" the international community to arrest the accused, the prosecutor had himself imposed an obligation to get results, which until this day never materialized. The ICC prosecutor's intervention seemed to be a response to political reasons discussed above: pressured to act by the states that support politically and financially the new court, he was in a hurry to demonstrate the legitimacy of his institution. By indicting the LRA, the prosecutor paradoxically put the ICC in a vulnerable position. As Myriam Revault d'Allonnes notes, "authority, unlike power, goes beyond the command/obey relationship to depend on both the recognition and legitimacy that is awarded it."[26] In this particular case, the ICC's pressing need for international legitimacy led the prosecutor to intervene on a fragile legal basis, undermining the legitimacy that the ICC needed in Uganda to be recognized as an authority.

Not only has the ICC's competence been open to debate, but the prosecutor's penal strategy has been scrutinized as well. He has intervened at the request of President Museveni against the LRA, although the government troops have also committed crimes against the Acholi people but have not been indicted. The ICC runs the obvious risk of appearing as the judicial arm of the Ugandan government. Some have even accused the ICC of being transformed into the Ugandan president's "attack dog": "Many well intentioned Africans, including this author, are unconvinced that a government that has been accused of committing atrocities against the very people it claims to protect should exploit the loopholes in the international justice system to quench political rebellion at home by using international bodies such at the ICC as an attack-dog."[27] The logical conclusion, according to this analysis, is that the action of international justice will be fouled by the indictments against the LRA because, far from the ideals to which it pretends, the Court will be totally manipulated by one of the parties of the conflict.

In the name of impartiality, Human Rights Watch has asked the prosecutor to widen the inquiry to include all suspected of serious crimes: "It is imperative that the ICC conducts an impartial investigation in Uganda. The ICC has the authority to investigate crimes committed by all sides in the conflict, not just the Lord's Resistance Army."[28]

The prosecutor has publicly justified his penal strategy, both in the name of his mandate and the modest resources given him to carry it out. He has said that he has barely enough resources to concentrate on the most serious crimes, those of the LRA, even if the Court does not totally exclude future charges against the Ugandan Army.[29] No doubt it would be particularly difficult for the prosecutor to obtain cooperation from the Ugandan authorities if he simultaneously launched charges against the Ugandan Army.

The result is paradoxical. On one side, it is undeniable that the ICC's action on behalf of the people in northern Uganda suffering abuse from the LRA and, to a lesser degree, from government forces, has been problematic in that it has reinforced one side to the detriment of the other. The credibility of the Court has been further weakened by President Museveni's use of the ICC as a sword of Damocles to force the heads of the LRA to the negotiating table, only to flip-flop with the proposal of amnesty that is forbidden by the Rome Statute.[30] The Ugandan president has used the ICC for his political agenda, offering the Court credibility that it badly needs, only to attempt to take it back as abruptly.[31] On the other side, from the perspective of conflict resolution, the ICC's intervention has not been a failure but has been a partial success: the Court has effectively restructured the conflict by modifying the power struggle. It has intimidated the leaders of the LRA, to the point of accelerating—for a time—the peace process. It has created a new space for negotiation, making the question of amnesty an issue of internal deliberation between the different groups in Uganda.

But this is not the perception that prevails for the mediators, a part of the Acholi elite, and opponents of the ICC. They criticize the prosecutor's supposed partiality and the Court's (relative) ineffectiveness, which led to the radical interpretation of its illegitimacy. Numerous observers, Ugandan officials, and Acholi representatives consider the international court ill adapted to adjudicate in Africa, because it contravenes local approaches to conflict resolution. The Court's handling of the LRA's crimes has brought to light the denunciation of the international court and its supposed imperialist spirit, both of which deserve careful examination.

The ICC: Universal or Neocolonial?

The anti-imperialist argument against the ICC intervening in Uganda can be made in three stages. First, the Court's opponents dispute the ICC's right to intervene in Uganda. Second, they argue that the ICC's indictments undermine the search for peace. As Betty Bigombe, the government's negotiator with the LRA, puts it: "We are talking about ending the war and you cannot end the war if the LRA leadership is not involved in the process. . . . It is now extremely difficult for me to talk meaningfully to the LRA leadership when they know they are being hunted down to be locked up behind bars in Europe." In Bigombe's opinion, the irresponsibility of the prosecutor's office comes from the fact that it consists of "bureaucrats sitting comfortably in their offices in The Hague." Betty Bigombe denounces the international court for being abstract, disembodied, and, above all, out of reach of any of the possible consequences of its actions.[32]

The third and final step of the argument involves looking at Africa as a proving ground for the West's latest organization techniques. As Adam Branch writes:

> Africa is once again serving as a guinea pig for the West, again at her own expense. Whether as the subject for risky medical procedures, unconventional weapons, or aggressive economic restructuring, Africa has for over a century been the unwilling, and often unwitting, subject of experimentation by the West, the place where scientists, strategists, and technocrats can try untried techniques without being accountable to those experimented upon. The most recent experiment is not being carried out by shadowy CIA operatives or ruthless scientists, but by the organisation that is supposed to usher in a new regime of accountability, an end to impunity, and a global rule of law: the International Criminal Court.[33]

Branch's argument is not completely unwarranted. The international court has been called into Africa more than elsewhere: the weakness of Africa's nation-states and the profound dysfunction of many of its judicial systems make them incapable of investigating the mass crimes that have occurred in several countries on the continent. Judicial urgency has, in effect, given priority to intervention in Africa's most fragile states and most dramatic situations and nowhere else. For the rest, Branch's criticism stems from the ICC's initial difficulty in applying to particular cases a rule that was designed to be generalized. This is the real issue for international justice: the ICC must not become an African criminal court.

Adam Branch, however, draws a radically different conclusion: the universality preached by the ICC is only a mask that must be torn away. The ICC, he says, is only the expression "at best, of paternalism and, at worst, of a new imperialism" of the West's relationship to Africa.[34] Branch explains the Court's ineffectiveness and disconnection from local realities that were noted by Betty Bigombe in this way: the ICC has donned the new clothes of Western imperialism.

Branch's argument concludes with the conviction that Africa has its own ways of handling conflict resolution; it has, as the African NGOs insist, judicial systems that are socially more effective than those of criminal justice, which "fail to encourage confession, conciliation or timely justice."[35] Africa, then, has its own concept of justice. Cultural relativism may triumph as the demonstration of judicial imperialism has already been established.[36] According to Sudanese scientist John Akec, it remains only to ask the West to respect "African values": "It is time for the West to respect African values. What Africa needs is Western support to solve its problems, not propagation of confusion as the ICC is currently doing for 'the good of Uganda.' It should go without saying that not every Western bureaucrat in missionary clothes is taken at face value anymore in 21st century Africa."[37]

From here, it is an easy step to adopt the slogan of the Organization of African Unity: "African solutions for African problems." This cultural vision has become dominant in the current debate, opposing African restorative justice to criminal justice—inevitably, Western. The analysis of Helena Cobban, published in *Transitional Justice Forum*, is revealing of this dominant prism:

> Much of the debate has become lodged somewhere between these two approaches to justice: restorative and retributive. The international community, with its own origins and preconceived notions resting squarely within the realm of retributive justice, continues to push for the kinds of institutions it has always used: Nuremberg style trials and tribunals of the kind created to deal with the Rwandan genocide. But evidence has shown and continues to show that this kind of mechanism is not at all suited to the kinds of violent conflict that have taken place in Northern Uganda and elsewhere.... Clearly,

the lessons that are drawn from the resolution of the conflict which now center around the Acholi, might have broader implications.[38]

The assumption that the essence of any culture is fixed and unchanging is obviously debatable, not least because it is historically false. Some Western countries (Spain, for example) have chosen strategies of impunity; others, in particular the regimes of Eastern and Central Europe in transition from Communist dictatorships, have opted for mechanisms of truth-seeking (for example, opening archives) and non-penal punishment (for example, lustration laws). Some African countries, in contrast to the "restorative justice/African values" argument, have chosen policies of punishment. Indeed, one of the reasons that Rwanda's Kigali government was against the creation of the International Criminal Tribunal for Rwanda (ICTR) was that it found the court too merciful: ICTR statutes forbid the death penalty, advocated by the Kagame government. In addition, the Rwandan government has kept more than a hundred thousand presumed criminals behind bars for more than ten years. African restorative justice could be a distant dream.

In addition, the cultural vision obscures the fact that the ICC owes its existence in part to Africa. An African nation, Senegal, was the first to ratify the ICC Statutes, and 30 out of the 106 countries that have ratified the ICC to date are African. In addition, these countries have supported the ICC because of pressure from their own societies and local NGOs that wanted a safeguard against weak national courts. Without Africa, the ICC would never have been established so quickly, if at all. Mass crimes are a modern phenomenon wherever they occur, and it does not insult the Rwandan survivors to see in the genocide machine "a tropical fascism of a nature completely different from what Rwanda had known until then"—in particular, the anti-Tutsi massacres of 1959 and 1973.[39] This modernity of mass crimes creates the need to find new legal remedies such as the ICC.

The cultural vision, then, is false, for it sends Africa back to a pre-political world, to a mystique of the African community and supposedly intangible values, as if these had been fixed once and for all. The promotion of "African values" also obscures the fact that culture tends to collapse after crimes against humanity and that one of the stakes involved in social reconstruction is to invent a new vocabulary to recount and reappropriate the tale of crime and its resolution. Indeed, sometimes under the conduct of authoritarian regimes, as in Rwanda with the setting up of the *gacacas* (neotraditional justice which was used to deal with thousands of alleged *génocidaires*), it leads to the reinvention of peasant's justice. As Christine Deslaurier notes with caution: "Questions remain about the recuperation of traditional legitimacy and about the capacity for adaptation of an autonomous and local system of negotiation along formal standards of modern judicial system, whether it is national or international."[40]

The resort to justice mechanisms originating from the tradition, but modified to suit the new political and social environment, tends to ignore individual responsibility in favor of community procedures. They can, nevertheless, be beneficial. What is important is the capacity of a society to restructure itself politically, whether by reinvention of traditional culture (for example, *ubuntu* in South Africa or the Acholi rituals in Uganda) or through a court of international justice.

A Profit-Loss Calculation

If the Refugee Law Project—the human rights program in the law school of Makere University in Uganda—is correct, and a number of Acholi leaders would have preferred an amnesty approach, it is not for cultural reasons of reconciliation and pardon but in the name of an interpretation of power politics unfavorable to the ICC. The political analysis of the situation by the Acholi religious leaders expressed by Monsignor Matthew Odongo, vicar general of the Roman Catholic Church of the district of Gulu Gulu, confirms this: "As religious leaders, we are concerned about the announcement by Interpol. The ICC and Interpol should hold on and give room to negotiations and see how far this dialogue can go. This is like throwing a stone in water to think that there is no contingency plan for the ICC or Interpol to arrest Kony and his commanders when the government, with an army, has failed for the past 20 years."[41]

In reality, the dilemma posed between international criminal justice and local restorative justice is misleading. The cultural argument merely confuses a simple observation: when international criminal justice is purely declaratory, when it limits itself to indictments, the logic of seeking peace, including through amnesty policies, also regains the upper hand. It is a rational choice made by political players, whatever their origins. In the Acholi case, the purification ceremony known as *Nyono Tonggweno ki Opobo* (literally, "stepping on the egg and opobo branch") proceeds from a logic of amnesty and social reintegration; it is this local justice that the Acholi elite prefer, for it offers political gains superior to the ICC, whose indictments of the LRA chiefs without any prospect of their arrest have appeared counterproductive. According to anthropologist Rosalind Shaw, the ICC compromises traditional mechanisms of social reintegration without offering alternative benefits.[42]

This does not mean that criminal justice, international or not, is, theoretically, inappropriate in Africa. The judicial system, indeed, has always filled a function of order and stability. Cherif Bassiouni notes that "if societies, like human beings, had a genetically imprinted survival instinct, it would be the 'rule of law.' . . . The putative instinct of social survival cannot be biologically demonstrated, but historical empirical evidence points in that direction. History records that a legal system has existed in every one of the 40 or so world civilizations over the past 7,000 years."[43] Vengeance puts society's existence in peril, says René Girard: "Vengeance constitutes an infinite, interminable process. Every time that it flares up anywhere in a community, it tends to spread and provoke a veritable chain-reaction with rapidly fatal consequences" for society as a whole.[44] But societies can protect themselves against this danger "if [the judicial system] limits [vengeance] effectively to a single reprisal carried out by a sovereign authority specialized in its domain. The decisions of the judicial authority always assert themselves as the last word on vengeance."[45]

Sometimes, however, an exclusively judicial approach is impossible because the central power and international justice are too weak, because society still so polarized by the recent conflict that trials could reignite conflict, and because of the many, many criminals.[46] In this case, non-criminal justice that aims for the reintegration of the perpetrators of crimes makes up for this impossibility of the judicial path. Its objective is, however, identical: to end the cycle of vengeance. This is transitional justice's substantial finality: to restructure the political community.

The Ugandan case is important because it brings into competition authorities that are superficially total opposites: the Western modernity of the ICC versus Acholi tradition; international vs. local; the expert language of the law as a purification ritual vs. rites coming from the dawn of time readapted to today's conflict; punishment vs. pardon; and so on. In reality, these authorities, each in their own way, have the same goal. But international criminal justice has until now shown itself incapable of bringing benefits that meet the expectations raised (the arrest and trial of war criminals), while the policies of

amnesty and traditional justice dazzle with a peace-at-hand and the possibility of immediate political gains. For exhausted people, locked in sordid camps
for twenty years, they give hope that the suffering is almost over. In these conditions, it is not surprising that community leaders have a political interest in
choosing amnesty by harkening back to Acholi culture while insisting that
this in no way equates to impunity for criminals. According to the survey made
by the Refugee Law Project, many Acholis share the opinion expressed by this
elder:

> I think amnesty is not very different [from our] traditional ways, because here,
> the Acholi do not have corporal punishment. We believe that a wrong doer will
> not be punished by death because he will not realize the effect. We want him to
> be alive to see—let him feel the shame. . . . So the amnesty is the same because
> it pardons people in the same way the Acholi culture does. You are free, but you
> feel the weight of what you've done. However, you don't let that person go to-
> tally free, he has some mild punishment, which involves the whole clan. The
> whole clan feel the effect because they have to contribute toward the compensa-
> tion for the bereaved family.[47]

But has traditional justice, conceived for dealing with minor offenses, adapted
to punishing the murder of tens of thousands of men, women, and children?
Let me be careful in answering positively. The discourse of traditional justice
only expresses an urgent need to find a peaceful environment. It does not
mean, however, that pardon has truly been granted, as anthropologist Sverker
Finnstrom writes: "Perhaps it is even too early to talk about reconciliation or
justice. Reconciliation can come in only at a later stage in any future peace
process."[48] More importantly, it might be "an act of romantic willful naiveté,"
as anthropologist Richard Wilson has shown in the case of the South African
Truth and Reconciliation Commission, "to conclude that African discourses
on reconciliation alone are capable of bringing peace to a social setting suffering from long-term armed conflicts or extreme political oppression."[49] Acholi
justice is perhaps only a useful coating to justify an amnesty approach that
allows hope for restructuring the local community. In other words, for what
are no doubt excellent political reasons, the cultural argument has been used
to excess.

   In reality, all victims are far from adhering without reservation to an amnesty process. They are often divided between contradictory feelings, seeking
naturally to create the best conditions for peace and security for the future but

without easily giving up on the idea of punishing those at the top who are responsible for such abominable crimes. A poll taken by the International Center for Transitional Justice between 20 April and 2 May 2005, which surveyed 2,585 people in four districts affected by the war (two Acholi and two non-Acholi), indicated that local communities were far from monolithic in their approach to justice and peace.[50] Even the act of polling people is significant, for it establishes a plurality of opinions and takes the monopoly of speech and representation away from the local elite.

The poll concluded that, for the majority of the people surveyed, the quest for justice and peace was not "an exclusive objective." More than three-fourths of those polled (76 percent) affirmed that those who had committed crimes must "be held accountable." Two-thirds of them were in favor of punishment (trial, prison, the death penalty) for the criminal leaders. But there is a hierarchy of needs: 71 percent were disposed to amnesty for all criminals if it were the only option for reestablishing peace. In all, 54 percent preferred peace with trials versus 46 percent who preferred peace and amnesty. The Acholi (44 percent for trials, 56 percent for amnesty) favored amnesty more than the Teso and the Lango did (61 percent for trials and 39 percent for amnesty). In addition, 84 percent of the people polled wished that the international community would be involved in the justice process.[51] A more recent survey conducted between April and June 2007 reached similar conclusions: "More than two-thirds of the respondents (70%) said it was important to hold accountable those responsible for committing violations of human rights and international humanitarian law in northern Uganda. Half of the respondents said the LRA leaders should be held accountable, and 48% said all of the LRA. As many as 70% of respondents said the UPDF committed war crimes and human rights abuses in northern Uganda, and 55% said they should be put on trial. At the same time, there was an important new emphasis on truth-seeking as necessary for victims and an increased willingness to compromise through amnesties or pardons in order to allow the peace process to succeed. Most respondents (65%) said those who received amnesties should first apologize before returning to their communities."[52]

Such polls can reveal a number of lessons. The first evidence, which validates the anticultural analysis, is the absence of a homogeneity of viewpoints among the populations: the number of opinions in favor of penal punishment (a bit less than one out of two among the Acholi people and a bit more than half among the non-Acholis) is significant, whereas international criminal justice has not been effective.[53] The studies by the Refugee Law Project and the International Center for Transitional Justice indicate a gap between the people's desire for some kind of penal sanction and the elite's more prudent attitude.

At the end of analysis, it is clear that international criminal justice is not the expression of judicial "colonialism." In Uganda the prosecutor was trying to reinforce by a primary judicial action the ICC's legitimacy, even if it meant intervening based on debatable authority. He justified his intervention by his ability to "galvanize" the will of the international community to capture the main perpetrators of crimes against humanity, something that has never been tested. The rejection of the ICC by a part of the population came not from its imperialist character but from fear that the Court's action, in particular the ban on amnesty for crimes against humanity, would lead the LRA leaders to continue in their madness, for lack of any alternative. If the indictments by the ICC had meant the swift arrest of the LRA leaders and the end of the war, the number of supporters of criminal justice would be much greater. International justice is no less adapted for Uganda than for Bosnia. The only difference—albeit a big one—is in the discrepancy between the legal norms and their effectiveness.

To this day, the ICC's balance sheet yields two radically different interpretations. Either it is a failure, in that the International Court of Justice of The Hague has been incapable of completing its mission; or it is a success in that the ICC has been the authority that convinced the leaders of the LRA to engage like never before in negotiations with the Ugandan government. There is now hope that the peace process will lead to an accord that guarantees at long last security and a return to normal life for millions of Ugandans. If that happens, the ICC prosecutor may bow out, but the Court will have played its part. In certain respects, the Court, manipulated by one and all, seems to have been reduced to a judicial weapon shorn of its ethical ambition. But the finality of its intervention is the return to peace, not to fulfill an idealistic vision of a new world order. In its role as authority, even if it is strongly contested by some, the Court has changed the behavior of the belligerents, restructured the conflict, and given some momentum to the peace process. If peace takes hold, the principle of triangulation will have triumphed. Uganda's path will have passed by The Hague, and international criminal justice will have functioned as a regulating idea, re-articulating the special relationship to the universal.

Archbishop Desmond Tutu was right to remind us that it is the Ugandans who will live with the political consequences of whatever justice they choose: "When all is said and done, it is up to the Ugandans themselves to decide on the best solution for themselves. But, whatever it may be, this solution must not hamper reconciliation and healing, nor on the other hand, encourage impunity and revive the suffering of the victims."[54]

Conclusion

A PROFOUND PARADOX lies at the heart of transitional justice. On the one hand, it has a role in the process of rebuilding society and the state. On the other, as a product and as an agent of neoliberal globalization, the most destructive effects of which it seeks to mitigate, transitional justice siphons off a part of the state's own legal, political, and symbolic power. In these pages, I will examine this paradox more closely, as well as the challenges it raises.

By breaking down market barriers, globalization contributed to the blurring of national boundaries, and with them, traditional references. The rise in power of hypernationalism, ethnicity, and fundamentalism from the former Yugoslavia to Kenya, from Rwanda to the Caucasus Mountains, is a sign of a political crisis in fragile societies. National identities are being pulled between the dynamics of fragmentation—of which the politics of ethnic cleansing is the most poisonous form—and supranational dynamics. Having lost their bearings, societies search for new identities: around what narrative, what memory, what values, should a nation project and reconstruct itself?

This task is all the more difficult in that violence is no longer a state monopoly: paramilitaries, militias, private companies in the security business, and transnational terrorist movements are the most visible expressions of these new local and global players. To them can be added political confrontation and organized crime—and the environment becomes propitious to the massive violation of human rights.

Transitional justice seeks to reconstruct the social fabric of these torn societies. This is the objective of the double reconciliation sought by the promoters of transitional justice, that is, the horizontal reconciliation between violently opposed groups and the vertical reconciliation between society and the machinery of the state that has persecuted them. With these strategies, which simultaneously contain violence and offer a way out of conflict, the action of transitional justice aims to reinforce social cohesion and to reestablish the state of law.

It was in the name of this logic of reconstruction that the International Criminal Tribunal for the former Yugoslavia (ICTY), Morocco's Equity and Reconciliation Commission (ERC), the Durban Conference, and the International Criminal Court (ICC) were all conceived. In spite of the radical differences between their historic situations, these examples share a common point: with different degrees of success, the promoters of transitional justice have in each case invented a particular model to respond to the challenge of massive violations of human rights.

From the purification rituals of Acholi justice to the action of the ICC and the truth commissions, we have seen the extraordinary adaptability of the tools of transitional justice at work and how this adaptability has given rise to fierce debate within the political class and society as a whole concerning the best approach. We have observed how the human rights community was divided in Morocco concerning the truth commission. In Uganda we have witnessed the competition between the ICC and traditional justice. Depending on the power struggle, contexts, and political objectives of the different actors, an entire range of tools and institutions is now available. But the question is not whether the mechanisms of transitional justice should be used, but which ones should be used and at what moment.

If transitional justice participates in the reconstruction of a state by putting an end to chaos and violence, it also participates in the shrinking of that state's influence. This shrinking has taken legal, political, and symbolic forms. Note, first of all, that the international tribunals—as seen with the ICTY—were established on the basis of Chapter VII of the UN Charter, which in the name of peace and international security allows the transgression of the boundaries of national sovereignty. Note also that the new law, formalized in the 1990s, has stripped states of some of their prerogatives. Thus, according to the number of bodies and jurisdictions internationalized, states can no longer—at least, in theory—give amnesty to war crimes, crimes against humanity, and genocide. In 1999, the United Nations forbade its mediators to guarantee peace accords that include blanket amnesties for the most serious crimes. In the resolution of conflicts and the handling of mass crimes, state power is, henceforth, curbed. In addition, the principle of universal jurisdiction and the globalization of criminal law have broken the, until then, virtually umbilical link binding the state and its territory, as the Pinochet case well illustrated.

The judicialization of international relations has had profound political effects, notably in the transformation of the relation between war and justice. The ICTY's indictment of Serbian president Slobodan Milosevic in 1999 and, even more so, that of Liberian president Charles Taylor at the very moment when he was on his way to participate in peace negotiations supported by the United Nations and attended by five heads of state, indicate the concrete effects of this new judicial diplomacy.

The shrinking of the state's role can be seen even in the manner in which the nation speaks to itself. The state now wears the face of Janus: it not only presents itself as heroic, seeing in the convulsions of history a nation emerging and building, but it may also describe itself, in the dark moments of its past, as criminal. The innumerable words of repentance—whether reserved for the fate of indigenous people, for the abandonment and persecution of Jews and Roms during World War II, for the Tutsis during the Rwandan genocide, or for the massacre at Srebrenica and many other places—are not mere words of recognition. They also indicate the weakening of the state, admitting in public its historical responsibility. The reparations awarded to the victims of the violations of human rights (whether by Morocco, Argentina, Chile, or the ICC), the demands for pardon, the critical rewriting of the history books, the multiplication of days of commemoration for once persecuted groups, all participate in this process to reevaluate the place of the state in the international system. This reevaluation should not be understood as masochism on the part of political power, a willing acceptance of its own emasculation, but the effects of neoliberal globalization that I noted earlier.

As the mirror image and agent of globalization, transitional justice forges new links between the particular and the universal. In the name of moral imperative—the struggle against impunity, the respect of human rights—it participates in a redefinition of national sovereignty, and nations that have known massive human rights violations constitute laboratories for experimentation. So-called hybrid tribunals, combining a national and international dimension, incarnate new forms of sovereignty. Sierra Leone, East Timor,

Bosnia-Herzegovina, Kosovo, Cambodia, Lebanon, and, maybe tomorrow, Burundi are so many examples. Even concerning the principle of intervention, the ICC is based on the concept of sovereignty that is no longer absolute: states have the obligation to punish the perpetrators of mass crimes, and if they do not—whether due to an absence of political will or of capacity—the International Court of Justice in The Hague has the authority to intervene.[1] This union of the universal and the particular reflects the process of constituting a judicial space that is both global and unequal, since, for example, three of the five members of the UN Security Council (that is, China, the United States, and Russia) have stayed well away from ratifying the Statutes of the ICC. Also, the principle of universal competence has been up to now used against nationals from weak states, and it is hard to imagine a judge from a weak state attacking with any success the nationals of one of the Great Powers.

Even if international justice cannot abstract itself from power struggles, this is now the era of cross-fertilization, with the development of hybrid tribunals, the advent of the ICC, and the application of the principle of universal competence. Naomi Roht-Arriaza calls "the Pinochet effect" the political and legal product of these interactions at different levels of justice that continue to echo and to feed one another: a Spanish judge's indictment of the ex-dictator of Chile and his house arrest for 503 days in Great Britain spotlighted the effects thousands of kilometers away of the dynamic of transitional justice initiated in different European countries. These indictments have indirectly reactivated legal procedures in Argentina and Chile (via the abrogation of amnesty laws) and have stimulated the use of the principle of universal jurisdiction in extraterritorial cases—for example, against the ex-dictator of Chad, Hissène Habré, known as "the African Pinochet."

This union of the universal and the particular poses challenges that are both new and fundamental: How does a state carry out the distribution of tasks between the national and international? What are the minimal standards to respect in an era of the flexibility of transitional justice? To what degree are traditional courts, such as those in northern Uganda, adapted to judging mass crimes? Indeed, if transitional justice has rewritten the relationship with evil, if it has produced new values, new standards, and new institutions that are themselves inspired by new law, this reconfiguration has created significant challenges. I have identified four major ones.

Legal Ambiguity

As discussed above, transitional justice has given birth to new law. But pro-found ambiguities remain as to the application of these new rules. From now on, general amnesty is forbidden for the perpetrators of international crimes. But at what level of responsibility are criminals exempt from amnesty? Which crimes are subject to pardon and which should be excluded from pardon under any circumstances? The answer is not clear. As Christine Bell notes, the norms are vague: "There is no easy 'list' to hand to negotiators, and this means that clear instructions—the easier way to ensure that mediators play a normative role—is not possible."[2] This normative blur reflects, in part, the impossibility of transcending the tension between the search for justice and that of peace. On the one hand, the United Nations and the ICC insist on the impossibility of building a democratic society while the foundation of political power is built on the impunity of mass crimes. On the other hand, the United Nations balks at setting strict rules that risk limiting the outcome of eminently fragile peace accords. The new law has redrawn the approach of the international commu-nity in conflict resolution without bringing any clear response to the new di-lemmas that it raises. Negotiators and mediators must assume, as best they can, this normative vagueness.

The Competition for Victimhood

Transitional justice offers a treatment for history's wounds. But this redemp-tive vision of history restored is no guarantee of success, for it can also pro-duce a world where practically everyone can demand reparation for suffering endured by his or her ancestors, turning the political community into a com-munity of plaintiffs. Transitional justice has, in effect, brought about a trans-fer of sacredness from the state to the victims, and this symbolic benefit has proved to be an ambiguous success for the victims. Not only does this transfer of sacredness threaten to freeze the victims into fixed roles, transforming them into designated agents of national reconciliation or the guardians of the memory of persecution, but it also puts them into competition. Only those who are recognized in the public space as victims can obtain recognition and reparation, whether symbolic or financial. The danger is in creating a market of suffering, as the Durban Conference sadly illustrated, which could ulti-mately lead to a war of memories.

Justice Perverted by Politics

Transitional justice, as we have seen, can no more separate itself from politics than humans can live without oxygen. But to be credible and legitimate, transitional justice must achieve autonomy from the political power or powers that have created it. Transitional justice cannot be merely the judicial or commemorative arm of a government or military alliance, for governments may be tempted to use and manipulate it to various ends, whether to put pressure on one or several belligerents (for example, the belligerents in the former Yugoslavia or the LRA in Uganda) or to whitewash or criminalize a leader or a regime. The law of justice and peace in Colombia or the Commission for Reception, Truth and Reconciliation (CAVR) in Timor-Leste have been used to whitewash the reputations of men suspected of serious crimes (to the extent that the UN secretary-general Ban Ki-moon has forbidden the United Nations to collaborate with this commission). On the other hand, transitional justice can serve to demonize the adversary. No one denies that Saddam Hussein was one of the bloodiest tyrants of the twentieth century, in particular during the 1980s, when the West considered him to be an effective barrier against the regime of the mullahs of Tehran. Nevertheless, his trial was marred by deep dysfunctions, including the assassination of some of the lawyers for his defense, and the pedagogical value of such justice remains to be seen. It is indeed striking to note the difference in the UN Security Council's approach. The Security Council did not consider it worthwhile to create an international criminal court for conflicts during which millions of men, women, and children perished, as in Congo; but, in Resolution 1757 (30 May 2007), it installed the Hariri tribunal in the name of the former prime minister of Lebanon (assassinated 14 February 2005) to judge the perpetrators of his murder and a dozen other assassinations of Lebanese political figures. The United Nations has never been embarrassed by the blanket amnesty, adopted in the peace accord of Taef in 1991, which guaranteed impunity to the perpetrators of war crimes and crimes against humanity in the Lebanese civil war and subsequent wars that caused tens of thousands of deaths.

The Technocratic Illusion

Transitional justice is based on the idea of a "toolbox" to manage war crimes, associated with the idea of "closure," the need to close the dark pages of the past. In closure can be seen the understandable desire of politicians, as well as part of society itself, to bring to an end the calling up of the past and to "turn toward the future" once the violence has been brought under control. In radically different ways, it is this ambition that we have seen in the work of the IER in Morocco and the ICC in Uganda. However, neither the "toolbox" nor "closure" holds up under examination. All of these examples demonstrate the illusion of locking away the past. It is vain to impose a duty of justice on an improbable tribunal of history, as much as it is vain to wish to write the final word on judicial truth, historical truth, or truths seen by human memories, as if, in fact, these could merge. Over two decades, Argentina has tried it all: criminal trials, truth commissions, and presidential pardons, and then repeal of amnesty laws and a return to a penal approach. Paradoxically, the impossibility of closure is good news: what is really at stake is society's ability to return to the events that devastated and transformed it.

Thus, transitional justice faces danger from many directions, not the least of which is the evolution of international norms and values, marked notably by the questioning of the universality of human rights and by multilateralism exemplified in the marginalization of the UN system. For a while, there was a certain euphoria around transitional justice, symbolized by Fyodor Dostoyevsky's phrase in *The Brothers Karamazov*: "We are all responsible for one another." This euphoria was marked in several ways, with the false but reassuring idea of a reconciliation that is almost at hand, without requiring painful compromises. The extraordinary aura of the South African TRC beyond its borders contributed to this enthusiasm. This craze for justice found its peak in the 1999 Belgian law of universal jurisdiction that authorized the pursuit of any war criminal with no link whatsoever to Belgian territory. Unenforceable and facing the hostility of the United States, the most utopian provisions of this law were quickly abrogated, but they reveal a mood that, here and there, lingers.

I would like to present the case here for a humble form of transitional justice. The mechanisms of transitional justice are not products with a fixed life but, instead, a slow historical process, the effect of which permeates society, while mixing with other social and political facts. They have real force only to the degree that they are integrated into the effective reconstruction of a state of law and democracy. It would, however, be dangerous to exult in the hubris of international justice and the politics of reconciliation. The existence of an international tribunal has rarely held back so-called purifications. The massacres of Srebrenica, two years after the creation of the ICTY, are tragic proof.

Limited, fragile, subject to unrelenting political pressures from all sides, and in constant danger of manipulation, transitional justice mechanisms may, to the degree that peoples make them their own, constitute true liberation from the chains of the past. At a time of ethnic passions, they represent a rare source of hope.

Epilogue
The Challenge of Legitimacy

MANY DEVELOPMENTS HAVE occurred in the field of international relations and transitional justice since the publication of the initial French edition of *Judging War, Judging History* in autumn 2007.

The single act of the inauguration of the Obama Administration in January 2009 created a new international atmosphere. Obama's announcement of the closure of the prison at Guantánamo Bay, the ban on torture, the United States' return to multilateral diplomacy, and a more constructive approach to the International Criminal Court (ICC) were all signs of this change.

There have also been many developments in the field of international justice, whether in Latin America, Africa, Europe, or Asia. On 17 February 2009, the trial of "Duch," the former chief warden of the Khmer Rouge's sinister Tuol Sleng prison, began in the Extraordinary Chambers in the Courts of Cambodia; at the beginning of March, the Special Tribunal for Lebanon also opened. In addition to these two new hybrid criminal tribunals is the (imminent) trial of the ex-leader of the Bosno-Serbs, Radovan Karadzic, at the International Criminal Court for the former Yugoslavia (ICTY). The ICTY and the International Criminal Court for Rwanda (ICTR) are both now engaged in finishing their work. And the ICC itself has accelerated its indictments: on 4 March 2009, under intense criticism, it brought charges for the first time against an acting head of state, Sudanese president Omar al-Bashir, for war crimes and crimes against humanity.

In September 2009, two ambitious reports emanating from fact-finding missions on crimes committed in recent conflicts—the December 2008 to January 2009 conflict in Gaza and the five-day war between Georgia and

Russia in October 2008[1]—demonstrated the continued expansion of the role of truth mechanisms in international relations and also generated a number of questions about their methodology, their neutrality, and their right (or not) to determine if international crimes have been committed.

A discussion of the long list of these striking events might give the misleading impression that transitional justice and international justice in particular are developing according to a smooth and continuous process. Nothing could be further from the truth.

Impunity remains the reality for the vast majority of perpetrators of serious violations of international humanitarian law. Although more than one hundred countries are now parties to the ICC, others, like Iraq, Somalia, Zimbabwe and Burma, hide from international justice behind the walls of national sovereignty. Even when courts exist, they do not always accomplish the mandate entrusted to them. The ICTR has never indicted the perpetrators of the so-called revenge crimes following the 1994 genocide of the Tutsis.

I have noted the rise of the hybrid tribunals. They were meant to fill the deficiencies of the first generation of the UN ad hoc tribunals (ICTY and ICTR), but they were too expensive, too slow, too Western, too removed from the societies concerned, and with a too-feeble impact on the often failing judicial systems in those countries. However, the world now has six models of hybrid tribunals (in Sierra Leone, Bosnia-Herzegovina, Kosovo, East Timor, Cambodia, Lebanon), and the results are, for now, mixed. Certainly, this semi-international justice is a bit less expensive, but it is also subject to stronger political pressure. The Extraordinary Chambers of Cambodia have begun their work but are hampered by the inertia of local authorities who want to delay the trial.[2] In addition, the desired proximity with the people most concerned is not guaranteed: the flagship of hybrid justice, the trial of the ex-president of Liberia, Charles Taylor, is taking place thousands of kilometers from the victims, in The Hague and not in the halls of the Special Court for Sierra Leone (SCSL), which indicted him.[3] To avoid the risk of destabilizing Lebanon, and for security reasons, the Special Tribunal for Lebanon (STL) is headquartered in the Dutch capital. Hybrid justice's promise to be close to the victims, while benefiting from the independence of its semi-international character, has yet to be demonstrated.

The challenges identified in the preceding pages are still significant: legal ambiguity,[4] the competition for victimhood, or justice perverted by politics and technocratic illusions. To these difficulties are added one of the fundamental challenges of international justice: controversial legitimacy. This challenge is not a new one: Nazi dignitaries denounced the Nuremberg trials in 1946 as a justice of the victors. More recently, the former Serbian president, Slobodan Milosevic, and many other defendants also challenged the legitimacy of the ICTY, with the support of a large percentage of the Serbian and Croatian population who saw in the first international tribunal the judicial arm of NATO.

What is new is the bloc opposition by a major regional organization like the African Union (AU), composed of dozens of countries, some of them supporters of international justice. At the 2008 Sharm el Sheikh Summit, the AU warned the European Union (EU) that the indictment of African officials suspected of international crimes by the European tribunals in the name of universal competence would "have negative consequences for the relationship between the EU and the African side,"[5] considering Africa to be a victim of "politically selective" justice, which "evokes memories of colonialism."[6] Tensions between the AU and the EU were such that discussions were conducted in the first semester of 2009 to defuse future diplomatic crises.

Tensions hit a new peak on 4 March 2009 with the ICC's indictment of the acting president of Sudan for war crimes and crimes against humanity. Following Sudan's virulent criticism of the Court's "judicial neo-imperialism," the member states of the Islamic Organization Conference, the Arab League, the Non-Aligned Movement, and the African Union accused the Court of violating Sudanese sovereignty, of threatening chances for a peace accord,[7] of not respecting the immunity accorded heads of state, and of making it more difficult for aid workers to reach victims.[8] The indictment of the Sudanese president, as well as the timing of the indictment, unleashed a vast debate on the prosecutor's penal strategy. But beyond this controversy, the reaction to the indictment of Omar al-Bashir underlines the fact that the effectiveness of the courts internationally rests on their moral authority. In this particular case, the ICC's authority was openly put into question when the states of the AU invited—to their territory or to the AU summit—President al-Bashir, considered to be a presumed war criminal by the ICC. The snub was even worse when the AU announced at its summit in Libya in July 2009 that it intended to take no notice of the indictment of the Sudanese president by the court of The Hague.[9] But this snub also generated reaction. Former secretary-general of the United Nations Kofi Annan publicly denounced the African leaders who showed solidarity with presumed mass murderers instead of with their victims: "One must begin by asking why African leaders shouldn't celebrate this focus [of the ICC] on African victims. Do these leaders really want to side with the alleged perpetrators of mass atrocities rather than their victims?"[10]

This hardening of the African Union toward international justice is a reversal, for it was thanks to many African countries that the ICC was able to enter into action in July 2002 by crossing the fatal barrier of sixty ratifications. Another sign of this change in attitude: although thirty African states ratified the Statutes in 2009, with one exception (South Africa), none of these countries had incorporated its provisions in its own national law, making the work of the ICC more difficult. This African hardening translates into the South's growing mistrust of the mechanisms of truth and justice that they denounce as judicial neo-imperialism. This rejection is all the stronger due to its North-South dimension, honed by the old relations of domination of the colonial era. It is symptomatic that in June 2009, the South bloc supported the Sri Lankan government's rejection of the request by the UN High Commissioner for Human Rights, backed by the governments of the West, to create a commission of inquiry into the deaths of thousands, if not tens of thousands, of civilians in the conflict between the Sri Lankan army and the Tamil Tigers.[11]

Multiple factors explain the hardening of the southern states: in addition to the solidarity that binds the members of regional groups, some authoritarian governments fear that international justice could one day turn on them. Many confront their own rebel movements and do not want the interference of a court investigating possible violations committed by their armed forces. The indictment of President al-Bashir was in this sense a dangerous precedent.

To the security factor is added political and ideological factors. The International Criminal Court has the ambition to be universal, but it is not. Thus, three of the five permanent members of the UN Security Council (China, the United States, Russia)[12] have not ratified the Statutes, exonerating themselves of any prosecution thanks to the veto of the Security Council, unlike other states. This double standard is considered all the more unacceptable in that the nations of the West that have posed as the champions of human rights are now in decline. Their ability to lobby their ex-colonies has weakened, while that of China, attached to an inflexible conception of its national sovereignty, has grown in strength and plays a major role in Africa and Asia.

Exasperation with the West is reinforced by the fact that it poses as a teacher while, during the "war against terror," it has often put security imperatives above certain constraints of the law—for example, the Bush Administration's policy of rendition of "illegal combatants" whereby it "subcontracted" torture to its allies in the South.

The governments of the South, in particular the Arab world and Africa, can better exploit their peoples' resentment of Europe, where the courts most active in international justice sit today and which is composed of countries that carry colonial baggage. Neither transitional justice nor *a fortiori* international justice has ever taken into account the evils of slavery and colonialism. Reparations have been exceedingly rare and hardly conclusive.[13] In addition, the historical experience of law in the colonized countries was that of an instrument, not of liberation and equality as in the West; law was a tool serving the European powers "to create a racial hierarchy, to dehumanize the local populations, to institutionalize the inequality and to dispossess the resources of these countries."[14]

More than elsewhere, the challenges of international justice are exacerbated in the Middle East. The colonial legacy, the persistence of many conflicts, foreign military intervention, and the lack of democracy make the work of international tribunals and commissions of inquiry more difficult there. Despite this, the spread of international justice has also been extended to this part of the world. This development has not yet received the attention it deserves because it is new, complex, and protean. In this region, where political and security concerns prevail over legal considerations, what are the effects of newly created courts and commissions of inquiry?

This is the example with which I would like to conclude this epilogue, because it shows—sometimes in caricature—a willingness to exploit international justice. However, and surprisingly, it appears that the political effects of these judicial and extrajudicial efforts are multiple and ambiguous. If strategic legalism can fill some of the original political goals set by its initiators, in the long term the politico-judicial dynamic thus engaged is difficult to control in the public arena. They may even encourage strategies of resistance and organizing against powers, reflecting the values of equality and justice preached.

First, note the impressive number of mechanisms for international justice related to the Middle East—and the list here is not exhaustive—that have been seized or created since 2000, the extent of which merits consideration:

- The International Court of Justice (ICJ), which on 9 July 2004 delivered an advisory ruling, "The Legal Consequences of the Wall Built on the Palestinian Occupied Territories";
- The International Criminal Court, which has accused the perpetrators of international crimes for atrocities committed in Darfur (Sudan), and which in spring 2009 conducted a preliminary examination on the Israeli-Palestinian conflict in Gaza of December 2008 and January 2009;
- The Special Tribunal for Lebanon, the first hybrid tribunal whose mandate is to punish the perpetrators of terrorism related to the attack that killed former prime minister Rafik Hariri on 14 February 2005;
- The Iraqi Special Tribunal for Crimes Against Humanity (IST), which is strictly an Iraqi court, although it was supported by the United States, both in search of the defendants and in the judicial process. It was established by the U.S.-appointed Iraq Governing Council on 10 December 2003. Paul Bremer, the U.S. administrator in Iraq, signed the statute into law on behalf of the Coalition Provisional Authority. On 11 August 2005, the Iraqi Transitional National Assembly adopted a new Statute of the Iraqi Special Tribunal, which changed its name to the High Criminal Court;
- The Scottish Court in the Netherlands (3 May 2000–14 March 2002), which ruled on the alleged perpetrators of the attack against Pan Am 103, the flight that exploded over Lockerbie on 21 December 1988;
- The United Nations Fact-Finding Mission to investigate all violations of international human rights law and international humanitarian law that might have been committed in the Gaza conflict of December 2008 and January 2009; and
- The national courts in Belgium, Great Britain, New Zealand, and Spain, acting under the principle of universal jurisdiction and seeking to punish politicians and Israeli soldiers suspected of war crimes and crimes against humanity.

With the exception of the ICJ, the work of these tribunals and commissions of inquiry relates to international crimes (war crimes, crimes against humanity, and acts of terrorism). To describe their work, the terms of transitional justice are ill adapted; none of these countries are in the sort of post-conflict situation known in post-apartheid South Africa, the former military dictatorships in Latin America, or the former communist regimes in Central and Eastern Europe. With the exception of the Scottish court dealing with the attack against the Pan Am jet, all others (Iraq, Sudan, Israel, Palestine, and, to a lesser extent, Lebanon) affect societies still in conflict.

As does humanitarian aid, justice in a time of war participates in the general waging of the conflict. The former judge of the ICTY, Georges Abi-Saab, noted that international justice does not exist, like an astronaut, in a state of weightlessness outside power struggles, but in the real world, breathing the oxygen of politics. In a conflict, the belligerents and their allies use these instruments of justice to support the legitimacy of their cause, to isolate, weaken, and criminalize the enemy and impose their narrative in the public arena.

In the Middle East (and elsewhere), this desire to exploit the law for political ends has resulted in the establishment of a made-to-measure mandate, aiming to render selective justice. This explains the mistrust and even the opposition of the vast majority of Arab states and Israel to international justice and, in particular, the ICC. Their joint opposition is evident in the fact that the Arab states constituted the bulk of the twenty-one countries that abstained from voting on the Statute of the ICC in 1998, and that three of the seven countries that opposed the Statute were Bahrain, Israel, and Qatar. Eleven years later, only three (and Palestine since January 2009) of the fifty-seven member countries of the Islamic Conference Organization were parties to the ICC, while one hundred and ten countries have now ratified the Rome Statute.

In a specific context and in terms of the specific policy objectives, governments—whether through their political clout, through alliances, or through their numerical majority—manage to create judicial institutions and commissions of investigation, imagining that they can control these instruments. However, the evolution of the balance of power, local and international contexts, and the movement toward the independence of judicial bureaucracies enable the internationalized courts to escape, at least partially, the objectives of their creators. Experience shows that the ICTY, which was established as an alibi court, set a precedent: it generated considerable jurisprudence and launched a political momentum and legal revolution that no one could have anticipated.

Chaired by Richard Goldstone, the first prosecutor of the ICTY, the Fact-Finding Mission on the Gaza Conflict (27 December to 18 January 2009) also deserves attention. The objective of the states that established this mission was to criminalize the Israeli government. But here again, the many developments of this fact-finding mission illustrate how truth mechanisms can often be difficult to control and have results that differ greatly from the initial obective.

The initial impulse for this mission came from Cuba, Egypt (on behalf of the Arab and African groups), and Pakistan (on behalf of the Organization of the Islamic Conference). On 12 January 2009, Cuba, Egypt, and Pakistan sponsored Resolution S-9/1 in the Human Rights Council (HRC), asking the United Nations to investigate "all violations of international human rights law and international humanitarian law by the occupying power, Israel, against the Palestinian people throughout the Occupied Palestinian Territory, particularly in the occupied Gaza Strip, due to the current aggression." The Israeli authorities immediately refused to cooperate.

A number of prominent experts refused to chair the commission, on the grounds that only one side would be investigated. In April 2009, Richard Goldstone did agree to chair the commission, but only if the mandadte were made more balanced. This request was granted by the HRC's president, Martin Ihoeghian Uhomoibhi, who expanded the mandate to investigate international crimes committed during the Gaza conflict, independently of the nationality of their authors.[15]

In the end, the Goldstone report did not beome the political victory that the sponsors of Resolution S-9/1 expected. On the one hand, the Israeli authorities (which rejected the report outright as politically biased) were accused of war crimes and possibly of crimes against humanity. But Hamas was also accused of the same charges.

Moreover, the main recommendation of the Goldstone report placed the Arab states in an ideological contradiction. If the two sides did not investigate crimes committed by their own combatants, the Security Council would refer the situation (i.e., the crimes committed during the Gaza conflict) to the International Criminal Court. But the Arab states had been for years the most critical voices against the ICC's "neo-imperialism." They now found themselves, for opportunistic reasons, approving a report that they would have fought in other circumstances.

Although it would be going too far to say that the Goldstone report was a model of a fact-finding mission, it did demonstrate that "truth mechanisms" can deliver results unanticipated by the political sponsors of such missions.

Even where such courts or commissions remain docile instruments at the service of the political power that has shaped them, once they operate in the public arena, their creators may not be able to control their impact. What prevails in the end is not the verdict but the interpretation made by the international audience.

A brief analysis of the effects of the trial of Saddam Hussein gives a glimpse of surprising results: The long hunt for the former Iraqi tyrant and his arrest by American troops, his trial, and his hanging, all under the media spotlight, sought to legitimize the U.S. military intervention in Iraq. Nevertheless, the merits of this intervention were disputed by a large part of Western and Arab public opinion. The former tyrant was tried by the Iraqi Special Tribunal (IST), which was funded by the Iraqi Governing Council appointed by the United States, and worked with logistical and technical support from the United States. Ultimately, not only was the trial's political objective not achieved, but the IST was criticized for not affording the former dictator a fair trial.[16] In addition, the Bush Administration became the target of criticism and even lawsuits (with no result so far) for the use of torture and the treatment of prisoners at Abu Ghraib and Guantánamo, which were carried out in the name of human rights and the restoration of democracy in Iraq and then embodied by the IST. Undoubtedly, the memory of U.S. policy played a part: having supported Saddam Hussein when he committed his worst atrocities,[17] the United States became, after the invasion of Kuwait, the strongest proponent of sanctions, with dramatic consequences as it struck the most vulnerable among the Iraqi people.[18] Legal strategies can backfire on their creators who find themselves accountable to public opinion for their own acts.

The makers of the constitution of the Special Tribunal for Lebanon (STL), like the IST, had political objectives. Created by the UN Security Council on 2 May 2007 in response to the assassination of former prime minister Rafik Hariri on 14 February 2005, the STL was the first hybrid tribunal with an "anti-terrorist" mandate. Its supporters, members of the pro-Western coalition of 14 March led by Saad Hariri and Walid Jumblatt, saw in it an instrument of protection against attempts at destabilization coming from Damascus and as a means to regain Lebanese sovereignty in disposing of Syrian guardianship.[19] They received strong support from the Security Council of the French government and the Bush Administration, which was then in favor of "regime change." At the time, Syria figured on the list of states sponsoring terrorism. All Western countries and their allies in the Security Council supported the resolution.[20] The five countries that abstained (China, Russia, South Africa, Indonesia, and Qatar) held that the STL exceeded its powers by encroaching on the sovereignty of Lebanon. Opposed to the creation of the STL were the Hezbollah; the Amal, whose leader, Nabih Berri, is the Speaker of the Parliament; and their ally, the Christian general Michel Aoun of the Free Patriotic Movement. They denounced the fact that the STL's political purpose was to weaken the Syrian regime.[21]

No one can predict the ability of the STL to fulfill the mandate entrusted to it by the Security Council, as regional political factors seem decisive, and because its legitimacy is questioned by a part of Lebanese society that opposes the constitution of this court for the murder of one man, whereas the Lebanese civil war (1975–1989) was concluded by widespread impunity with the amnesty of 1991, in spite of the 145,000 dead, 180,000 wounded, and 17,000 missing.[22] The fact that after the elections on 7 June 2009, slightly more than four years after the assassination of his father, Saad Hariri became prime minister helps to raise concerns about the court. Wadad Halwani, a human rights activist who criticized this selective justice, says: "Why should justice be confined to officials and leaders? . . . It is very important to know who killed Hariri, but it is also important to know where all the kidnapped people are. . . . How come international justice differentiates between victims?"[23]

Despite, but perhaps also in order to establish, its still controversial legitimacy, the STL will need to clarify legal concepts, and in a highly focused and strategic area: What are the criteria that determine that a political murder—in this case, that of Rafik Hariri, who was no longer prime minister at the time of the crime—is a "terrorist act," a definition that has divided lawyers, public opinion, and governments for decades? What if the victim is considered a "terrorist" by one authority and a "freedom fighter" by another authority? And what about the notion of "state terrorism"? What about reconciling a fair trial and a trial in absentia in such sensitive cases?[24]

Never before has a trial in absentia been allowed in international and hybrid courts, opening new possibilities of action at the STL but fueling even more fears of the politicization of justice. The STL is engaged in a process of development of the law, the repercussions of which could have an impact, in terms of international security, far beyond the borders of Lebanon and the Middle East. This means that the STL can produce limited effect in criminal cases that it investigates while establishing law with major political effects.

Like the IST and the STL, the Palestinian Authority ratified the Statute of the ICC in January 2009 in order to address political goals. Insofar as the Court accepts jurisdiction—a highly controversial point[25]—it could investigate alleged crimes committed by the Israeli army in Gaza in January 2009. In spring 2009 the ICC prosecutor announced the opening of a pre-investigation.

The legal option was not new to the supporters of the Palestinian cause. In March 2002, twenty-three survivors of the massacres of Sabra and Shatila in Lebanon filed a complaint in Belgium against, notably, Israeli prime minister Ariel Sharon. Via the use of universal jurisdiction, the political issue of the complaint was to isolate and criminalize Israel, using the court as a media echo chamber. More recently, on 14 September 2009, a London court issued an arrest warrant against Tzipi Livni, the Israeli minister of foreign affairs at the time of the Gaza conflict, for alleged war crimes. As stressed by Laurie King-Irani, who served as the North American coordinator for the International Campaign for Justice for the Victims of Sabra and Shatila,

> prosecuting war crimes and crimes against humanity through the principle of universal jurisdiction is first and foremost a judicial endeavor. But it is often a profoundly political undertaking as well. Universal jurisdiction cases frequently heighten diplomatic tensions, and alter the course of political events and usually raise troubling questions about state sovereignty. These cases can also engender new forms of political power by consolidating transnational coalitions of activists, parliamentarians, scholars, journalists and legal specialists.[26]

The Palestinian legal offensive in turn led to intense diplomatic pressure from the Jewish state, which—with American support—was awarded the abandonment of complaints against the responsible Israeli politicians in Belgium and Spain, as well as the narrowing of laws concerning universal jurisdiction in these two countries.[27] Here again, it would be reductive to read the impact of these courts only through the prism of power relations. The outcome of the purely judicial battle is only one aspect of a broader field of confrontation that aims to impose its narrative in the public space and to marginalize its opponent.

It is interesting to note that in turning to the courts and commissions of inquiry, the Palestinian Authority (PA) also left itself open to attack. In wanting to criminalize the enemy, the PA acknowledged the legitimacy of a court that may one day turn against it. Indeed, if the ICC decides to recognize its jurisdiction, the Court could not only investigate serious violations of international humanitarian law against Palestinians but also violations that they have perpetrated. In different terms, this is what happened with the Goldstone Commission. Thus, unwittingly, and even in spite of themselves, the legal strategies adopted by the initiators of the Goldstone Commission have led to an extension of accountability[28] in the Middle East.

This desire of the Palestinian Authority to use the law, and the ICC in particular, has already led to unexpected political effects. With the exception of Jordan, the members of the Arab League are opposed to international justice, which they perceive as threatening, being in the pay of the West, and diverting attention from the continuing injustice of the occupation of Palestinian territories by Israel. Libya even denounced the ICC as "a terrorist organ."[29] But by calling on this same Court, the Palestinians, who embody "the sacred cause of the Arab world," undermine (with Jordan) the Arab refusal of the Court. Indeed, in June 2009 the Arab League sent to the prosecutor of the ICC his fact-finding report on crimes committed in Gaza, thereby legitimizing a court which it has never spared criticism.

There is a strange irony in the development of international justice and commissions of inquiry in the Middle East. The presupposition of the initiators of these mechanisms of justice joined that of the followers of the toolbox in their purely instrumental vision. True, their goals are radically different: the first seek to criminalize the opponent, while the latter believe that the cathartic effect of these mechanisms allows the restoration of national unity. Both believe that they can control the effects of international justice. However, this reasoning suffers from a lack of humility. One side effect of globalization is that all societies now have a thirst for accountability. And they are neither fools nor unfounded critics, nor do they want mere show trials. We have seen in the Middle East and elsewhere that the political effect of the courts, the truth commissions, and the commissions of inquiry in societies proves uncontrollable over time. Thus, not only are criminals made accountable for their actions, but so, too, are those who judge them.

Reference Matter

Notes

Book epigraphs: Antjie Krog, *Country of My Skull* (Johannesburg: Random House, 1998), 36; Hannah Arendt, "Le procès d'Auschwitz," in *Auschwitz et Jérusalem*, 2nd ed. (Paris: Deuxtemps Tierce, 1997), 257–258.

Prologue

1. I reported this incident in an article for the French daily, *Libération*, "With the ICRC in ex-Yugoslavia," 19 October 1993. I was able to attach myself to the activities of its delegates for several weeks. We calculated body mass index by measuring the weight of each prisoner, subtracting 2 kilos for clothing, and dividing the result by height. We found that 6.7 percent of the prisoners were in immediate danger of death (a BMI of less than 16), 55 percent suffered from severe malnutrition (a BMI between 16 and 20), and a third remained just above this level.

2. While I was gathering testimonies in the months and years that followed the genocide, thousands of Hutu men, women, and children who had taken refuge in Kivu (Congo) were killed in reprisal. However, these crimes were not made part of the mandate of the International Criminal Tribunal Rwanda. International justice revealed both its weak dissuasive power and its limits in preventing mass crimes.

3. I was in Chad to make the documentary film *Chasseur de dictateur (The Dictator Hunter)*, about the application of universal jurisdiction in the charges brought against Hissène Habré (Paris-Geneva: ARTE, TSR, Article Z, 2000).

4. Julie Mertus, "Only a War Crimes Tribunal: Triumph of the International Community, Pain of Survivors," in *War Crimes: The Legacy of Nuremberg*, ed. Belinda Cooper (New York: TV Books, 1999).

5. Jean-Michel Chaumont, *La concurrence des victimes*, 2nd ed. (Paris: La Découverte, 2002).

Introduction

1. Jacques Le Goff, *La naissance du purgatoire* (Paris: Gallimard, 1991), 5.

2. Ariel Colonomos, *La morale dans les relations internationales* (Paris: Odile Jacob, 2005), 71.

3. Francis Fukuyama, *The End of History and the Last Man* (New York: Free Press, 1992).

4. In his Fourteen Points address delivered before the U.S. Senate on 8 January 1918, President Woodrow Wilson affirmed his will to break with the tenets of traditional European diplomacy—secret diplomacy, leadership of the Great Powers, refusal of the principle of nationality—in favor of peace founded on democracy, self-determination, multilateralism, and liberalism. These values were reactivated at the end of the Cold War.

5. See David Luban's review of the book by Jon Elster, *Closing the Books: Transitional Justice in Historical Perspective* (Cambridge: Cambridge University Press, 2004), in *Ethics* 116.2 (January 2006): 409.

6. This conference resulted in a seminal three-volume work edited by Neil Kritz, *Transitional Justice: How Emerging Democracies Reckon with Former Regimes* (Washington, DC: United States Institute of Peace, 1995).

7. Desmond Tutu, foreword to *Reconciliation After Violent Conflict: A Handbook*, ed. David Bloomfield, Teresa Barnes, and Luc Huyse (Stockholm: Institute for Democracy and Electoral Assistance, 2003), i.

8. Ibid.

9. Ruti Teitel, "Transitional Justice Genealogy," *Harvard Human Rights Journal* 16 (Spring 2003): 69.

10. Paul Ricoeur, *Philosophie de la volonté. Finitude et culpabilité, la symbolique du mal* (Paris: Aubier-Montaigne, 1960), 11–30.

Chapter 1

1. The Tokyo trials never had anywhere near the same impact as those conducted at Nuremberg, either in the West or in the rest of Asia.

2. Opening address by Robert Jackson, in *Trial of the Major War Criminals Before the International Military Tribunal*, vol. 2, *Proceedings of 11/14/1945–11/30/1945* (Nuremberg: International Military Tribunal, 1947), 98–102. Jackson stressed the moral imperative to prosecute the war criminals to protect "civilization": "Unfortunately the nature of these crimes is such that both prosecution and judgment must be by victor nations over vanquished foes. The worldwide scope of the aggressions carried out by these men has left but few real neutrals. Either the victors must judge the vanquished or we must leave the defeated to judge themselves. After the first World War, we learned the futility of the latter course."

3. Robert Jackson refers to this moral authority in his first speech: "The former high station of these defendants, the notoriety of their acts, and the adaptability of their conduct to provoke retaliation make it hard to distinguish between the demand for a just and measured retribution, and the unthinking cry for vengeance which arises from the anguish of war. It is our task, so far as humanly possible, to draw the line between the two." Ibid.

4. *Trial of the Major War Criminals Before the International Military Tribunal*, vol. 2, *Proceedings of 11/14/1945–11/30/1945* (Nuremberg: International Military Tribunal, 1947), 98–102.

5. Ibid., 98–102.

6. For more detail, see Florent Brayard, ed., *Le Génocide des Juifs: entre procès et histoire, 1943–2000* (Brussels: Complexe, 2000), in particular, the article by Michael R. Marrus, "L'histoire de l'Holocauste dans le prétoire," 25–55.

7. Maurice Bardèche (brother-in-law of writer Robert Brasillach, who was executed for collaboration in 1945) contested the Allies' legal and moral right to judge the officials of the Third Reich for acts that they "may have" committed. His revisionist ideas earned him a year's sentence in prison for "apology for war crimes," and his book, *Nuremberg, ou la terre promise* (Paris: Les Sept Couleurs, 1948), was banned. Pardoned by President René Coty, Bardèche served only a few weeks in Fresnes. He persisted in 1952 with a second book, *Nuremberg II, ou les faux-monnayeurs* (Paris: Les Sept Couleurs, 1952).

8. See Richard Overy, "The Nuremberg Trials: International Law in the Making," in *From Nuremberg to The Hague: The Future of International Criminal Justice*, ed. Philippe Sands (Cambridge: Cambridge University Press, 2003), 1–29.

9. Ibid., 26.

10. Ibid., 23.

11. In the final memorandum of the Nuremberg Statutes, the judges—under American pressure—introduced a "highly political" comma, which affected the legal definition of the new grounds for indictment for crimes against humanity. This comma inferred the restriction of crimes against humanity only in a time of war: "Article 6c: Crimes against humanity: murder, extermination, enslavement, deportation, and other inhumane acts committed against civilian populations, before or during the war; or persecutions on political, racial or religious grounds in execution of or in connection with any crime within the jurisdiction of the tribunal, whether or not in violation of the domestic law of the country where perpetrated." Nuremberg Trial Proceedings, vol. 1, Charter of the International Military Tribunal.

12. However, it was pursued as a charge in a handful of trials for crimes committed during World War II.

13. Karl Jaspers, *La culpabilité allemande* (Paris: Éditions de Minuit, 1990), 33.

14. John Torpey, ed., *Politics and the Past: On Repairing Historical Injustices* (New York: Rowman and Littlefield Publishers, 2003), 2.

15. See Lily Gardner Feldman, "The Principle and Practice of 'Reconciliation' in German Foreign Policy Relations with France, Israel, Poland and the Czech Republic," *International Affairs* 75.2 (April 1999): 333–356.

16. In 1998 the Statutes of the International Criminal Court created a voluntary fund to benefit the victims.

17. From the Knesset, Menachem Begin launched a violent diatribe against reparations: "Nations worthy of the name have mounted the barricades for less than this. We, members of the last generation of the redeemed; we who have heard the din of the death trains, who have seen our fathers dragged to the gas chambers, who have seen our elderly father thrown into the river under our eyes with 500 other Jews in

the glorious community of Brisk, Lithuania, until the water ran red with blood; we, who have seen our old mother murdered with our own eyes in a hospital; we who have witnessed these events unprecedented in history—are we now going to be afraid to risk our lives to stop negotiations with the murderers of our parents? If we do not stand up to this, nothing remains to us but to hide our faces in shame. . . . This is the final appeal I make from the Knesset floor: 'Stop this new genocide of the Jews!'" Tom Segev, *Le Septième Million: Les Israéliens et le génocide* (Paris: Liana Lévi, 1993), 265 (*The Seventh Million: The Israelis and the Holocaust* [New York: Hill & Wang, 1993]).

18. Ibid., 264.

19. See Peter Maguire, *Law and War: An American Story* (New York: Columbia University Press, 2001).

20. Protocol had not required Willy Brandt to kneel, and the gesture came as a total surprise.

21. Vladimir Jankélévitch, *L'Imprescriptible* (Paris: Le Seuil, 1986), 25. Jankélévitch chose the book's title in 1956 when he expressed for the first time, in *La Revue administrative*, the arguments contained in *Pardonner*. The complete text of *Pardonner* first appeared in 1971, Éditions Le Pavillon. *L'Imprescriptible* also comprises the essay "Dans l'honneur et la dignité," published in 1948 in *Les Temps Modernes*.

22. UN General Assembly, Resolution 2583 on 15 December 1969, Resolution 2840 on 18 December 1971, Question of Punishment of War Criminals and of Persons Who Have Committed Crimes Against Humanity, and Resolution 3020 on 18 December 1972, Principles of International Cooperation in the Detection, Arrest, Extradition and Punishment of Persons Guilty of War Crimes and Crimes Against Humanity.

23. The Convention on the Imprescriptibility of War Crimes and Crimes Against Humanity, adopted by the UN General Assembly as Resolution 2391, 26 November 1968. The Convention entered into force on 11 November 1970.

24. UN General Assembly, Resolution 3068, International Convention on the Suppression and Punishment of the Crime of Apartheid, adopted 30 November 1973, and entered into force on 18 July 1976.

25. Tom Segev evokes the words of Ben-Gurion in 1961: "They [the Sephardes] had been living in Asia or Africa and didn't have the slightest idea what Hitler had done. It was necessary to explain all that to them, starting from zero." "Le tournant du procès Eichmann," *Le Monde diplomatique* (April 2001): 10–11.

26. Gidéon Hausner, *Justice à Jérusalem: Eichmann devant ses juges* (Paris: Flammarion, 1966), 383. See also analysis on the same topic by Annette Wievorka, *L'ère du témoin* (Paris: Hachette, 2002).

27. Geoffrey Hartman, "Apprendre des survivants: remarques sur l'histoire orale et les archives video de témoignages sur l'holocauste à l'université de Yale," in *Le Monde Juif. Revue d'histoire de la Shoah* (January–April 1994): 68; also cited by Wieworka, *L'ère du témoin*, 97.

28. Peter Novick, *The Holocaust in American Life* (Boston: Houghton Mifflin, 1999), 127–145.

29. Tom Segev, *The Seventh Million*, 330.

30. Among Israelis and the Jewish world as a whole, Ben-Gurion's commemoration policy unleashed vigorous debate along the fault line separating those who held a universal memory of genocide from those who sought to emphasize the Jewish martyrdom. In a famous debate, Hannah Arendt argued that the capture of Eichmann must serve as a lesson to the entire world, for all humanity was hurt by the genocide. Hannah Arendt believed in the capacity to fight the state by creating "embarrassing situations" and by mobilizing public opinion. She was one of the first to formalize "the law of din" which would become one of the most effective communication techniques used by NGOs working in human rights. At the very moment that the writings of Hannah Arendt were sparking violent debate, Amnesty International was created in London. There was no direct link between the two events. However, it showed that the question of the repression of state crimes was no longer the privilege of governments alone but was in the public domain, including for new players. A corollary was that the image of the victim began to change. Heretofore absent or with a mere walk-on part in political debate, their voices and those of their representatives now made themselves heard.

31. Referring to Menachem Begin's letter, Israeli writer Amos Oz responds: "Mister Prime Minister, Adolf Hitler is already dead." See Tom Segev, "Nazis! Nazis!" *Haaretz*, 29 March 2002.

32. The Nakbah (literally, "catastrophe" in Arabic) was the term for the ethnic cleansing perpetrated by the Zionists against the Palestinians during the creation of Israel in 1948.

33. Avishai Margalit and Gabriel Motzkin, "The Uniqueness of the Holocaust," *Philosophy and Public Affairs* 25.1 (Winter 1996): 80.

34. Pierre Vidal-Naquet, Préface, in *La culpabilité allemande* by Karl Jaspers (Paris: Editions de Minuit, 1990), 17.

35. Carine Gilloin, *Une histoire des grands hommes: Anthropologie historique de la communauté herero, 1840–1993 (Namibie)* (Paris: EHESS, 1999), 188–192.

36. Frédéric Mégret, "Three Dangers for the International Criminal Court," *Finnish Yearbook of International Law* 12 (2001), 193–247.

37. Ibid.

38. Ibid.

Chapter 2

1. See, for example, Desmond Tutu, *There Is No Future Without Forgiveness* (New York: Doubleday, 1999); Michael P. Scharf, "The Case for a Permanent International Truth Commission," *Duke Journal of Comparative and International Law* 7 (1997): 375–398; Naomi Roht-Arriaza, ed., *Introduction to Impunity and Human Rights in International Law and Practice* (New York: Oxford University Press, 1995); Richard Dicker and Elise Keppler, "Beyond The Hague: The Challenges of International Justice,"

in *Human Rights Watch World Report* (New York: Human Rights Watch, 2004), http://www.hrw.org/en/news/2004/01/26/beyond-hague-challenges-international-justice; Juan Mendez, "Comments on Prosecution: Who and for What?" in *Dealing with the Past: Truth and Reconciliation Commission in South Africa*, ed. Alex Boraine, Janet Levy, and Ronel Scheffer, 87–90 (Cape Town, South Africa: IDASA, 1994); Alex Boraine and Janet Levy, eds., *The Healing of a Nation? Justice in Transition* (Cape Town, South Africa: IDASA, 1994); Martha Minow, *Breaking the Cycles of Hatred: Memory, Law, and Repair* (Princeton, NJ: Princeton University Press, 2003); Priscilla B. Hayner, *Unspeakable Truths: Confronting State Terror and Atrocity* (New York: Routledge, 2001); Eric Stover and Harvey Weinstein, eds., *My Neighbor, My Enemy: Justice and Community in the Aftermath of Mass Atrocity* (Cambridge: Cambridge University Press, 2004).

2. See Cherif Bassiouni, ed., *Post-Conflict Justice* (New York: Transnational Publishers, 2002); and Alex Boraine, "Transitional Justice as an Emerging Field," presented at the "Repairing the Past: Reparations and Transitions to Democracy" Symposium, Ottawa, 11 March 2004, http://www.idrc.ca/uploads/user-S/10829975041revised-boraine-ottawa-2004.pdf.

3. See Thomas Carothers, "The End of the Transition Paradigm," *Journal of Democracy*, 13.1 (January 2002): 1–21.

4. Guillermo O'Donnell and Philippe C. Schmitter, *Transitions from Authoritarian Rule: Tentative Conclusions About Uncertain Democracies* (Baltimore: Johns Hopkins University Press, 1986).

5. See Ruti Teitel, *Transitional Justice* (New York: Oxford University Press, 2000), 3.

6. Robert I. Rotberg and Dennis Thompson, eds., *Truth v. Justice: The Morality of Truth Commissions* (Princeton, NJ: Princeton University Press, 2000), 8.

7. Aspen Institute, *State Crimes: Punishment or Pardon,* Papers and Reports of the Conference, November 4–6, 1988, Wye Centre, Maryland.

8. On the history of the truth commissions, see Hayner, *Unspeakable Truths*.

9. Historically, the establishment of the first Latin American Truth Commissions, in Argentina and Chile, was the result of a standoff between the outgoing elite and the incoming elite, between the will to keep silent and the will to hold wrongdoers accountable.

10. Rotberg and Thompson, *Truth v. Justice*, 69.

11. Reed Brody, "Justice: The First Casualty of Truth?" *Nation*, April 12, 2001, http://www.thenation.com/doc/20010430/brody.

12. Ronald C. Slye, "Amnesty, Truth, and Reconciliation: Reflections on the South African Amnesty Process," in Rotberg and Thompson, *Truth v. Justice*, 170–188; quotation from p. 80.

13. The truth commissions had another advantage, according to their promoters: they provided "closure" for the families of the victims, psychologically, in that they could at last begin their process of grief and stop hoping for an unlikely return of the disappeared; and, legally, in that they would have a clear status (widows, orphans), which would give them elementary rights (pensions, remarriage, and so on).

14. The Trauma Centre for Victims of Violence and Torture in Cape Town estimates that, of the hundreds of people with whom it has worked, between 50 and 60 percent have experienced serious psychological problems after giving their testimonies or have said they regretted having taken part in the Truth and Reconciliation Commission hearings; see Hayner, *Unspeakable Truths*, 144. A certain number of them have been "retraumatized" to the point that Trudy de Ridder, one of the psychologists who worked with victims who testified before the TRC, wonders if the political benefits society retains are superior to the suffering created in victims by the hearings of the Truth Commission. See Trudy de Ridder, "The Trauma of Testifying: Deponents' Difficult Healing Process," *Track Two* 6.3/4 (December 1997), http://ccrweb.ccr.uct.ac.za/archive/two/6_34/p30_deridder.html.

15. Eric Brahm, *Trauma Healing*, January 2004, http://www.beyondintractability.org/essay/trauma_healing.

16. Ervin Staub and Laurie Anne Pearlman, "Healing, Reconciliation, and Forgiving After Genocide and Other Collective Violence," in *Forgiveness and Reconciliation: Religion, Public Policy, and Conflict Transformation*, ed. Raymond G. Helmick and Rodney L. Petersen, 195–217 (Philadelphia: Templeton Foundation Press, 2001), http://restorativejustice.org/rj3/Reviews/Helmick/collectiveviolence.htm.

17. Judith Lewis Herman, *Trauma and Recovery* (New York: Basic Books, 1992), l.

18. Mauro Bottaro, *Se réconcilier au nom de quel passé? Seuils et franchissements historiques dans les usages politiques et symboliques de l'Islam au Maroc* (Paris: Mémoire non publié présenté à l'EHESS, 2005), 54.

19. Tutu, *No Future Without Forgiveness*, 31. Tutu ties the ethic of responsibility to the ethic of conviction, the strategic pardon to religious forgiveness: "We South Africans can only survive and get ahead together. Blacks and whites, tied together by circumstances and history, by fighting to get out of the quagmire that was apartheid. Neither of these two groups can get ahead alone. God has tied us together, chained us together." It is, he insists, a way of putting into practice what Martin Luther preached: "If we cannot learn to live together, as brothers and sisters, then we shall die as imbeciles." The president of the TRC inscribed what appears to be a strategic pardon into an effective pardon linked to African culture.

20. Dele Olojede, "Truth or Consequences: Biko's Widow Opposes S. Africa Commission's Policy on Pardon," *Newsday*, 2 February 1997.

21. *Azanian People Organisation (AZAPO) and Others v. The President of the Republic of South Africa*, Case CCT 17/96, 15 July 1996.

22. Ronald Slye, "Amnesty, Truth, and Reconciliation," 31.

23. "The aim of reconciliation should not be seen as seeking some comprehensive social harmony, whether psychological or spiritual," insist Amy Gutmann and Dennis Thompson, in Rotberg and Thompson, *Truth v. Justice*, 32.

24. Cited in Sandrine Lefranc, *Politiques du pardon* (Paris: PUF, 2002), 46.

25. Paul Ricoeur, *La mémoire, l'histoire, l'oubli* (Paris: Seuil, 2000), 58.

26. Cited in Rony Brauman and Eyal Sivan, *Eloge de la désobéissance. À propos d' "un spécialiste," Adolf Eichmann* (Paris: Le Pommier, 1999), 52.

27. Freeman Dyson, "Rocket Man," *New York Review of Books* 55, no. 1 (17 January 2008).

28. Rodolfo Mattarollo, "Recent Argentine Jurisprudence in the Matter of Crimes Against Humanity," in *Review of the International Commission of Jurists: Impunity, Crimes Against Humanity and Forced Disappearance*, ed. Louise Doswald-Beck, 62–63 (September 2001); quotation from p. 17.

29. Cited in Mattarollo, "Recent Argentine Jurisprudence," 17.

30. Louis Joinet, *Lutter contre l'impunité: Dix questions pour comprendre et pour agir* (Paris: La Découverte, 2002), 9. See also UN Commission on Human Rights, Forty-ninth session, *The Realization of Economic, Social and Cultural Rights: Final Report on the Question of the Impunity of Perpetrators of Human Rights Violations* (E/CN.4/Sub.2/1997/20/Rev.1).

31. Pierre Allan and Alexis Keller, "The Concept of a Just Peace, or Achieving Peace Through Recognition, Renouncement and Rule," in *What Is a Just Peace?* ed. Pierre Allan and Alexis Keller, 195–216 (Oxford: Oxford University Press, 2006), 200.

32. However, the analysis of the repression in situations as different as those in Morocco, northern Uganda, or South Africa clearly shows that the systematic discrimination of economic, social, and cultural rights was exacerbated by tensions and worsened the conflict. In 2006, Louise Arbour, the UN High Commissioner for Human Rights, suggested that transitional justice includes the latter rights from now on. See her speech, "Economic and Social Justice for Societies in Transition," New York University School of Law, October 25, 2006, 26.

33. Mary Kaldor, *New and Old War: Organized Violence in a Global Era* (Cambridge, MA: Polity Press, 2001), 153.

34. *Report of the International Criminal Court to the United Nations*, 1 August 2005, A/60/177, http://www.amicc.org/docs/ICCReportToGA%20August2005.pdf.

35. Antonio Cassese, "A Big Step Forward for International Justice," Crimes of War Project, December 2003, http://www.crimesofwar.org/icc_magazine/icc-cassese.html.

36. Office of the National Security Advisor, "A National Security Strategy of Engagement and Enlargement" (Washington, DC: The White House, February 1996).

37. For more information on the Clinton Administration's foreign policy, see Bill Clinton, *My Life* (New York: Random House, 2004); Alvin Z. Rubinstein, Albina Shayevich, and Boris Zlotnikov, eds., *The Clinton Foreign Policy Reader: Presidential Speeches with Commentary* (Armonk, NY: M. E. Sharpe, 2000); William G. Hyland, *Clinton's World: Remaking American Foreign Policy* (Westport, CT: Praeger, 1999); Jewett Aubrey and Marc Turetzky, "Stability and Chance in President Clinton's Foreign Policy Beliefs, 1993–1996," *Presidential Studies Quarterly* 28 (1998): 638–665; Douglas Brinkley, "Democratic Enlargement: The Clinton Doctrine," *Foreign Policy* 106 (Spring 1997): 110–127.

38. There were, no doubt, tactical considerations in this signing as well, as it allowed the United States to negotiate the final modalities in the creation of the ICC. President Bush "unsigned" the Statute in 2006.

39. John Bellinger, legal counsel for U.S. secretary of state Condoleezza Rice, speaking at the Institute of International Humanitarian Law in San Remo (Italy), 8 September 2006. Oral intervention.

40. David Scheffer (speech, "Human Rights and International Justice," Dartmouth College, Hanover, New Hampshire, 23 October 1998), http://www.findarticles .com/p/articles/mi_m1584/is_10_9/ai_53461439.

41. Wole Soyinka, *The Burden of Memory, the Muse of Forgiveness* (Oxford: Oxford University Press, 1999), 1.

42. The WJC wanted to obtain restitution of the money left by the victims of the Nazis. President Bill Clinton charged his undersecretary of state, Stuart Eizenstat, with participating in the resolution of the dispute. The former president of the Federal Reserve Bank, Paul Volcker, was mandated to direct the investigation into the archives of the Swiss banks. In December 1998, Secretary of State Madeleine Albright organized an international conference of fifty states to identify "the possessions stolen during the Holocaust." Washington Conference on Holocaust-Era Assets, http://www .state.gov/www/regions/eur/wash_conf_material.html.

43. Jacques Derrida, "Le siècle et le pardon," reported by Michel Wievorka, *Le Monde des débats*, December 1999.

44. See Antoine Garapon and Ioannis Papadopoulos, *Juger en Amérique et en France* (Paris: Odile Jacob, 2003), 77.

45. Ibid. The application of plea bargaining by the ad hoc tribunals raises fundamental questions. Under plea bargaining, a defendant may negotiate the charges with the prosecutor. But is there a place for transactional logic when crimes against humanity are involved? Should not crimes against humanity—by definition, imprescriptible—remain beyond any form of negotiation? See Garapon and Papadopoulos, *Juger en Amérique.*

46. Paul W. Kahn, "Why the United States Is So Opposed," Crimes of War Project, December 2003, http://www.crimesofwar.org/icc_magazine//icc-kahn.html.

47. Jürgen Habermas, *L'espace public* (Paris: Payot, 1993), 63. See also "What Makes the World Hang Together? Neo-Utilitarianism and the Social Constructivist Challenge," *International Organization* 52.4 (Autumn 1998): 855–885; Martha Finnemore and Kathryn Sikkink, "International Norm Dynamics and Political Change," *International Organization* 47.4 (Autumn 1998): 887–917; Alexander Wendt, "Anarchy Is What States Make of It: The Social Construction of Power Politics," *International Organization* 46.2 (Spring 1992): 391–425.

48. Antonio Cassese, "A Big Step Forward."

49. They are the soul added to globalization that creates as much wealth as inequality. The actions of the humanitarian and human rights NGOs are reminders of the oneness of the human condition in a world where the mesh of information has never been so dense but where social differences have never been so great. Their names reflect the new values of globalization, the critique of the all-powerful state within its borders, the celebration of transparency, and the struggle for human rights

and justice: Doctors Without Borders, Transparency International, Physicians for Human Rights, International Center for Transitional Justice, and the World Organization Against Torture. Significantly, Amnesty International, created in 1961, bears a name that is countercurrent to this new era. The time is no longer one of amnesty for political prisoners but of the stigmatization of their persecutors.

50. Naomi Roht-Arriaza, *The Pinochet Effect: Transnational Justice in the Age of Human Rights*, Pennsylvania Studies in Human Rights series (Philadelphia: University of Pennsylvania Press, 2005), 197–198.

51. Ibid., 197–198.

52. Reed Brody, interview with author, Geneva, 16 November 2006.

53. Other countries, like Switzerland, judged ordinary nationals of the former Yugoslavia and Rwanda, although the connection was weak: neither the victims nor the criminal acts had any connection to Swiss territory, except that the presumed perpetrator happened to be there.

54. Rony Brauman, *Penser dans l'urgence: parcours critique d'un humanitaire* (Paris: Seuil, 2006), 67.

55. Ibid., 89.

56. Stanley Hoffmann, "Clash of Globalizations," *Foreign Affairs* 81.4 (July/August 2002): 104–126. In substance, the author explains, economic globalization was the source of growth and wealth creation but also produced profound inequality between states and within them, generating its share of the poor and migrants in search of a better life. Cultural globalization brought a reaction of introversion and of identity and religious crisis in the face of American hegemony perceived as the expression of neo-imperialism leveling differences. Political globalization fed on the effects of the two earlier globalizations and could be seen in the rise in ultranationalism and "ethnism," bringing in its wake the multiplication of conflicts.

57. Olivier Corten, "Humanitarian Intervention: A Controversial Right," *Le Courrier de l'UNESCO* (June 1999), http://www.unesco.org/courier/1999_08/uk/ethique/intro.htm.

58. UN General Assembly, Implementation of Resolution 60/251 of 15 March 2006, called "right to truth," UN High Commission for Human Rights, Report A/HRC/5/7, 7 June 2007, 3; see also the UN study on the right to truth, E/CN.4/2006/91, 8 February 2006, which concludes that "the right to truth implies knowing the full and complete truth as to the events that transpired, the specific circumstances, and how participated in them."

59. Agnès Lejbowicz, *La philosophie du droit international* (Paris: PUF, 1999), 277.

60. Elazar Barkan, *The Guilt of Nations: Restitution and Negotiating Historical Injustices* (New York: W. W. Norton and Company, 2000), x; see also, in a similar vein, Alan Cairns's *Politics and the Past: On Repairing Historical Injustices* (Lanham, MD: Rowman and Littlefield, 2003), in which he evokes a "post-imperial" international order, which, thanks to these mechanisms of apology and reparation, allows people without voice to claim their history and reconcile with their past.

61. First report by the president of the ICTY before the UN General Assembly, 29 August 1994, A/49/342, S/1994/1007, paragraph 15, http://www.un.org/icty/rappannu-e/1994/AR94e.pdf.

62. Alain Finkielkraut, interview with the author, "Regards croisés sur les espoirs et les dangers de la justice internationale," *Le Temps* (Geneva), 6 December 1999.

63. Reed Brody, "Justice: The First Casualty of Truth?" *Nation*, April 12, 2001, www.thenation.com/doc/20010430/brody.

64. Ibid.

65. Between 1993 and 2006, the cost of ICTY and the ICTR was about $1.6 billion, or the equivalent of 15 percent of the UN's ordinary budget. By the end of 2006, the ICTY had judged one hundred accused. By the end of 2009, only two defendants were still at large, in particular the former military Bosnian Serb leader Ratko Mladic. See the ICTY's Web site, http://www.un.org/icty/glance-ff/index.htm. Between 1994 and 2006, the ICTR judged twenty-two people; see the ICTR's Web site, http://www.ictr.org/.

66. Eric Stover and Harvey Weinstein, eds., *My Neighbor, My Enemy: Justice and Community in the Aftermath of Mass Atrocity* (Cambridge: Cambridge University Press, 2004).

67. The concept of "soft power" was introduced by Joseph S. Nye, Jr., in *Bound to Lead: The Changing Nature of American Power* (New York: Basic Books, 1990). For Nye, soft power is the capacity to make others accept as universal a particular vision of the world so that domination by the one who exercises it is considered legitimate. In the preface of *Soft Power: The Means to Success in World Politics* (Boston: Public Affairs, 2004), Nye defines soft power as "the capacity to get what we want by seduction rather than by coercion or money. When our policies are considered legitimate, our soft power is reinforced."

68. Kahn, "Why the United States Is So Opposed."

69. Ibid.

70. Ibid.

71. George W. Bush, "Address to a Joint Session of Congress and the American People" (address, United States Capitol, Washington, DC, 20 September 2001).

72. Ariel Meyerstein, "The United States Vetoes Bosnian Peace-Keeping Resolutions in Protest Against International Court," Crimes of War Project, 1 July 2002, http://www.crimesofwar.org/onnews/news-peacekeep.html.

73. Senate Bill 3930, Military Commissions Act of 2006 (as passed by Congress), S.3930, 22 September 2006.

74. Cherif Bassiouni, "The Institutionalization of Torture Under the Bush Administration," *Case Western Reserve Journal of International Law* 38 (2006): 389–425.

75. Julien Cantegreil, "Lutte antiterroriste: une chance pour les valeurs de l'Europe," *Le Temps* (Geneva), 9 November 2006.

76. Paul van Zyl, in *Dealing with the Past and Transitional Justice: Creating Conditions for Peace, Human Rights and the Rule of Law* (Bern: Swisspeace, 2005), 30.

77. Cassese, "A Big Step Forward."

78. Cassese comments: "States no longer have unfettered freedom to regulate their relations, peremptory norms now constitute a major stumbling block to that freedom. Even more significantly, States are no longer allowed to make unilateral decisions about how to react to alleged breaches of legal standards by other States. Nor, it follows, are they permitted to employ forcible means (for instance, armed reprisals) for imposing compliance with whose legal standards." Ibid.

Chapter 3

1. Mary Robinson, Nelson Mandela, The Visionary Declaration, World Conference Against Racism, Racial Discrimination, Xenophobia, and Related Intolerance, in "Durban 2001, United Against Racism" OHCHR, December 2000, http://www.hurights .or.jp/wcar/E/doc/wcrnewsletter1.pdf.

2. Ibid.

3. Mary Robinson, interview with the author, "Durban piégé par l'antiracisme et le sionisme," *Libération* (Paris), 25 August 2001.

4. Ibid. For Mary Robinson, the vision of a past "at peace" is part of a larger plan of action destined to counterweight inequality reinforced by the process of global deregulation: "At the time of globalization, it is natural that human rights standards be laid down in counterpoint to the rules of the World Trade Organization (WTO) and the Bretton Woods institutions (the IMF and the World Bank). It is intolerable, for example, that countries in which a fourth of the population have HIV do not have a decent health system."

5. United Nations, "Le Secrétaire general exhorte la conference de Durban à répondre aux attentes du monde entier en lançant un appel à l'action contre le racisme," press release, SG/SM/7933, RD/930, 31 August 2001.

6. Ibid. It is significant that Kofi Annan, once in charge of UN peacekeeping operations, participated in this "spirit of repentance." A few months before the Durban Conference, he had publicly apologized for the United Nations' nonintervention to stop the genocide of the Tutsis in Rwanda and the massacres in Srebrenica in the former Yugoslavia.

7. Denis Sassou Nguesso, UN press release DR/D/14, 1 September 2001.

8. Nelson Mandela and Mary Robinson, "Tolerance and Diversity: A Vision for the 21st Century," *UN Chronicle* 38.2 (June–August 2001), 40.

9. Mary Robinson, interview with the author, 25 August 2001.

10. In his opening speech of the conference, Kofi Annan emphasized "the symbolism of this moment—the conjunction of theme, of time and of place. For decades the name of this country was synonymous with racism in its vilest form. But today, Mr. President, you and your fellow citizens have transformed its meaning—from a byword for injustice and oppression, into a beacon of enlightenment and hope, not only for a troubled continent, but for the entire world. Where else, my friends, could we hold this conference? Who could teach us how to overcome racism, discrimination

and intolerance, if not the people of this country?" United Nations, press release, SG/SM/7933, RD/930, 31 August 2001.

11. For three years, the pharmaceutical companies blocked a new South African law that sought to import or produce generic drugs for the country's 4.7 million people infected with HIV, that is, 11 percent of the population. In April 2001, the thirty-nine companies withdrew their complaint to the Johannesburg court in the face of negative public opinion: the NGOs had successfully opposed "the right to profit" with "the right to life."

12. In "Tolerance and Diversity," Mary Robinson and Nelson Mandela reaffirm the existence of "one human family . . . self-evident because of the first mapping of the human genome."

13. UN General Assembly, Fifty-fifth Session, Point 87, *"Comprehensive Review of the Whole Question of Peacekeeping Operations in All Their Aspects,"* A/55/305–S/2000/809, 21 August 2000.

14. Rosa Amelia Plumelle-Uribe, *La férocité blanche, des non-blancs aux non-aryens, génocides occultés de 1492 à nos jours* (Paris: Albin Michel, 2001), 79.

15. Aimé Césaire, introduction to *Esclavage et colonisation* by Victor Schoelcher (Paris: Presses Universitaires de France, 1948), 17–18. In *Discours sur le colonialisme* (Paris: Présence africaine, 1955), Césaire returns to the West's different treatment of crimes committed against the Jews and crimes against Africans: "Yes, it would be worth studying, in clinical detail, the step-by-step approach of Hitler and Nazism and to reveal to the very distinguished, very humanist, very Christian bourgeois of the 20th century that he bears within himself an unrecognized Hitler, that Hitler lives within himself, that Hitler is his demon, that if he rants against him, it is through a lack of logic, and that, at the bottom, what he cannot forgive in Hitler is not the crime in itself, the crime against mankind, it is not the humiliation of Man himself, it is the crime against the white man and for having applied to Europe colonial procedures that, until then, had been used to raise only the Arabs of Algeria, the coolies of India and the niggers of Africa."

16. The term comes from the title of the book by Plumelle-Uribe, *La férocité blanche, des non-blancs aux non-aryens, génocides occultés de 1492 à nos jours.* Ibid.

17. Cited by Nadja Vuckovic, "Qui demande des réparations et pour quels crimes," in *Le livre noir du colonialisme, XVIe–XXIe: de l'extermination à la repentance,* ed. Marc Ferro (Paris: Robert Laffont, 2003), 771. The figure of 50 million, put forward by the Black Panthers, is not based on any study. Historians put the figure between 10 and 20 million. Marc Ferro, for example, estimates that 13.2 million people were enslaved by Europeans between the sixteenth and nineteenth centuries; Ferro, *Le livre noir du colonialisme,* 107.

18. Robert Roth, "Le juge et l'histoire," in *Crimes de l'histoire et réparations: les réponses du droit et de la justice,* ed. Laurence Boisson de Chazournes, Jean-François Quéguiner, and Santiago Villalpando (Brussels: Editions de l'Université de Bruxelles, 2004), 3.

19. "Focus on the Slave Trade," BBC News, 2 September 2001, http://news.bbc.co
.uk/1/hi/world/africa/1523100.stm.

20. Thomas Lantos, "The Durban Debacle: An Insider's View of the UN World
Conference Against Racism," *Fletcher Forum of World Affairs* 26:1 (Winter/Spring
2002): 31–52.

21. According to the United Nations' classification, the Arab-Islamic group is not
a regional group, but these countries act in a coordinated fashion through the Organization of the Islamic Conference, to which most of them belong.

22. Given the partly foreseeable slant of a North-South clash, only a handful of
heads of state came to Durban, all from the African continent except for Cuba's Fidel
Castro, the presidents of Poland and the Baltic states, and the president of the Palestinian Authority, Yasser Arafat. By contrast, although they had planned to attend,
British prime minister Tony Blair and French foreign minister Hubert Védrine canceled their trips, as did Colin Powell—the first descendant of a slave to become a U.S.
secretary of state—whose presence would have been a powerful symbol of the vitality
of American democracy.

23. Pierre Hazan, "Esclavage et colonialisme: le spectre des demandes de réparations," *Le Temps* (Geneva), 1 September 2001.

24. Samir Amin, "World Congress Against Racism," *Solidarités* (Geneva), 10
November 2001, 17.

25. Hans Morgenthau, *In Defense of the National Interest: A Critical Examination
of American Foreign Policy* (New York: Knopf, 1951), 19.

26. Carl Schmitt, *The Concept of the Political* (Chicago: University of Chicago
Press, 1996).

27. *Apartheid Lives On in the Land of Zionism*, flyer distributed during the conference at Durban by the Free Palestine Campaign Committee and Islamicforum.

28. See Dialo Diop, "Réparations des crimes contre l'humanité en Afrique," in
Boisson de Chazournes, Quéguiner, and Villalpando, eds., *Crimes de l'histoire et
réparations*, 266.

29. Ibid.

30. Holocaust Victim Assets Litigation, United States District Court, Eastern District of New York, Case no. CV 96-4849 (ERK) (MDG). To better understand the political context in Switzerland, see Pierre Hazan, *Le mal suisse* (Paris: Stock, 1998). Strictly
speaking, this case was not about the origins of compensation, but its use. However,
more than a third of this money was used to compensate hundreds of slave workers
under the Third Reich, employed or not by Swiss firms, as well as hundreds of Jews
who were turned away at the Swiss border.

31. I remember an anecdotal but most revealing incident: an outburst between
two delegates, one Arab, the other Israeli, each calling the other "Nazi."

32. Pascal Bruckner, *La tyrannie de la pénitence* (Paris: Grasset, 2006), 146.

33. Article 24: "Recognizing that globalization is a historically uneven process
based on colonial and imperialist integration of the world economy and on maintaining and deepening unequal power relations between countries and regions of

the world that exacerbates global inequalities and conditions of poverty and social exclusion." Article 21 affirmed "the right to self-determination of all peoples, including the Hawaiian, Kurdish, Kashmiri, West Sumatran, West Papuan, Achenese, Sri Lankan Tamils, Tibetans, Roma and Travelers, the non-independent territories of the Americas, such as Puerto Rico, Martinique, and Guadalupe."

34. In the same vein, Article 162 affirms: "We declare Israel as a racist, apartheid state in which Israel's brand of apartheid as a crime against humanity has been characterized by separation and segregation, dispossession, restricted land access, denationalization, 'bantustanization' and inhumane acts."

35. Article 118 "call[s] for the reinstitution of UN Resolution 3379 determining the practices of Zionism as racist practices which propagate the racial domination of one group over another."

36. The resolution continued: "We call on all concerned African nations to take formal action to obtain the return of stolen cultural artifacts, gold, money, mineral wealth and the return of occupied land on the continent and call on the international community to support such actions."

37. On this point, see the debate on the Web site http://www.icare.to, and, in particular, the articles of Erika Harriford, "The Death of the European Caucus," and of Mutombo Kanyana, "Y a-t-il une volonté des ONG juives de diviser le mouvement anti-raciste mondial?," posted there.

38. The delegates from the Arab-Islamic countries backed out of their oral agreement with Mary Robinson before the opening of the conference. They tried to bring back a resolution adopted by the General Assembly on 10 November 1975 that was abrogated in 1991 under U.S. pressure.

39. Yasser Arafat, president of the executive council of the Palestinian Authority, speech, 31 August 2001, distributed without quote.

40. "After having assassinated six million Jews, they now want to deny their deaths. During this conference, we have witnessed vile attempts to generalize and multiply the use of the word 'Holocaust' in order to drain it of its meaning as a reference to a unique historical event that carries a clear and essential message for all Humanity. . . . Those who cannot bring themselves to pronounce the word Holocaust and who refuse to see anti-Semitism for what is most nefarious, want us to condemn 'the racist practices of Zionism.' Has a single Arab country that has participated in the elaboration of this obscenity taken a look at its own actions? Or . . . given any thought to the situation of Jews and other minorities living in their own countries? These countries would have us believe that they are not anti-Semitic but anti-Zionist, a lie that has been demonstrated again and again. Are we those despicable caricatures published by the Arab media and distributed here at this conference?" Declaration by Rabbi Michael Melchior, Israel's undersecretary of foreign affairs, given by Ambassador Mordechai Yedit, head of the Israeli delegation, 3 September 2001, distributed without quote.

41. Pierre Hazan, "A Durban, Américains et Israéliens claquent la porte de la Conférence contre le racisme," *Le Temps* (Geneva), 4 September 2001.

42. The representative of the African Descendants Caucus estimated that "the depart of the American delegation from Durban showed a lack of respect for millions of Americans of African origin who were victims of slavery and the slave trade, as well as Africans as a whole." She accused the U.S. government of dodging "the essential question" concerning compensation by hiding behind the question of attacks against Israel.

43. Interview with the author, Washington, DC, 23 June 2006.

44. The temptation to taunt the West was all the stronger in that some governments, like Zimbabwe, had driven their countries to economic and social catastrophe. The thirst for vengeance on the West was in proportion to the fact that the West wrapped itself in morality and human rights. The aim was to tear away this position as giver of lessons, using the only card available: crimes of the past. See "Mugabe Blames Jews," *Sunday Times* (Cape Town), 2 September 2001.

45. Ali Mohamed Osman Yacin, minister of justice, Sudan, UN press release DR/D/20.

46. Then Tanzanian minister of foreign affairs, Jakaya Kikwete, stated that the absence of compensation for crimes committed against Africans could be explained only by racism, an additional sign of contempt with which the West treats its victims. See Jakaya Kikwete, minister of foreign affairs of the United Republic of Tanzania, press release, RD/D/24, 2 September 2001. "Payment of reparation and compensation are logically the best way of demonstrating that justice has been done to those who have been wronged. After all, it is common practice everywhere—why not apply it to Africa? The Germans paid compensation to Europe for crimes against humanity during World War I. The Jews are being compensated for crimes committed against them during the Holocaust. There are many such examples. We do not understand why there is a total hostility to the idea of reparation and compensation to Africa. What is blasphemous about it? Is it because Africa does not deserve it? Or is it the difficulty of determining the compensation? Africans deserve this—it is a matter of principle. What form that reparation and compensation will take is a matter that can be discussed."

47. According to Jakaya Kikwete: "Slavery and colonialism are responsible in a big way, for poverty, underdevelopment, marginalization and economic disparity in Africa and among people of African descent in the diaspora. After several hundred years of slavery and colonialism, the legacy of those obnoxious systems are so deeply rooted that the consequences live on and will continue to be felt for many years to come. Tanzania supports the proposal that States which benefited from slavery, the slave trade and colonialism should acknowledge responsibility for their past injustices and provide reparations and compensation to the victims." See Kikwete, UN press release.

48. Oulai Siene, minister of justice and public liberty, Ivory Coast, press release, RD/D/24, 2 September 2001.

49. The president of Senegal opposed financial compensation. See http://www.droitshumains.org/Racisme/durb_conf_05.htm.

50. Yoweri Kaguta Museveni, president of the Republic of Uganda, speech, distributed during the Durban Conference, without quotation.

51. Olusegun Obasanjo, president of Nigeria, press release, DR/D/14, 1 September 2001.

52. Vuckovic, "Qui demande des réparations et pour quels crimes," 771.

53. For Nelson Mandela, compensation to the victims of slavery could take the form of a development plan for Africa; UN press release (DR/D/14).

54. See notably Plumelle-Uribe, *La férocité blanche.*

55. Francisco Proaño Arandi, representative of Ecuador, UN press release, DR/D/24, 3 September 2001.

56. United Nations, press release, 31 August 2001. Kofi Annan emphasizes Mary Robinson's position that an act of repentance should not open the question of compensation. Mary Robinson stated: "The international community should express itself in stronger terms. The words 'deep regrets' and the expression of 'remorse' are no doubt preferable to 'apologies' in the sense that the States express them in common accord. Apologies are no doubt even more preferable at the bilateral level." Mary Robinson, interview with the author, 25 August 2001.

57. "Africa demands that we listen to it so that the world will honour the memory of the crime of slavery and colonialism in its recent history and assume the responsibility. If not, the black people will continue to be perceived as an object whose value fluctuates in function of supply and demand," Enoch P. Kavindele, vice president of the Republic of Zambia, UN press release, DR/D/20, 2 September 2001.

58. "Speakers on Slavery Practically at Impasse," in *Business Day,* 5 September 2001.

59. The Nuremberg tribunals used retroactively, if parsimoniously, "crimes against humanity," but a direct link existed between the victims and the accused.

60. Charles Josselin, minister delegate to the International Organization of la Francophonie, speech, distributed at the Durban Conference without quote, 1 September 2001.

61. On Tuesday, 4 September, the fifteen EU countries threatened to "pack their suitcases within 24 hours" if an acceptable compromise text was not submitted. Jacob Zuma, advisor to the South African president, lambasted this ultimatum: "The Europeans are acting like colonial masters!" However, the Europeans were supported by French prime minister Lionel Jospin, who on 5 September also threatened that the EU participants would leave Durban before the end of the conference if "Zionism is assimilated as a form of racism."

62. Pierre Sané, introduction to Boisson de Chazournes, Quéguiner, and Villalpando, eds., *Crimes de l'histoire et réparations,* xii.

63. Richard Holbrooke, in *Le Monde* (Paris), 5 September 2001. Others, like Elie Wiesel, saw here the demonstration of the cowardice of the international community to deal with the free expression of anti-Semitism: "This conference against hate has become a conference of hate. Shame on those who organized it in this manner, shame on those who have not followed the United States and Israel in their protest. How could civilized nations accept to remain there?" *Le Monde* (Paris), 5 September 2001.

64. Pierre-André Taguieff, *Prêcheurs de haine. Traversée de la judéophobie planétaire* (Paris: Mille et Une Nuits, 2004), 340. See also Alain Finkielkraut, who

adopted this view, writing that "the Durban Conference has inaugurated a period when anti-Semitism is stripped of its racist filth to roll in the fine, immaculate idiom of anti-racism." Rony Brauman and Alain Finkielkraut, *La discorde, Israël-Palestine, les juifs, la France* (Paris: Mille et Une Nuits, 2006), 36.

65. Louis Salas-Molins, "Esclavage: Peut-on juridiquement envisager de ne pas réparer?" in Boisson de Chazournes, Quéguiner, and Villalpando, *Crimes de l'histoire et réparations*, 182–184.

66. Véronique Nahoum-Grappe, "Vertige de l'impunité, ou l'impasse du rêve de justice," in Boisson de Chazournes, Quéguiner, and Villalpando, *Crimes de l'histoire et réparations*, 13.

Chapter 4

1. According to ERC president Driss Benzekri, "There is growing interest in the Moroccan experience, notably in North Africa, the Middle East and Africa for it represents a model." "IER: l'expérience marocaine de réconciliation suscite beaucoup d'intérêt," *L'Opinion* 1 (4 February 2005).

2. In the early 1990s a best-seller by Gilles Perrault, *Notre ami, le Roi* (Paris: Gallimard, 1990) revealed a number of subjects: the twenty-year house arrest of the children of General Oufkir; the existence of the secret prison of Tazmamart; and the visit of Amnesty International in 1990, which denounced serious human rights abuses. Amnesty International, *Maroc: tortures, "disparitions," emprisonnement politique* (Paris: Editions francophones d'Amnesty International, 1991).

3. In the early 1990s, the radical wing in Algerian society, the "eradicateurs," wanted to repress the Islamists.

4. Moroccan authorities banned the publication of this 144-page letter, although it circulated widely in Moroccan society.

5. Robert Pape counts 62 militants of Al-Qaeda who committed transnational suicide attacks between 1995 and 2003, of whom 34 were Saudis, 12 Moroccans, 4 Turks, 3 Afghans, and 3 Indonesians. Robert Pape, *Dying to Win: The Strategic Logic of Suicide Terrorism* (London: Random House, 2005).

6. The *dahir* (royal decree) specified that the ERC was "considered to be a commission of truth, equality and reconciliation." *Dahir* no. 1.04.42 of 19 *safar* 1425 (10 April 2004) approving the statutes of the Equity and Reconciliation Commission, http://www.ier.ma/_ar_article.php?id_article=221.

7. Ibid.

8. This commission that prefigured the ERC only partially accomplished its work and was strongly criticized.

9. Salah El-Ouadie, interview with the author, Rabat, 26 January 2005.

10. Ibid.

11. Salah El-Ouadie, "Lettre ouverte à mon tortionnaire," *Libération* (Casablanca), 16 April 1999, http://www.acat.asso.fr/dudh/tortionr.html.

12. Driss Basri, "Me juger, c'est juger Hassan II," *La Vérité* 195 (21–27 January 2005).

13. Last, but not least, the ERC had only consultative power and could only give recommendations. It had decisional power only in the area of compensation. The mechanism to lock up the truth commission was now in place.

14. This is the CCDH's recommendation concerning the creation of the ERC, previously available at http://www.ier.ma/article.php3?id_article=24.

15. This is the entire text of the speech given by the king on the creation of the ERC, available at http://www.ier.ma/_ar_article.php?id_article=23.

16. See http://www.maghreb-ddh.org/article.php3?id_article=163.

17. Human Rights Watch, "Morocco's Truth Commission: Honouring Past Victims During an Uncertain Present," *A Human Rights Watch Report*, Vol. 17, No. 11(E), November 2005, 12, http://www.hrw.org/reports/2005/morocco1105/4.htm/.

18. United Nations Development Programme, *Arab Human Development Report: Towards Freedom in the Arab World* (New York: UNDP, 2004), http://www.rbas.undp.org/ahdr_2004/ahdr2.cfm?menu=3&submenu=3&subsubmenu=2.

19. Driss el Yazami, interview with the author, Rabat, 25 January 2005.

20. See Abdellatif Agnouche, "Contribution à l'étude de stratégies de légitimation du pouvoir autour de l'institution califienne" (thesis, Casablanca College of Law, Economics and Social Science, 1986), cited by Mauro Bottaro, *Se réconcilier au nom de quel passé? Seuils et franchissements historiques dans les usages politiques et symboliques de l'Islam au Maroc* (Paris: Mémoire non publié présenté à l'EHESS, 2005), 23.

21. In the Middle Ages, the term *makhzen* referred to the "warehouses" of the state treasury and, by extension, the administration in charge of the treasury. In Morocco today, the term refers to the government and the system of power, including the informal system, that accompanies it.

22. See, for example, Bush's remarks to the National Endowment for Democracy: "Governments across the Middle East and North Africa are beginning to see the need for change. Morocco has a diverse new parliament; King Mohammed has urged it to extend the rights to women. Here is how His Majesty explained his reforms to parliament: 'How can society achieve progress while women, who represent half the nation, see their rights violated and suffer as a result of injustice, violence, and marginalization, notwithstanding the dignity and justice granted to them by our glorious religion?' The King of Morocco is correct: The future of Muslim nations will be better for all with the full participation of women." *President Bush Discusses Freedom in Iraq and Middle East, Remarks by the President at the 20th Anniversary of the National Endowment for Democracy, United States Chamber of Commerce, Washington, DC,* 6 November 2003, http://www.whitehouse.gov/news/releases/2003/11/20031106-2.html.

23. Mohammed VI, speech given at Agadir on the opening of the ERC, 7 January 2004, http://www.ier.ma/_fr_article.php?id_article=23.

24. Ibid.

25. Abdelhay Moudden, interview with the author, Rabat, 4 February 2005.

26. On the theme of pardon and reconciliation in Morocco, see Mauro Bottaro, who explores what he calls the "contradictions" of the ERC in *Se réconcilier au nom de quel passé?*

27. As Driss Benzekri said, "In my opinion, Morocco is engaged in a progressive process of democratization which should, in a relatively short time, lead to the establishment of a form of constitutional monarchy. This would mean the limitation of executive power, the strengthening of legislative power and a strict separation of power, by breaking the link between the executive and the judiciary. But, of course, it is for the monarchy, parliament and the political class to choose the form of Morocco's government." Driss Benzekri, speech at the National Endowment for Democracy, Washington, DC, 19 January 2006.

28. Mohammed VI, speech at Agadir.

29. Hypothesis formulated by Bottaro, *Se réconcilier au nom de quel passé?*

30. Malika Zeghal, interview with the author, 18 November 2005.

31. Their number has never been great (a hard core of a few hundred militants), but they have significant political weight.

32. According to the recommendations of the International Center for Transitional Justice (ICTJ), the victims had been debriefed, had spoken with a psychiatrist, and had had a rapid medical examination to ensure their psychic and physical resistance.

33. The victims could be divided into two categories—the militants and the other, barely politicized unfortunates who suffered terrible abuse simply because they were related to opponents or because they organized a strike at their school or participated in a protest.

34. Pierre Hazan, "Le Maroc exorcise ses années de plomb," *Le Temps* (Geneva), 12 February 2005.

35. Bottaro, *Se réconcilier au nom de quel passé?*, 77.

36. Moroccan Human Rights Association, "Témoignages en toute liberté pour la vérité," 12 February 2005, http://www.amdh.org.ma/html/act_pub.asp.

37. To cite but a few: Ahmed Marzouki, *Tazmamart, Cellule 10* (Paris: Paris-Méditérannée 2001); Abdelaziz Mouride, *On affame bien les rats* (Paris: Paris-Méditérannée, 2001); Jaouad M'didech, *La chambre noire* (Casablanca: Eddif, 2001); Malika Oufkir and Michèle Fitoussi, *La prisonnière* (Paris: le Livre de Poche, 2000); Tahar Ben Jelloun, *Cette aveuglante absence de lumière* (Paris: Le Seuil, 2000); Christine Daure Serfaty, *Tazmamart* (Paris: Stock, 1992); Midhat René Bourequat, *Mort vivant* (Paris: Pygmalion, 2001).

38. Lahcen Moutik, interview with the author, Layoune, 3 December 2005.

39. On 23 April 2004, these independence fighters sent a memorandum to the ERC criticizing the mandate's "negative points," among them the absence of truth, the non-invocation of individual responsibility, the continuation of impunity, and the continuation of violations after 1999. Memorandum submitted to the Equity and Reconciliation Commission, Layoune, 23 April 2004.

40. According to lawyer Mohamed Bouhali: "I was a Sahrawi militant against the Spanish colonial power. I studied law in Rabat, then, I was arrested by the Moroccan

police because of my origins and my Sahrawi sympathies for Polisario Front. I spent 15 years and three months in prison from 1976 to 1991, at Derboulay Chérif, Hagdaz and Kalaat M'Gouna. I was never tried, nor charged, nor have I ever signed any statement. I received 1.470.000 *dirhams*, that is, two times less than the compensation to prisoners in Tazmamart. This is unacceptable and unjust. I want to assert my rights to the Moroccan State. As a victim, I demand respect for my rights. I remain a partisan of self-determination and the current Intifada shows that nothing has been settled. We were in favor of a public hearing, if we could choose those who would expose the violations of human rights, without censorship, without keeping quiet about the names of the torturers, we want to unmask them in full daylight, we are against impunity, and for trials. The ERC hand-picked the victims, choosing those that suited it, the human rights violations continue, the unjust trials, the harassment, the repression," interview with the author, Layoune, 4 December 2005.

41. Iguilid Hammoud, interview with the author, Layoune, 3 December 2005.

42. Djmi el Ghali, interview with the author, Layoune, 4 December 2005.

43. The ERC has never publicly admitted the political reasons for the hearing's cancellation.

44. Balghlal Adbelmjid, a member of the AMDH who described himself as Moroccan first and Sahrawi second, deplored the ERC's "lack of courage": "We have lost a lot because of the public hearing's cancellation. This hearing was very important symbolically: it would have freed speech and given legitimacy to the suffering of the past. The taboo of past repression has not been broken. The ERC did not have enough courage. It has not completed the work begun," Balghlal Adbelmjid, interview with the author, Layoune, 3 December 2005. Eddymaoui Lahabib had been approached to speak during the hearing that was finally canceled. A Polisario sympathizer, he was imprisoned for five years from 1977 to 27 May 1982. He was one of the few Sahrawis to have had a trial: "If I had testified, there would have been two parts to my testimony: first, about our right to self-determination, what we are not allowed to say here and what the Moroccans can not understand anyway. Second, about the reality of the massive human rights violations: the wells poisoned to force the population to sedentarize, the herds of camels and gazelles killed, the aerial bombing, the massive and blind arrests, the antipersonnel mines that are still killing people, the theft of our phosphates and fish." Eddymaoui Lahabib, interview with the author, Layoune, 5 December 2005.

45. In Sierra Leone, the majority of the population is Muslim. In South Africa, there is an important Muslim minority, especially in the Durban area.

46. Desmond Tutu explains the meaning of *ubuntu* as "my humanity is inextricably linked to yours" in Desmond Tutu, *Il n'y a pas d'avenir sans pardon* (Paris: Albin Michel, 2000), 39. Archbishop Tutu also gives the political and practical reasons for dismissing criminal proceedings, while, in his public statements, he emphasizes only the spiritual dimension of pardon.

47. See the entire text of the royal speech given at the conclusion of the ERC's mandate and the presentation of the report on development in Morocco at http://www.ier.ma/_fr_article.php?id_article=1531.

48. Ibid.

49. Consider the position of Salah El-Ouadie: "I did not want a few individuals to pay for the State's responsibility. Individualizing punishment would have relieved the State of its responsibility and that was exactly what I wished to avoid. Those who stick to extreme positions are mistaken." According to this reasoning, it would be an error to judge men for the crimes committed, when a criminal system was the real guilty party. Salah El-Ouadie reverses the rationale for prison: that punishment has value of an exemplary nature and that the stigmatization of evil permits the "purging" of a criminal system and also participates in the process of "purifying" society. Salah El-Ouadie, interview with the author, Rabat, 26 January 2005.

50. In December 2005, when French judge Patrick Ramel, in a commission rogatory, asked that some twenty people linked to the Ben Barka affair (including Generals Hosnni Benslimane and Abdelhak Kadiri) be located, the presiding Moroccan judge Jamal Serhane coolly replied that he had no idea where they lived. In addition to such political blockages, the crimes were committed long ago and much of the evidence had been lost. In fear of losing sight of the main objective, Driss Benzekri says: "We are carrying out a work of remembrance ten, twenty, or thirty years after the fact. We can not throw out names into the public domain outside a proper judicial setting. Human rights are not a supermarket where one can dismiss, at an opportune moment, the presumption of innocence. . . . Our work would slip into slander, political accusations and counter-accusations. . . . We are not looking for individual responsibility. We do not have enough proof to be able to pin the superiors who gave the orders. We are working from the testimony of victims, and the victims have no information about the people who gave the orders." Cited in Human Rights Watch, "Morocco's Truth Commission," 27.

51. Abdelhay Moudden, interview with the author, Rabat, 4 February 2005.

52. See Human Rights Watch, "Morocco's Truth Commission," 27.

53. Jonathan S. Gration, Maghreb round table series, Center for Strategic and International Studies, Washington, DC, 16 February 2006. Along with a dozen countries in North Africa, the United States had launched the Trans-Sahara Counter Terrorism Initiative to stop terrorist networks from settling in the "Saharan corridor," where state power hardly existed.

54. A top official in the Ministry of Interior speaking off the record, interview with the author, Rabat, 3 December 2005.

55. The commission's final report notes repeatedly that the ERC had been unable to clarify certain historical facts because of the lack of cooperation from the police, army, gendarmerie, and security forces.

56. "Le Maroc, poubelle de la CIA," *Le Journal-Hebdo* 237 (Casablanca) (31 December 2005). On 6 January 2006, the paper also stated: "Dick Marty, the Swiss Senator in charge of investigations of so-called 'black sites,' places of secret detention in Europe that are managed by the CIA, revealed that the prisoners had been transferred to Morocco," http://www.lejournal-hebdo.com/article_print.php3?id_article=6394.

57. Abdelhay Moudden, interview with the author, 8 December 2005.

58. The report is available only in Arabic.

59. Instance Equité et Réconciliation, *Fiches de synthèse* (Rabat: IER, 2006), http://www.ier.ma/?lang=fr.

60. "Que peut faire le roi?" *Journal-Hebdo* (Casablanca) (15 February 2006), http://www.lejournal-bedo.com/article_print.php3?id_article=6488. This publication quotes one of the "bosses" of the army, who had shouted at his interrogator about the ERC, "The next time riots erupt, he (the king) had better not count on us to shoot into the crowd."

61. Figure given by Toby Shelley, journalist with *Financial Times* and author of *Endgame in the Western Sahara* (London: Zed Books, 2004), during the public hearing organized by the U.S. Congress, Washington, DC, 17 November 2005.

62. IER, Synthèse du rapport final, 2006, http://www.ier.ma/article.php3?id_article=1496.

63. Abdelhay Moudden, interview with the author, Rabat, 8 December 2005.

64. Mohammed VI, speech at the end of the ERC's mandate, 6 January 2006, http://www.ier.ma/_fr_print.php?id__article=1531. In an interview in *El Pais*, the king reaffirmed: "There are neither judges nor people judged. We are not before a tribunal. It is a question of examining, without complex or shame, this page of our history." "SM le Roi à El Pais: L'objectif des auditions publiques est de 'réconcilier le Maroc avec son passé,'" *El Pais*, 16 January 2005, http://www.ier.ma/article.php3?id_article=742.

65. Narjis Reghaye, interview with Mohamed Elyazghi, "L'Instance Equité et Réconciliation n'a pas à écrire l'histoire politique du Maroc" (Rabat: USFP), 26 September 2005, http://www.usfp.ma/article.php?t=4&id=49.

66. Mohammed VI, speech at the end of the ERC's mandate.

67. The criteria for compensation remain obscure and appear arbitrary in the eyes of many victims. Decisions left no possible recourse. In addition, the Commission, too close to the Palace, did not get to the end of its work in identifying the victims, in particular the Sahrawis. Last, but not least, the Commission, at least when it proceeded to compensation, did not have the mandate to reveal the circumstances of the human rights violations. Many victims refused to testify, for they considered that the Commission's manner of functioning amounted to "buying their silence."

68. Concerning reparations, the ERC listed 16,891 claims as receivable. Of these, 6,385 ex-victims received financial compensation (that is, 37.9%), 1,895 received financial compensation and reparations for other wrongs (11.2%), and 1,499 people (8.9%) received recommendations for reparations.

69. Driss el Yazami, interview with the author, 15 January 2008.

70. Louise Arbour, "Economic and Social Justice for Societies in Transition," New York University School of Law, October 26, 2006.

71. Driss Benzekri, presentation to the National Endowment for Democracy, Washington, DC, 19 January 2006. The former president of the ERC summed up the reforms he proposed: "We have recommended constitutional and legislative changes,

whose objective is to advance on the path to democracy and a State of law and economic and social development. We have recommended the reinforcement of fundamental rights and liberties, with a revision of those that affect freedom of expression, the banning of racism and xenophobia, the equality of men and women, the banning of crimes against humanity. We have also recommended that the police, the gendarmery and the army be placed under better control. We believe necessary also that the laws and regulations frame better the action of security agencies in crisis situations and in the control of demonstrations. We also propose that the government be held responsible for the actions of the security services. It is for Parliament to legislate, so that these agencies be held accountable. We also recommend that Parliament use the procedures that exist but which are not used, such as creating a commission of Parliamentary inquiry to reinforce the role of elected officials. It is also necessary to put a stop to the executive domination of the judiciary. It is absurd that the Minister of Justice be president of the Supreme Court. The president should come from the magistracy. And we propose that the Superior Council also include members of civil society, notably from human rights NGOs. We have proposed the ratification of the statutes of the ICC, abolition of the death penalty, reinforcement of sanctions in the newly introduced law banning torture, we consider that agents must refuse to obey illegal orders, we propose also to revise the code of procedure and criminal legislation."

72. Mohammed VI, speech at the end of the ERC's mandate.

73. Ahmed A. Benchemsi, "Années noires: Banco Royal," *TelQuel*, No. 208 (Casablanca), 14 February 2006, http://www.telquel-online.com/208/couverture_208_1.shtml.

74. Bottaro, *Se réconcilier au nom de quel passé?*, 80.

75. Cited in Florence Beaugé, "Driss Benzekri, opposant hier, partenaire aujourd'hui," *Le Monde*, 14 February 2006.

76. "How can the ERC, then, write in a report meant to enlighten Moroccan public opinion on one of the most serious crimes committed during the years of lead, that 'there is no suspicion of the implication of the Moroccan secret service'? How can it minimize in such a caricatural way the Moroccan responsibility in this political crime? Why didn't the ERA recall the condemnation pronounced by a French court of a Moroccan minister in office and of agents of the Moroccan special services? In refusing to point to the real responsibilities that led to the kidnapping and murder of Mehdi Ben Barka, in refusing to specify the obstacles raised in the name of State security for the past 40 years, in trying to avoid the insufficiencies of its investigative work in this affair, in confiding to an organization that is not up to the job, the ERC has taken the risk of seeing buried definitively the dossier without shining all the light on the circumstances of the disappearance of the victim nor on his grave. This is not the best way to honor the memory of Mehdi Ben Barka and his political work, nor the path by which the Moroccan people can make a lasting peace with its past. Collective memory is nourished by truth and clarity." Statement made in the name of the family of Mehdi Ben Barka: Bachir Ben Barka, Belfort, 19 January 2006.

77. The president of the ERC was received at the White House, French diplomacy praised the work of the truth commission, and the British Parliament "congratulated King Mohammed VI and the government of Morocco for having supported the recommendations of the Commission . . . , for having accorded reparations to 16,000 citizens, and for having reinforced democracy and the legal framework concerning human rights in Morocco." "The action of His Majesty the King Mohammed VI in reinforcing the State of law in Morocco is an example to follow for the rest of the Arab world," affirmed Mme. Trinidad Jiménez, secretary of international relations of the Spanish Workers Party (PSOE). Trinidad Jiménez, "L'action de SM le Roi pour le renforcement de l'Etat de Droit au Maroc un exemple à suivre par le reste du Monde Arabe (PSOE)" (Madrid: PSOE press release, 12 January 2006), http://www.ier.ma/article.php3?id_article=1545&var_recherche=jimenez.

78. Aboubakr Jamaï, Catherine Graciet, Ali Amar, and Mouaad Rhandi, "Que peut faire le roi," *Journal-Hebdo* (Casablanca), 15 February 2006.

79. Abdallah El Harif, in Florence Beaugé, "Driss Benzekri le pardon malgré tout," *Le Monde* (Paris), 14 February 2006. The mistrust of the ERC was reinforced by the fact that it did not communicate in a satisfactory manner. It never had a spokesperson. Some NGOs severely criticized the ERC for its lack of transparency. It should be said that some commissioners feared that a too-public communication could lead the security services to reduce the Commission's margin of maneuver. See Human Rights Watch, "Morocco's Truth Commission," 37.

80. Lahcen Daoudi, interview with the author, Rabat, 1 December 2005.

81. Abdelhamid Amine, in Florence Beaugé, "Driss Benzekri."

82. Prince Moulay Icham, "Démocratie et sacralité sont inconciliables," *TelQuel* No. 156–157 (Casablanca) (25 December 2004–7 January 2005): 94–97, http://www.telquel-online.com/156/interrogatoire_156.shtml.

Chapter 5

1. United Nations Association of the United States of America, "Information Concerning the Situation in Northern Uganda to the Prosecutor of the International Criminal Tribunal," March 2004.

2. Human Rights Watch, "Uprooted and Forgotten: Impunity and Human Rights Abuses in Northern Uganda," *A Human Rights Watch Report*, Vol. 17, No. 12(A), September 2005, http://hrw.org/reports/2005/uganda0905/5.htm#_Toc114146485.

3. Olara Otunnu, "The Silent Genocide," *Foreign Policy* 3 (July/August 2006). See also John A. Akec, "Ugandan Double Stand and ICC Threaten Juba Talks," *Sudan Tribune*, 1 October 2006, http://www.sudantribune.com/spip.php?page=imprimable&id_article=17887: "Every week a thousand people die in IDP's camps. Like Hitler's industrial complexes that succeeded in eclipsing Auschwitz and Holocaust crimes from the world's radar for a considerable amount of time, the profits and money to be made in peaceful parts of Uganda knocked at the doors of the rich and powerful far louder than the moral imperative to act, to prevent further suffering and death of the

international displaced refugees living in government's concentration camps in Northern Uganda. . . . There are issues of injustice and inequitable distribution of national
resources that need to be addressed."

4. Jan Egeland, UN under-secretary for humanitarian affairs, lamented in 2003,
"The conflict in Northern Uganda is the biggest, forgotten, neglected humanitarian
emergency in the world today." "War in Northern Uganda World's Worst Forgotten
Crisis UN," *Agence France-Presse*, 11 November 2003, http://www.reliefweb.int/rwb
.nsf/AllDocsByUNID/elfl76894430fdeec1256ddb0056ea4c.

5. Edward Hallett Carr, *The Twenty Years' Crisis, 1919–1939: An Introduction to
the Study of International Relations* (New York: Harper & Row, 1964), 100.

6. See also Reinhold Niebuhr, *Moral Man and Immoral Society: A Study of Ethics
and Politics* (Louisville, KY: Westminster John Knox, 2001).

7. In 1876 the International Committee for the Relief of the Wounded took the
name of the International Committee of the Red Cross (CICR).

8. Gustave Moynier, "La création d'une institution judiciaire internationale, propre à prévenir et à réprimer les infractions à la Convention de Genève," *Bulletin international des sociétés de secours aux militaires blessés*, no. 11 (Geneva: April 1872):
122–131.

9. *United States v. Ohlendorf*, IV Trials of War Criminals, Case No. 9.

10. Jean Barrea, *Théorie des relations internationales* (Paris: Artel, 1994), 5.

11. Ibid., 6.

12. Hans J. Morgenthau, *Politics Among Nations: The Struggle for Power and Peace*,
5th ed., revised (New York: Alfred A. Knopf, 1978), 4–15.

13. Diane Orentlicher, "Settling Accounts: The Duty to Prosecute Human Rights
Violations of a Prior Regime," *Yale Law Journal* 1100.8 (June 1991): 2537–2615; quotation from p. 2559. See also Benjamin Ferencz, *An International Criminal Court: A Step
Towards World Peace* (Dobbs Ferry, NY: Oceana, 1975), 1–61, 1980, 46: "The establishment of a permanent international criminal court was opposed on the basis that its
existence 'might even impair the possibilities of peace by interfering with the process
of political conciliation.'"

14. David Crane, interview with the author, Washington, DC, 3 March 2006. The
Ghanians refused to comply and gave Taylor a presidential plane to return quickly to
Liberia. The Ghanian president declared that "he felt betrayed by the international
community. . . . Five African presidents were meeting in Accra to find ways of kick
starting the Liberian peace process, and Mr. Taylor had been invited as president of
Liberia. . . . 'I felt betrayed [by this indictment] by the international community.'" Interview in *New African* (March 2004), http://www.ghanacastle.gov.gh/president/
castle-newsp-details.cfm?EmpID=195. The Libyan leader, Mu'ammar Al-Qadhafi, expressed the views of many African leaders when he denounced the Taylor arrest,
declaring, "It means that every head of state could meet a similar fate. This sets out a
serious precedent." Sarah Grainger and John James, "Head Hunted," *Focus on Africa*
(October–December 2006): 16. To date, the ICC has not succeeded in concluding a
Memorandum of Understanding with the African Union.

15. Stanley Hoffmann, "Peace and Justice: A Prologue," in *What Is a Just Peace?*, ed. Pierre Allan and Alexis Keller, 12–18 (Oxford: Oxford University Press, 2006).

16. Richard Goldstone, "Bringing War Criminals to Justice During an Ongoing War," in *Hard Choices: Moral Dilemmas in Humanitarian Intervention*, ed. Jonathan Moore, 195–211 (Lanham, MD: Rowman and Littlefield, 1998).

17. Ibid., 204.

18. Luc Coté, "Reflections on the Exercise of Prosecutorial Discretion in International Criminal Law," *Journal of International Criminal Justice* 3 (2005): 9, 162–186.

19. Frédéric Mégret, "Three Dangers for the International Criminal Court," *Finnish Yearbook of International Law* 12 (2001): 201.

20. Rome Statute of the International Criminal Court, A/CONF.183/9, 17 July 1998.

21. I. William Zartman and Victor Kremenyuk, eds., *Peace Versus Justice: Negotiating Forward- and Backward-Looking Outcomes* (Lanham, MD: Rowman and Littlefield, 2005), 3.

22. Kofi Annan, *The Rule of Law and Transitional Justice in Conflict and Post-Conflict Societies*, UN Document S/2004/616, 3 August 2004, paragraph 21.

23. Ibid.

24. Katherine Southwick, "Investigating War in Northern Uganda: Dilemmas for the International Criminal Court," *Yale Journal of International Law* (Summer–Fall 2005): 108.

25. Statement by ICC chief prosecutor Luis Moreno Ocampo, 24 October 2006, 4–5, http://www.icc-cpi.int/library/organs/otp/speeches/LMO_20051024_English.pdf.

26. See Myriam Revault d'Allonnes, "De l'autorité à l'institution: la durée publique," *Revue Esprit* (August 2004): 42–64; quotation from p. 46.

27. Akec, "Ugandan Double Stand."

28. Human Rights Watch, "Court Needs to Investigate Crimes by All Sides in Northern Uganda's Conflict," press release, 29 July 2004, http://www.hrw.org/en/news/2004/02/04/icc-investigate-all-sides-uganda.

29. Ocampo states: "In Uganda, the criterion for selection of the first case was gravity. We analyzed the gravity of all crimes in Northern Uganda committed by all groups. The LRA, the UPDF and other forces. Our investigations indicated that the crimes committed by the LRA were of dramatically higher gravity. We therefore started with an investigation of the LRA. At the same time, we have continued to collect information on allegations concerning other groups to determine whether other crimes meet the stringent thresholds of the Statute and our policy" (Statement by ICC chief prosecutor Luis Moreno Ocampo, 7). But at the same time, the prosecutor declares: "A resource-driven approach would mean that a situation involving hundreds of crimes, such as killings and rapes, may have to be set aside in the interest of focusing on a competing situation involving thousands of killings and rapes" (9).

30. "It was agreed with the government of southern Sudan that the defeated LRA terrorists be given the option of a soft landing. This would take the form of peace talks that would lead them to abandon terrorism and come out of the bush.

This option is open for a period of two months starting May"; "Uganda: U.S. Government Demands Trial for Rebel Leaders," *Irin News*, 6 July 2006. Having solicited the ICC in December 2004, Museveni asked the ICC in December 2004—without getting it—for the unilateral retraction of charges against the LRA. The Ugandan government offered in exchange the surrender of the LRA leaders, and an internal process of "reconciliation." Two years later, in 2006, the Ugandan government officially gave the LRA leaders two months (from May 2006) to surrender in exchange for total amnesty.

31. The ICC prosecutor was in a position all the more delicate in that he needed the cooperation of the Sudanese authorities to apprehend the leaders of the LRA who were in their territory, while he was simultaneously investigating crimes against humanity and war crimes committed by the Sudanese forces and Janjaweed militia that they supplied in Darfur. With Resolution 1593 on 31 March 2005, the UN Security Council had, in effect, transmitted to the ICC prosecutor the case of some two hundred thousand dead and millions displaced in Darfur.

32. See Apolo Kakaire, "Ugandan Mediator Critical of ICC Indictments," Institute for War and Peace Reporting, 15 April 2006, http://www.globalpolicy.org/component/content/article/164/28551.html.

33. See Adam Branch, "The ICC Should Stop Immediately Its Investigations in Uganda," 1 January 2005, http://www.monitor.co.ug/archives/a2005/jan/oped/0113/oped1133.php.

34. Adam Branch, "International Justice, Local Injustice," *Dissent* 51:3 (2004), http://www.dissentmagazine.org/article/?article=336.

35. Barney Afako, *Seeking Alternatives in Justice: The Experience of Northern Uganda* (London: African Rights, 2001), 8.

36. Cultural relativism affirms that values and norms are neither absolute nor universal but emerge from social customs. A certain number of Asian and Islamic states judge that human rights are not universal for they reflect Western values and norms.

37. Akec, "Ugandan Double Stand."

38. Helena Cobban, "Thoughtful Writing About TJ in Uganda," *Transitional Justice Forum*, 5 October 2005, http://th-forum.org/archives/001486.html.

39. Jean-Pierre Chrétien, "L'Afrique continue de souffrir de notre vision exotique," *Libération*, 31 January–1 February 2004.

40. Christine Deslaurier, "Le 'Bushinganthe' Peut-il Réconcilier le Burundi?" *Politique Afrique* 92 (December 2003): 93.

41. Jonathan Edelstein, "A Stick Too Many," *Transitional Justice Forum*, 2 June 2006, http://th-forum.org/archives/001955.html.

42. "There was little popular support for bringing such a commission to Sierra Leone, since most of the people preferred a 'forgive and forget' approach. . . . Social forgetting is a cornerstone of established processes of reintegration and healing for child and adult ex-combatants. Speaking of this war in public after undermines these processes, and many believe it encourages violence." Rosalind Shaw, *Rethinking Truth*

and Reconciliation Commissions: Lessons from Sierra Leone, Special Report 130 (Washington, DC: United States Institute of Peace, February 2005).

43. Cherif Bassiouni, "The Perennial Conflict Between International Criminal Justice and Realpolitik," *Georgia State University Law Review* 22.3, No. 136 (Spring 2006), http://digitalarchive.gsu.edu/colpub_review/136.

44. René Girard, *La violence et le sacré* (Paris: Payot, 2002), 29.

45. Ibid.

46. In the 1980s, the fear of a new military takeover in Argentina made the government abandon criminal charges in favor of a truth commission.

47. Refugee Law Project, "Whose Justice? Perceptions of Uganda's Amnesty Act of 2000; the Potential for Conflict Resolution and Long Term Reconciliation," Working Paper no. 15: 27 (Kampala: Refugee Law Project, February 2005), http://www.refugeelawproject.org/working_papers/RLP.WP15.pdf.

48. Sverker Finnstrom, "Where Is Uganda Going? Peace Talks with Kony Are Worth Everything," 9 July 2006, http://www.monitor.co.ug/artman/publish/debate/Peace_talks_with_Kony_are_worth_everything_49187.shtml.

49. Sverker Finnstrom, "Peace Talks Are Worth Everything," *Monitor Online* (10 July 2006), http://www.monitor.co.ug/artman/publish/debate/Peace_talks_with_Kony_are_worth_everything_49187.shtml.

50. It is nevertheless necessary to point out that the desire of the people is difficult to evaluate due to the difficulties of translating concepts as general as "justice" and "reconciliation" and that the responses depend in part on the manner in which the questions are formulated as well as the attitude of the pollsters.

51. International Center for Transitional Justice and Human Rights Center, "Forgotten Voices: A Population-Based Survey on Attitudes About Peace and Justice in Northern Uganda," New York: ICTJ, July 2005. According to this survey, 32 percent said that the international community should be in charge of justice, but only 27 percent had heard about the ICC at the time.

52. International Center for Transitional Justice, "When the War Ends: A Population-Based Survey on Attitudes About Peace, Justice, and Social Reconstruction in Northern Uganda," Human Rights Center, Payson Center for International Development, December 2007, 3. This survey was a joint project of UC Berkeley's Human Rights Center, Tulane's Payson Center for International Development, and the New York–based International Center for Transitional Justice.

53. Marc Lacey, "Offering Olive Branch to a Brutal Uganda Foe," *New York Times*, 19 April 2005: "Some war victims are urging the international court to back off. They say the local people will suffer if the rebel command feels cornered. They recommend giving forgiveness more of a chance, using an age-old ceremony involving raw eggs. 'When we talk of arrest warrants, it sounds so simple,' says David Onen Acana II, chief of the Acholis, the dominant tribe in the war-riven North. 'But an arrest does not mean the war will end.'" Helena Cobban, *Transitional Justice Forum* (15 September 2005), http://tj-forum.org/archives/001447.html.

54. Desmond Tutu, *There Is No Future Without Forgiveness* (New York: Doubleday, 1999).

Conclusion

1. For example, the ICC delivered an arrest warrant against Mathieu Ngudjolo on 6 July 2007, although his movement had received a general amnesty from the Congo in 2006.

2. Christine Bell, "The New Law of Transitional Justice," paper presented at "Building a Future on Peace and Justice" conference, Nuremberg, June 25–27, 2007.

Epilogue

1. European Union, Independent International Fact-Finding Mission on the Conflict in Georgia, 30 September 2009, http://www.ceiig.ch/Report.html.

2. See, in particular, Cesare Romano, A. Nollkaemper, and J. Kleffner, eds., *Internationalized Criminal Courts and Tribunals: Sierra Leone, East Timor, Kosovo and Cambodia* (Oxford: Oxford University Press, 2004).

3. The trial is presided over by the SCSL but is on the premises of the ICC.

4. Mark Freeman, *Necessary Evils: Amnesties and the Search for Justice* (New York: Cambridge University Press, 2009).

5. The AU-EU expert report titled "The Principle of Universal Jurisdiction," Council of the European Union, Brussels, 16 April 2009, 4.

6. Ibid., 36.

7. The Arab League and the African Union have requested—in vain—the application of Article 16 of the Statutes of Rome to suspend the arrest warrant against the Sudanese president.

8. Denouncing "a selective justice" by the West, Jean Ping, president of the AU Commission, accused the ICC at the meeting in Addis Ababa in June 2009 of perpetuating the myth that African governments and leaders are criminals by nature. "La 'justice sélective de la CPI' dénoncée par Jean Ping," *Afrique en ligne*, 27 January 2009, http://www.afriquejet.com/actualites/politique/la-%22justice-selective%22-de-la-cpi-denoncee-par-jean-ping-2009012720597.html.

9. "African Union in Rift with Court," BBC, 3 July 2009.

10. Kofi Annan, "Africa and the International Court," *International Herald Tribune*, 30 June 2009.

11. During the special session on Sri Lanka of the UN Human Rights Council in May, the UN High Commissioner for Human Rights, Navi Pillay, said that an "independent and credible international investigation into recent events should be dispatched to ascertain the occurrence, nature and scale of violations of international human rights and international humanitarian law, as well as specific responsibilities." Peter Capella, "UN Rights Chief Presses for Sri Lanka Probe," *Agence France Presse*, 27 May 2009.

12. It is interesting to note that in 2008 and 2009 more than three thousand communications from Russia concerning presumed war crimes committed by the Georgian forces were sent to the ICC prosecutors.

13. One exception is, in the words of Human Rights Watch, the "dirty deal" concluded in 2009 between Italy and Libya, by which Italy would pay financial compensation to Tripoli for the colonial period in exchange for gas and active collaboration by the Libyan authorities to stop clandestine immigration to Italy. Human Rights Watch, "Italy/Libya: Gaddafi Visit Celebrates Dirty Deal: Italy and Libya Join Forces to Prevent Boat Migrants from Leaving or Seeking Asylum," press release, June 2009, http://www.hrw.org/fr/news/2009/06/09/italylibya-gaddafi-visit-celebrates-dirty-deal.

14. Hugo van der Merve, comment during the experts' seminar on "Transitional Justice and Human Rights: New Challenges and Perspectives" (University Carlos III, Madrid, 28–29 May 2009). See also Zinaida Miller, "Effects of Invisibility: In Search of the 'Economic' in Transitional Justice," *International Journal of Transitional Justice* 2 (2008): 266–291.

15. "Richard Goldstone Appointed to Lead Human Rights Council Fact-Finding Mission on Gaza Conflict," press release, United Nations, 3 April 2009, http://www.unhchr.ch/huricane/huricane.nsf/view01/2796E2CA43CA4D94C125758D002 F8D25?opendocument.

16. See, in particular, Amnesty International, "Iraq: Amnesty International Deplores Death Sentences in Saddam Hussein Trial," press release, 5 November 2006, http://www.amnesty.org/en/library/info/MDE14/037/2006 and Human Rights Watch, "Judging Dujail: The First Trial Before the Iraq High Tribunal," 19 November 2006.

17. At that time the UN Security Council refused to denounce Iraq, despite the unanimous conclusions of a report of experts sent to the region to verify the truth of allegations of the use of chemical weapons by Saddam Hussein's regime.

18. The panel established by the UN Security Council to report on the humanitarian situation in Iraq noted in 1999 that "in marked contrast to the prevailing situation prior to the events of 1990–1991, infant mortality rates in Iraq today are among the highest in the world, low infant birth weight (less than 2.5 kg) affects at least 23 percent of all births, chronic malnutrition affects every fourth child under five years of age." UN Security Council, *Report of the Humanitarian Panel of the United Nations Security Council*, 30 March 1999, Document S/1999/356, Annex II, paragraph 43. In its annual report for 2000, the International Committee of the Red Cross (ICRC) noted: "Ten years after the Gulf war and the imposition of international trade sanctions, daily life for ordinary Iraqis was a struggle for survival. The tragic effects of the embargo were seen in the steady deterioration of the health system and the breakdown of public infrastructure," ICRC, *ICRC 2000 Annual Report*, 196.

19. In this perspective, see Nadim Shehadi and Elizabeth Wilmhurst: "Failing to set up the Tribunal would have been interpreted as a green light for assassinations and terrorism to continue with impunity in Lebanon. Any political cost involved in setting up the Tribunal will be offset by the higher cost of not doing so." Nadim Shehadi and Elizabeth Wilmhurst, "The Special Tribunal for Lebanon: The UN on Trial?" *Middle East International Law Briefing Paper* (London: Chatham House, July 2007), 1.

20. The co-sponsors of the initial resolution were the United States, Britain, France, Belgium, Slovakia, and Italy. Other states like Ghana and Peru voted in favor of the resolution.

21. An analysis shared by Mona Yacoubian, a former intelligence analyst for the State Department and a special adviser on the Muslim World Initiative at the USIP, holds that "in many ways, the tribunal represents almost an existential threat to the Syrian regime." Mona Yacoubian, "Yacoubian: Linkages Between Special UN Tribunal, Lebanon, and Syria," Council on Foreign Relations, 1 June 2007, http://www.cfr.org/publication/13512/yacoubian.html. For a more detailed discussion on the creation of the tribunal, see Frédéric Mégret, "A Special Tribunal for Lebanon: The UN Security Council and the Emancipation of International Criminal Justice," *Leiden Journal of International Law* 21 (2008): 485–512.

22. For more detail, see Marieke Wierda, Habib Nassar, and Lynn Maalouf, "Early Reflections on Local Perceptions, Legitimacy and Legacy of the Special Tribunal for Lebanon," *Journal of International Criminal Justice* 5 (2007): 1065–1081. According to Amnesty International, the tribunal was "politically selective" and should address the serious crimes committed in particular during the civil war. Amnesty International, "The Special Tribunal for Lebanon 'Selective Justice,'" 24 February 2009, http://www.amnestyusa.org/document.php?id=ENGMDE180012009&lang=e.

23. Wadad Halwani, interview with Lynn Maalouf, Beirut, June 1997, in Wierda, Nassar, and Maalouf, "Early Reflections," p.1072.

24. See Paola Gaeta, "To Be (Present) or Not to Be (Present): Trials in Absentia Before the Special Tribunal for Lebanon," *Journal of International Criminal Justice* 5 (2007): 1165–1174.

25. The affair is politically and judicially sensitive because the Court's jurisdiction in the Israeli-Palestinian conflict remains subject to intense controversy: if the judges hold that Palestine does not constitute a state, at least at the present time, the lack of jurisdiction will be interpreted in the Arab-Islamic world as a political decision that validates their suspicions toward this Court. On the other hand, recognizing Palestine as a state would provoke reactions equally negative in Israel. Whatever decision the Court makes, it will be criticized and likely considered illegitimate by the belligerents.

26. Laurie King-Irani, "Does International Justice Have a Local Address? Lessons from the Belgian Experiment," *Middle East Report* 229 (Winter 2003): 20–35; quotation on p. 21. See also http://www.indictsharon.net.

27. Associations close to Israel have also filed a complaint against the president of the Palestinian Authority, which has also been judged inadmissible by Belgium.

28. On 3 April 2009, the president of the Human Rights Council established an international independent fact-finding mission with the mandate "to investigate all violations of international human rights law and international humanitarian law that might have been committed at any time in the context of the military operations that were conducted in Gaza during the period from 27 December 2008 [to] 18 January 2009, whether before, during or after." "Richard J. Goldstone Appointed to Lead Hu-

man Rights Council on Fact-Finding Mission on Gaza Conflict," UN press release, 3 April 2009.

29. Mouammar Kadhafi, quoted by Thijs Bouwknegt, "L'Afrique boude la CPI," Radio Nederland (12 June 2009), http://www.rnw.nl/fr/afrique/article/l'-afrique-boude-la-cpi.

Bibliography

Afako, Barney. *Seeking Alternatives in Justice: The Experience of Northern Uganda.* London: African Rights, 2001.

Akande, Dapo. "International Law Immunities and the International Criminal Court." *American Journal of International Law* 98.3 (July 2004): 407–433.

Akhavan, Payam. "Beyond Impunity: Can International Criminal Justice Prevent Future Atrocities?" *American Journal of International Law* 95.1 (January 2001): 7–31.

———. "The Lord's Resistance Army Case: Uganda's Submission of the First State Referral to the International Criminal Court." *American Journal of International Law* 99.2 (April 2005).

Aldana-Pindell, Raquel. "An Emerging Universality of Justiciable Victims' Rights in the Criminal Process to Curtail Impunity for State-Sponsored Crimes." *Human Rights Quarterly* 26.3 (2004): 605–685.

Allan, Pierre, and Kjell Goldmann, eds. *The End of the Cold War: Evaluating Theories of International Relations.* 2nd ed. Dordrecht: Kluwer Law International, 1995.

Allan, Pierre, and Alexis Keller, eds. *What Is a Just Peace?* Oxford: Oxford University Press, 2006.

Amin, Samir. "World Congress Against Racism." *Solidarités* (Geneva), 10 November 2001.

Amnesty International. "Iraq: Amnesty International Deplores Death Sentences in Saddam Hussein Trial." Press release, 5 November 2006, http://www.amnesty.org/en/library/info/MDE14/037/2006.

Annan, Kofi. "Africa and the International Court." *International Herald Tribune*, 30 June 2009.

Aolain, Fionnuala, and Colm Campbell. "The Paradox of Transition in Conflicted Democracies." *Human Rights Quarterly* 27 (2005): 172–213.

Arbour, Louise. "Economic and Social Justice for Societies in Transition." New York University School of Law, October 25, 2006.

Arendt, Hannah. *Eichmann à Jérusalem.* Paris: Gallimard, 1991.

Aron, Raymond. *Introduction à la philosophie de l'histoire: essai sur les limites de l'objectivité historique.* Paris: Gallimard, 1938.

Arsanjani, Mahnoush, and W. Michael Reisman. "The Law-in-Action of the International Criminal Court." *American Journal of International Law* 99.2 (April 2005): 385–403.

Aubrey, Jewett, and Marc Turetzky. "Stability and Chance in President Clinton's Foreign Policy Beliefs, 1993–1996." *Presidential Studies Quarterly* 28 (1998): 638–665.

Austin, John Langshaw. *How to Do Things with Words: The William James Lectures Delivered at Harvard University in 1955.* Edited by J. O. Urmson. Oxford: Oxford University Press, 1962.

Azizi, Abdellatif El. "Années de plomb l'autre affaire Ben Barka." *TelQuel* 190 (Casablanca), 10 September 2005.

———. "Enquête: Al Adi Wal Ishane, l'international islamiste." *TelQuel* 185 (Casablanca), 16 July 2005.

Badie, Bertrand. *La diplomatie des droits de l'homme.* Paris: Fayard, 2002.

Ball, Terence, James Farr, and Russell L. Hanson, eds. *Political Innovation and Conceptual Change.* Cambridge: Cambridge University Press, 1989.

Bardèche, Maurice. *Nuremberg, ou la terre promise.* Paris: Les Sept Couleurs, 1948.

———. *Nuremberg II, ou les faux-monnayeurs.* Paris: Les Sept Couleurs, 1952.

Barkan, Elazar. *The Guilt of Nations: Restitution and Negotiating Historical Injustices.* New York: W. W. Norton and Company, 2000.

Barnett, Michael, and Martha Finnemore. "The Politics, Power, and Pathologies of International Organizations." *International Organizations* 53.4 (Autumn 1999): 699–732.

Bar-On, Dan. *Fear and Hope: Three Generations of the Holocaust.* Cambridge: Cambridge University Press, 1995.

Barrea, Jean. *Théorie des relations internationales.* Paris: Artel, 1994.

Barsalou, Judy. *Trauma and Transitional Justice in Divided Societies.* Special Report 135. Washington, DC: United States Institute of Peace, April 2005.

Bassiouni, Cherif, ed. "The Institutionalization of Torture Under the Bush Administration." *Case Western Reserve Journal of International Law* 38 (2006): 389–425.

———. *Post-Conflict Justice.* New York: Transnational Publishers, 2002.

Bell, Christine. "The New Law of Transitional Justice." Paper presented at "Building a Future on Peace and Justice" conference, Nuremberg, June 25–27, 2007.

Benchemsi, Ahmed A. "Bilan. 2005. Les grandes tendances se dessinent." *TelQuel* 187 (November 2005).

Bennani, Driss, and Abdellatif El Azizi. "Maroc/Algérie: Bluff et petites manoeuvres." *TelQuel* 189 (Casablanca), 3 September 2005.

Bloomfield, David, Teresa Barnes, and Luc Huyse. *Reconciliation After Violent Conflict: A Handbook.* Stockholm: Institute for Democracy and Electoral Assistance, 2003.

Boisson de Chazournes, Laurence, Jean-François Quéguiner, and Santiago Villal-pando, eds. *Crimes de l'histoire et réparations: les réponses du droit et de la justice*. Brussels: Editions de Université de Bruxelles, 2004.

Boraine, Alex. *A Country Unmasked: Inside South Africa's Truth and Reconciliation Commission*. Oxford: Oxford University Press, 2000.

Boraine, Alex, Janet Levy, and Ronel Scheffer. *Dealing with the Past: Truth and Reconciliation Commission in South Africa*. Cape Town, South Africa: IDASA, 1994.

Bottaro, Mauro. *Se réconcilier au nom de quel passé? Seuils et franchissements historiques dans les usages politiques et symboliques de l'Islam au Maroc*. Paris: Mémoire non publié d'EHESS, 2005.

Boukhari, Karim. "Droits de l'homme: les dossiers chauds de l'IER." *TelQuel* 194 (Casablanca), 8 October 2005.

Brahm, Eric. "Getting to the Bottom of Truth: Evaluating the Contribution of Truth Commissions to Post-Conflict Societies." Paper presented at Wisconsin Institute for Peace and Conflict Studies 20th Annual Conference, "Challenges and Paths to Justice." Marquette University, Milwaukee, Wisconsin, 6–8 October 2004.

Brauman, Rony. *Penser dans l'urgence: parcours critique d'un humanitaire*. Paris: Seuil, 2006.

Brauman, Rony, and Alain Finkielkraut. *La Discorde: Israël-Palestine, les Juifs, la France*. Paris: Mille et Une Nuits, 2006.

Brauman, Rony, and Eyal Sivan. *Eloge de la désobéissance: À propos d' "un spécialiste" Adolf Eichmann*. Paris: Le Pommier, 1999.

Brayard, Florent, ed. *Le Génocide des Juifs: entre procès et histoire, 1943–2000*. Brussels: Complexe, 2000.

Brinkley, Douglas. "Democratic Enlargement: The Clinton Doctrine." *Foreign Policy* 106 (Spring 1997): 110–127.

Brody, Reed. "Justice: The First Casualty of Truth?" *Nation*, April 12, 2001, http://www.thenation.com/doc/20010430/brody.

Brooks, Roy L. *Atonement and Forgiveness: A New Model for Black Reparations*. Berkeley: University of California Press, 2004.

Bruckner, Pascal. *La tyrannie de la pénitence*. Paris: Grasset, 2006.

Brumberg, Daniel. "Liberalization Versus Democracy: Understanding Arab Political Reform." Carnegie Paper 37. Washington, DC: Carnegie Endowment for International Peace, April 2003.

Cairns, Alain. *Politics and the Past: On Repairing Historical Injustices*. Lanham, MD: Rowman and Littlefield, 2003.

Cantegreil, Julien. "Lutte antiterroriste: une chance pour les valeurs de l'Europe." *Le Temps* (Geneva), 9 November 2006.

Carothers, Thomas. "The End of the Transition Paradigm." *Journal of Democracy* 13.1 (January 2002): 1–21.

Carr, Edward Hallett. *The Twenty Years' Crisis, 1919–1939: An Introduction to the Study of International Relations*. New York: Harper and Row, 1964.

Cassese, Antonio. "A Big Step Forward for International Justice." Crimes of War Project. December 2003, http://www.crimesofwar.org/icc_magazine/icc-cassese.html.

Center for Strategic International Studies. "The U.S., the EU, and Middle East Reform: What Can We Learn from Morocco?" *Middle East Program Morocco Trip Report* (March 2006).

Césaire, Aimé. Introduction to *Esclavage et colonisation* by Victor Schoelcher. Paris: Presses Universitaires de France, 1948.

Chaumont, Jean-Michel. *La concurrence des victimes.* 2nd ed. Paris: La Découverte, 2002.

———. "Du culte des héros à la concurrence des victimes." *Criminologie* 33.1 (2000).

Checkel, Jeffrey T. "The Constructivist Turn in International Relations Theory." *World Politics* 502 (1998): 324–348.

Clinton, Bill. *My Life.* New York: Random House, 2004.

Cohen, Craig. *Measuring Progress in Stabilization and Reconstruction.* Stabilization and Reconstruction Series. Washington, DC: United States Institute of Peace, 1 March 2006.

Cole, Elizabeth, and Judy Barsalou. *Unite or Divide? The Challenges of Teaching History in Societies Emerging from Violent Conflict.* Special Report 163. Washington, DC: United States Institute of Peace, June 2006.

Colonomos, Ariel. *La morale dans les relations internationales.* Paris: Odile Jacob, 2005.

Cooper, Belinda, ed. *War Crimes: The Legacy of Nuremberg.* New York: TV Books, 1999.

Corten, Olivier. "Humanitarian Intervention: A Controversial Right." *Le Courrier de l'UNESCO* (June 1999), http://www.unesco.org/courier/1999_08/uk/ethique/intro.htm.

Davis, David Brion. *Inhuman Bondage: The Rise and Fall of Slavery in the New World.* New York: Oxford University Press, 2006.

De Jong, Joop T. V. M., Ivan H. Komproe, Mark Van Ommeren, Mustafa El Masri, Mesfin Araya, Noureddine Khaled, Willem van de Put, and Daya Somasundaram. "Lifetime Events and Posttraumatic Stress Disorder in Four Postconflict Settings." *Journal of the American Medical Association* 286.5 (August 2001): 555–562.

de Ridder, Trudy. "The Trauma of Testifying: Deponents' Difficult Healing Process." *Track Two* 6.3/4 (December 1997), http://ccrweb.ccr.uct.ac.za/archive/two/6_34/p30_deridder.html.

Dicker, Richard, and Elise Keppler. "Beyond The Hague: The Challenges of International Justice." In *Human Rights Watch World Report.* New York: Human Rights Watch, 2004, http://www.hrw.org/en/news/2004/01/26/beyond-hague-challenges-international-justice.

Dickinson, Laura. "The Promise of Hybrid Courts." *American Journal of International Law* 97.2 (April 2003): 295–310.

Dimitrejevic, Nenad. "Justice Beyond Blame: Moral Justification of (the Idea of) a Truth Commission." *Journal of Conflict Resolution* 50.3 (June 2006): 368–382.

Elsea, Jennifer. "International Criminal Court: Overview and Selected Legal Issues." Washington, DC: Congressional Research Service, 5 June 2002.

——. "U.S. Policy Regarding the International Criminal Court." Washington, DC: Congressional Research Service, 3 September 2005.

Elster, John. *Closing the Books: Transitional Justice in Historical Perspective.* Cambridge: Cambridge University Press, 2004.

——. "Redemption for Wrongdoing: The Fate of Collaborators After 1945." *Journal of Conflict Resolution* 50.3 (June 2006): 324–338.

Encyclopedia of Genocide and Crimes Against Humanity 3. London: Macmillan Reference, 2004, 1045–1047.

European Union. Independent International Fact-Finding Mission on the Conflict in Georgia, 30 September 2009, http://www.ceiig.ch/Report.html.

Eze, Emmanuel Chukwudi. "Transition and the Reasons of Memory." *South Atlantic Quarterly* 10.3 (Fall 2004): 755–768.

Falk, Richard. "Criminal Accountability in Transitional Justice." *Peace Review* 12.1 (2000): 81–86.

Fanon, Frantz. *Les damnés de la terre.* Paris: La Découverte, 2002.

Feldman, Lily Gardner. "The Principle and Practice of 'Reconciliation' in German Foreign Policy Relations with France, Israel, Poland and the Czech Republic." *International Affairs* 75.2 (April 1999): 333–356.

Ferencz, Benjamin. *An International Criminal Court: A Step Towards World Peace.* Dobbs Ferry, NY: Oceana, 1975.

Ferro, Marc, ed. *Le livre noir du colonialisme, XVIe–XXIe: de l'extermination à la repentance.* Paris: Robert Laffont, 2003.

Ferry, Jean-Marc. *L'Ethique reconstructive.* Paris: Cerf, 1996.

Finnemore, Martha, and Kathryn Sikkink. "International Norm Dynamics and Political Change." *International Organization* 47.4 (Autumn 1998): 887–917.

Foucault, Michel. "La vérité et les formes juridiques." *Dits et écrits*, Vol. 1, *1954–1975.* Paris: Gallimard, 2001.

Freeman, Mark. *Necessary Evils: Amnesties and the Search for Justice.* New York: Cambridge University Press, 2009.

Friedman, Merle. "The Truth and Reconciliation Commission in South Africa as an Attempt to Heal a Traumatized Society." In *International Handbook of Human Response to Trauma*, edited by Arieh Shalev, Rachel Yehuda, and Alexander McFarlane, 399–411. New York: Plenum Publishers, 2000.

Frost, Mervyn. *Towards a Normative Theory of International Relations.* New York: Cambridge University Press, 1986.

Fukuyama, Francis. *The End of History and the Last Man.* New York: Free Press, 1992.

Gaeta, Paola. "To Be (Present) or Not to Be (Present): Trials in Absentia Before the Special Tribunal for Lebanon." *Journal of International Criminal Justice* 5 (2007): 1165–1174.

Garapon, Antoine. *Bien juger.* Paris: Odile Jacob, 2001.

——. *Des crimes qu'on ne peut ni punir ni pardonner: pour une justice internationale.* Paris: Odile Jacob, 2002.

——. "Jusqu'où la justice pénale internationale peut-elle être plurielle?" Conférence présentée devant la Cour Pénale Internationale, The Hague, 18 January 2007.

Garapon, Antoine, and Ioannis Papadopoulos. *Juger en Amérique et en France.* Paris: Odile Jacob, 2003.

Gavron, Jessica. "Amnesties in the Light of Developments in International Law and the Establishment of the International Criminal Court." *International Law and Comparative Quarterly* 51 (January 2002): 91–117.

Gibson, James L. "The Contributions of Truth to Reconciliation: Lessons from South Africa." *Journal of Conflict Resolution* 50.3 (June 2006): 409–432.

——. "The Truth About Truth and Reconciliation in South Africa." *International Political Science Review* 26.4 (2005): 341–361.

Gilloin, Carine. *Une histoire des grands hommes: Anthropologie historique de la communauté herero, 1840–1993 (Namibie).* Paris: EHESS, 1999.

Girard, René. *La violence et le sacré.* Paris: Payot, 2002.

Goldstone, Richard. "Bringing War Criminals to Justice During an Ongoing War." In *Hard Choices: Moral Dilemmas in Humanitarian Intervention*, edited by Jonathan Moore, 195–211. Lanham MD: Rowman and Littlefield, 1998.

Grainger, Sarah, and John James. "Head Hunted." *Focus on Africa* (October–December 2006).

Habermas, Jürgen. *L'espace public.* Paris: Payot, 1993.

Halpern, Jodi, and Harvey M. Weinstein. "Rehumanizing the Other: Empathy and Reconciliation." *Human Rights Quarterly* 26 (2004): 561–583.

Hartman, Geoffrey. "Apprendre des survivants: remarques sur l'histoire orale et les archives video de témoignages sur l'holocauste à l'université de Yale." In *Le Monde Juif. Revue d'histoire de la Shoah* (January–April 1994).

Hassner, Pierre, and Justin Vaïsse. *Washington et le monde: dilemmes d'une Superpuissance.* Paris: CERI/Autrement, 2003.

Hausner, Gidéon. *Justice à Jérusalem: Eichmann devant ses juges.* Paris: Flammarion, 1966.

Hayner, Priscilla B. *Unspeakable Truths: Confronting State Terror and Atrocity.* New York: Routledge, 2001.

Hazan, Pierre. "A Durban, Américains et Israéliens claquent la porte de la Conférence contre le racisme." *Le Temps* (Geneva), 4 September 2001.

——. "Avec le CICR dans l'ex-Yougoslavie." *Libération*, 19 October 1993.

——. "Esclavage et colonialisme: le spectre des demandes de réparations." *Le Temps* (Geneva), 1 September 2001.

——. *Justice in a Time of War: The True Story Behind the International Criminal Tribunal for the Former Yugoslavia.* College Station, TX: Texas A&M University Press, 2004.

——. *Le mal suisse.* Paris: Stock, 1998.

——. *Morocco Betting on a Truth and Reconciliation Commission.* Special Report 165. Washington, DC: United States Institute of Peace, July 2006.

——. "Regards croisés sur les espoirs et les dangers de la justice internationale," interview with Alain Finkielkraut, *Le Temps* (Geneva), 6 December 1999.

——. "The Revolution by the ICTY: The Concept of Justice in Wartime." *Journal of International Criminal Justice* 2 (2004): 435–540.

——. *The Victim's Guide to the International Criminal Court.* Paris: Reporters sans Frontières, 2001.

Herman, Judith Lewis. *Trauma and Recovery.* New York: Basic Books, 1992.

Hesse, Carla, and Robert Post, eds. *Human Rights in Political Transitions: Gettysburg to Bosnia.* New York: Zone Books, 1999.

Hoffmann, Matthew. "Entrepreneurs and Norm Dynamics: An Agent-Based Model of the Norm Life Cycle." In *Proceedings of Agent-Based Simulation 3 Conference,* edited by Christoph Urban, 32–37. Ghent, Belgium: SCS-Europe, 2002.

Hoffmann, Stanley. "Clash of Globalizations." *Foreign Affairs* 81.4 (July/August 2002): 104–126.

——. *The Ethics and Politics of Humanitarian Intervention.* Notre Dame, IN: Notre Dame University, 1996.

——. "Peace and Justice: A Prologue." In *What Is a Just Peace?,* edited by Pierre Allan and Alexis Keller, 12–18. Oxford: Oxford University Press, 2006.

Honeyman, Catherine, Shakirah Hudani, Alfa Tiruneh, Justina Hierta, Leila Chirayath, Andrew Iliff, and Jens Meierhenrich. "Establishing Collective Norms: Potentials for Participatory Justice in Rwanda." *Peace and Conflict: Journal of Peace Psychology* 10.1 (2004): 1–24.

Human Rights Watch. "Court Needs to Investigate Crimes by All Sides in Northern Uganda's Conflict." Press release, 29 July 2004, http://www.hrw.org/en/news/2004/02/04/icc-investigate-all-sides-uganda.

——. "Italy/Libya: Gaddafi Visit Celebrates Dirty Deal: Italy and Libya Join Forces to Prevent Boat Migrants from Leaving or Seeking Asylum." Press release, 9 June 2009, http://www.hrw.org/en/news/2009/06/09/italylibya-gaddafi-visit-celebrates-dirty-deal.

——. "Judging Dujail: The First Trial Before the Iraq High Tribunal." Report E1809 (19 November 2006), http://www.hrw.org/en/node/11112/section/2.

——. "The Meaning of 'The Interests of Justice' in Article 53 of the Rome Statute." Human Rights Watch Policy Paper, June 2005.

——. "Morocco: Human Rights at a Crossroads." *A Human Rights Watch Report.* Vol. 16, No. 6(E), October 2004, http://www.hrw.org/reports/2004/morocco1004/.

——. "Morocco's Truth Commission: Honoring Past Victims During an Uncertain Present." *A Human Rights Watch Report.* Vol. 17, No. 11(E), November 2005, http://www.hrw.org/reports/2005/morocco1105/4.htm/.

——. "Uprooted and Forgotten: Impunity and Human Rights Abuses in Northern Uganda." *A Human Rights Watch Report.* Vol. 17, No. 12(E), September 2005, http://hrw.org/reports/2005/uganda0905/5.htm#_Toc114146485.

Human Security Center. *Human Security Report 2005.* 2005.

Huntington, Samuel P. *The Third Wave: Democratization in the Late Twentieth Century.* Norman: University of Oklahoma Press, 1991.

Hyland, William G. *Clinton's World: Remaking American Foreign Policy.* Westport, CT: Praeger, 1999.

Ignatieff, Michael. *Human Rights as Politics and Idolatry.* Princeton, NJ: Princeton University Press, 2002.

Instance Equité et Réconciliation. "Déclaration de l'Instance Equité et Réconciliation." 11 January 2004, http://www.ier.ma/article.php3?id_article=222.

――――. "Public Briefings for Testimonies: Third Session." Figuig, Morocco: IER, 29 January 2005.

――――. *Résumé du rapport final.* Rabat: IER, 2005, http://www.ier.ma/_fr_article.php?id_article=1496.

International Center for Transitional Justice. "Algerian Charter Risks Reinforcing Impunity and Undermining Reconciliation." ICTJ Press Release, 26 September 2005, http://www.ictj.org/en/news/press/release/257.html.

――――. "The International Criminal Court and Conflict Mediation." New York: ICTJ, June 2005.

International Center for Transitional Justice and Human Rights Center. "Forgotten Voices: A Population-Based Survey of Attitudes About Peace and Justice in Northern Uganda." New York: ICTJ, July 2005, http://www.ictj.org/images/content/1/2/127/pdf.

――――. "When the War Ends: A Population-Based Survey on Attitudes About Peace, Justice, and Social Reconstruction in Northern Uganda." Human Rights Center, Payson Center for International Development, December 2007.

International Court of Justice. "The Legal Consequences of the Wall Built on the Palestinian Occupied Territories." Advisory opinion, 9 July 2004.

International Criminal Court. *Rapport de la Cour pénale internationale à l'Organisation des Nations unies.* The Hague: ICC, 1 August 1995, A/60/177.

International Federation for Human Rights. "Les commissions de vérité et de réconciliation: l'expérience marocaine." Regional Seminar Report. Rabat: IFHR, 25–27 March 2004.

――――. *Reflections on the Concept "Interests of Justice" in Article 53 of the Rome Statute.* Paris: FIDH, 20 June 2005.

James, Wilmot, and Linda van de Vuver, eds. *After the TRC: Reflections on Truth and Reconciliation in South Africa.* Athens: Ohio University Press, 2001.

Jankélévitch, Vladimir. *L'Imprescriptible.* Paris: Le Seuil, 1986.

Jaspers, Karl. *La culpabilité allemande.* Paris: Editions de Minuit, 1990.

Joinet, Louis. *Lutter contre l'impunité: Dix questions pour comprendre et pour agir.* Paris: La Découverte, 2002.

Kagan, Robert. "Power and Weakness: Why the United States and Europe See the World Differently." *Policy Review* 113 (June/July 2002): 1–18.

Kahn, Paul W. "Why the United States Is So Opposed." Crimes of War Project, December 2003, http://www.crimesofwar.org/icc_magazine//icc-kahn.html.

Kaldor, Mary. *New and Old War: Organized Violence in a Global Era.* Cambridge, MA: Polity Press, 2001.

Kaminski, Marek M., Monika Nalepa, and Barry O'Neill. "Normative and Strategic Aspects of Transitional Justice." *Journal of Conflict Resolution* 50.3 (June 2006): 295–302.

Katzenstein, Peter, ed. *The Culture of National Security: Norms and Identity in World Politics.* New York: Columbia University Press, 1996.

Katzenstein, Peter J., Robert O. Keohane, and Stephen D. Krasner. "International Organizations and the Study of World Politics." *International Organization* 52.4 (Autumn 1998): 645–685.

Keohane, Robert O., Joseph S. Nye, and Stanley Hoffmann, eds. *After the Cold War: International Institutions and State Strategies in Europe, 1989–1991.* Cambridge, MA: Harvard University Press, 1993.

King-Irani, Laurie. "Does International Justice Have a Local Address? Lessons from the Belgian Experiment." *Middle East Report* 229 (Winter 2003): 20–35.

Koskenniemi, Marrti. "Constitutionalism as a Mindset: Reflections on Kantian Themes About International Law and Globalisation." Paper presented at the Cegla Center International Conference "Critical Modernities: Politics and Law Beyond the Liberal Imagination." Tel Aviv University, 28–30 December 2005.

———. *The Gentle Civilizer of Nations: The Rise and Fall of International Law, 1870–1960.* Cambridge: Cambridge University Press, 2001.

Kritz, Neil, ed. *Transitional Justice: How Emerging Democracies Reckon with Former Regimes.* Vol. 1, *General Considerations.* Vol. 2, *Country Studies.* Vol. 3, *Laws, Ruling, and Report.* Washington, DC: United States Institute of Peace, 1995.

Ksikes, Driss. Débat; "Dans les Conditions actuelles, faut-il travailler *pour, avec,* ou *contre* le pouvoir?" *TelQuel* 187 (Casablanca), 1 August 2005.

———. "Et si le Maroc n'était pas en transition?" *TelQuel* 192 (Casablanca), 24 September 2005.

Lacey, Marc."Offering Olive Branch to a Brutal Uganda Foe." *New York Times,* 19 April 2005.

Lacina, Bethany, and Nils Petter Gleditsch. "Monitoring Trends in Global Combat: A New Dataset of Battle Deaths." *European Journal of Population* 21 (2005): 145–165.

Languin, Noëlle, Jean Kellerhals, and Christian-Nils Robert. *L'art de punir.* Geneva: Schultess, 2006.

Lantos, Thomas. "The Durban Debacle: An Insider's View of the UN World Conference Against Racism." *Fletcher Forum of World Affairs* 26.1 (Winter/Spring 2002): 31–52.

Lefranc, Sandrine. *Politiques du pardon.* Paris: PUF, 2002.

Le Goff, Jacques. *La naissance du purgatoire.* Paris: Gallimard, 1991.

Lejbowicz, Agnès. *La philosophie du droit international.* Paris: PUF, 1999.

Levi, Primo. *Si c'est un homme.* Paris: Julliard, 1987.

MacFarquhar, Neil. "In Morocco, a Rights Movement, at the King's Pace." *New York Times,* October 1, 2005, http://www.nytimes.com/2005/10/01/international/africa/01morocco.html.

MacPherson, Martin. *Open Letter to the Chief Prosecutor of the International Criminal Court: Comments on the Concept of the Interests of Justice.* Amnesty International, 17 June 2005.

Maghraoui, Abdeslam. "Depoliticization in Morocco." *Journal of Democracy* 13.4 (October 2002): 24–32.

Maghreb Arab Press. "La 3éme séance des auditions publiques des victimes des violations des droits de l'homme, le 29 Janvier à Figuig." Rabat: MAP, 25 January 2005.

Maguire, Peter. *Law and War: An American Story.* New York: Columbia University Press, 2001.

Mamdani, Mahmood. "Reconciliation Without Justice." *Southern African Review of Books* 46 (1996): 3–6.

Margalit, Avishai, and Gabriel Motzkin. "The Uniqueness of the Holocaust." *Philosophy and Public Affairs* 25.1 (Winter 1996): 65–83.

Marie, Gallois Pierre, and Jacques Vergès. *L'apartheid judiciaire: le tribunal pénal international arme de guerre.* Paris: L'Age d'Homme, 2002.

Marks, Susan. "Big Brother Is Bleeping Us—With the Message That Ideology Doesn't Matter." *European Journal of International Law* 12.1 (2001): 109–123.

Marks, Susan, and Andrew Clapham. *International Human Rights Lexicon.* New York: Oxford University Press, 2005.

Mattarollo, Rodolfo. "Recent Argentine Jurisprudence in the Matter of Crimes Against Humanity." In *Review of the International Commission of Jurists: Impunity, Crimes Against Humanity and Forced Disappearance,* edited by Louise Doswald-Beck, no. 62–63 (September 2001).

McCullough, Michael, Frank Fincham, and Jo-Ann Tsang. "Forgiveness, Forbearance, and Time: The Temporal Unfolding of Transgression-Related Interpersonal Motivations." *Journal of Personality and Social Psychology* 84.3 (2003): 540–557.

McWhorter, Stephanie. "Killing the Citizenry: Data on State Violence and Civilian Deaths." Prepared for Center for the Study of Civil War "Workshop on Techniques of Violence in Civil War," 20–21 August 2004.

Mégret Frédéric. "A Special Tribunal for Lebanon: The UN Security Council and the Emancipation of International Criminal Justice." *Leiden Journal of International Law* 21 (2008): 485–512.

——. "Three Dangers for the International Criminal Court." *Finnish Yearbook of International Law* 12 (2001): 193–247.

Meister, Robert. "Human Rights and the Politics of Victimhood." *Ethics and International Affairs* 16.2 (Fall 2002): 91–108.

Mertus, Julie, "Only a War Crimes Tribunal: Triumph of the International Community, Pain of Survivors." In *War Crimes: The Legacy of Nuremberg*, edited by Belinda Cooper. New York: TV Books, 1999.

Meyerstein, Ariel. "On the Advantage and Disadvantage of Truth Commissions for Life: Dreaming an Israeli-Palestinian Truth Commission." *Journal of Church and State* 45.3 (Summer 2003): 457–484.

——. "The United States Vetoes Bosnian Peace-Keeping Resolutions in Protest Against International Court." Crimes of War Project, 1 July 2002, http://www.crimesofwar.org/onnews/news-peacekeep.html.

Miller, Zinaida. "Effects of Invisibility: In Search of the 'Economic' in Transitional Justice." *International Journal of Transitional Justice* 2 (2008): 266–291.

Minow, Martha. *Between Vengeance and Forgiveness: Facing History After Genocide and Mass Violence*. Boston: Beacon Press, 1998.

Mohammed VI. "La commission équité et réconciliation et le rapport sur le développement humain au Maroc." *Discours royal*. Rabat, 6 January 2006.

Moore, Jonathan, ed. *Hard Choices, Moral Dilemmas in Humanitarian Intervention*. Lanham, MD: Rowman and Littlefield, 1998.

More, Sir Thomas. *Utopia*. Translated and edited by Robert M. Adams. New York: W. W. Norton and Company, 1975.

Morgenthau, Hans. *In Defense of the National Interest: A Critical Examination of American Foreign Policy*. New York: Knopf, 1951.

Moynier, Gustave. "La création d'une institution judiciaire internationale propre à prévenir et à réprimer les infractions à la Convention de Genève." Note au Comité international de secours aux militaires blessés, in *Bulletin international des sociétés de secours aux militaires blessés*, no. 11 (Geneva: April 1872): 122–131.

Muddell, Kelli. "Transitional Justice in Cambodia: Challenges and Opportunities." *Asia Society Symposium Report*, 9 September 2003, http://www.asiasource.org/asip/Cambodia_report.pdf.

Munoz-Rojas, Daniel, and Jean-Jacques Frésard. "The Roots of Behavior in War: Understanding and Preventing IHL Violations." International Committee of the Red Cross, October 2004.

Nahoum-Grappe, Véronique. "Vertige de l'impunité, ou l'impasse du rêve de justice." In *Crimes de l'histoire et réparations*, edited by Laurence Boisson de Chazournes, Jean-François Quéguiner, and Santiago Villalpando. Brussels: Editions de l'Université de Bruxelles, 2004.

Nichols, Hans. "Truth Challenges to Justice in Freetown." *Washington Times*, 5 January 2005.

Niebuhr, Reinhold. *Moral Man and Immoral Society: A Study of Ethics and Politics*. Louisville, KY: Westminster John Knox Press, 2001.

Novick, Peter. *The Holocaust in American Life*. Boston: Houghton Mifflin, 1999.

Nye, Joseph S., Jr. *Bound to Lead: The Changing Nature of American Power*. New York: Basic Books, 1990.

——. *Soft Power: The Means to Success in World Politics.* Boston: Public Affairs, 2004.

O'Connell, Jamie. "Gambling with the Psyche: Does Prosecuting Human Rights Violators Console Their Victims?" *Harvard International Law Journal* 46.2 (Summer 2005): 295–345.

Olojede, Dele. "Truth or Consequences: Biko's Widow Opposes S. Africa Commission's Policy on Pardon." *Newsday,* 2 February 1997.

Opgenhaffen, Veerle, and Mark Freeman. *Transitional Justice in Morocco: A Progress Report.* New York: International Center for Transitional Justice, November 2005.

Orentlicher, Diane. "Settling Accounts: The Duty to Prosecute Human Rights Violators of a Prior Regime." *Yale Law Journal* 1100.8 (June 1991): 2537–2615.

Ossipow, William. *La transformation du discours politique dans l'église.* Lausanne: L'Age d'Homme, 1979.

Otunnu, Olara. "The Silent Genocide." *Foreign Policy* 3 (July /August 2006).

Overy, Richard. "The Nuremberg Trials: International Law in the Making." In *From Nuremberg to The Hague: The Future of International Criminal Justice*, edited by Philippe Sands. Cambridge: Cambridge University Press, 2003.

Perrault, Gilles. *Notre ami, le roi.* Paris: Gallimard, 1990.

Pham, Phuong, Harvey Weinstein, and Timothy Longman. "Trauma and PTSD Symptoms in Rwanda: Implications for Attitudes Toward Justice and Reconciliation." *Journal of the American Medical Association* 292.5 (August 2004): 602–612.

Plumelle-Uribe, Rosa Amelia. *La férocité blanche, des non-blancs aux non-aryens, génocides occultés de 1492 à nos jours.* Paris: Albin Michel, 2001.

Posner, Eric, and Adrian Vermule. "Reparations for Slavery and Other Historical Injustices." *Columbia Law Review* 103.3 (April 2003): 689–748.

Refugee Law Project. "Peace First, Justice Later: Traditional Justice in Northern Uganda." Working Paper 17, July 2005, http://www.refugeelawproject.org/others/RLP .IDMC2.pdf.

——. "Whose Justice? Perceptions of Uganda's Amnesty Act of 2000, the Potential for Conflict Resolution and Long Term Reconciliation." Working Paper No. 15: 27. Kampala: Refugee Law Project, February 2005.

Revault d'Allonnes, Myriam. "De l'autorité à l'institution: la durée publique." *Revue Esprit* (Paris) (August–September 2004): 42–62.

Ricoeur, Paul. *La mémoire, l'histoire et l'oubli.* Paris: Seuil, 2000.

——. *Philosophie de la volonté: Finitude et culpabilité, la symbolique du mal.* Paris: Aubier Montaigne, 1960.

Rodella, Aude-Sophie. "L'expérience hybride de la Sierra Leone: De la Cour spéciale à la Commission Vérité et Réconciliation et au-delà." *Politique Africaine* 92 (December 2003).

Roht-Arriaza, Naomi, ed. *Introduction to Impunity and Human Rights in International Law and Practice.* New York: Oxford University Press, 1995.

――――. *The Pinochet Effect: Transnational Justice in the Age of Human Rights.* Pennsylvania Studies in Human Rights series. Philadelphia: University of Pennsylvania Press, 2005.

Rome Statute of the International Criminal Court. A/CONF.183/9, 17 July 1998, http://www.icc-cpi.int/NR.

Rotberg, Robert I., and Dennis Thompson, eds. *Truth v. Justice: The Morality of Truth Commissions.* The University Center for Human Values Series. Princeton, NJ: Princeton University Press, 2000.

Roth, Robert. "Le juge et l'histoire." In *Crimes de l'histoire et réparations: les réponses du droit et de la justice,* edited by Laurence Boisson de Chazournes, Jean-François Quéguiner, and Santiago Villalpando. Brussels: Editions de l'Université de Bruxelles, 2004.

Rousso, Henry, ed. *La hantise du passé.* Paris: Textuel, 1998.

Rubinstein, Alvin Z., Albina Shayevich, and Boris Zlotnikov, eds. *The Clinton Foreign Policy Reader: Presidential Speeches with Commentary.* Armonk, NY: M. E. Sharpe, 2000.

Rudolph, Christopher. "Constructing an Atrocities Regime: The Politics of War Crimes Tribunals." *International Organization* 55.3 (Summer 2001): 655–691.

Sa'Adah, Anne. "Regime Change: Lessons from Germany on Justice, Institution Building and Democracy." *Journal of Conflict Resolution* 50.3 (June 2006): 303–323.

Sahlins, Marshall. "Les lumières en anthropologie." Conférence prononcée 27 March 1997. Paris: Publication de la société d'ethnologie, 1999.

Salas-Molins, Louis. "Esclavage: Peut-on juridiquement envisager de ne pas réparer?" In *Crimes de l'histoire et réparations,* edited by Laurence Boisson de Chazournes, Jean-François Quéguiner, and Santiago Villalpando. Brussels: Editions de Université de Bruxelles, 2004.

Salzberger, Ronald P., and Mary C. Turck. *Reparations for Slavery: A Reader.* New York: Rowman and Littlefield, 2004.

Sands, Philippe, ed. *From Nuremberg to The Hague: The Future of International Criminal Justice.* Cambridge: Cambridge University Press, 2003.

Scharf, Michael P. "The Amnesty Exception to the Jurisdiction of the ICC." *Cornell International Law Journal* 32 (1999): 507–527.

Scheffer, David. "Human Rights and International Justice." Speech, Dartmouth College, Hanover, New Hampshire, 23 October 1998, http://www.findarticles.com/p/articles/mi_m1584/is_10_9/ai_53461439.

Schmitt, Carl. *The Concept of the Political.* Chicago: University of Chicago Press, 1996.

――――. "Swapping Amnesty for Peace: Was There a Duty to Prosecute International Crimes in Haiti?" *Texas International Law Journal* 31.1 (1996): 1–39.

Segev, Tom. "Nazis! Nazis!" *Haaretz,* 29 March 2002.

――――. *The Seventh Million: The Israelis and the Holocaust.* New York: Hill & Wang, 1993.

――――. "Le tournant du procès Eichmann." *Le Monde diplomatique* (April 2001), http://mondediplo.com/2001/04/13eichmann.

Shaw, Rosalind. *Rethinking Truth and Reconciliation Commissions: Lessons from Sierra Leone.* Special Report 130. Washington, DC: United States Institute of Peace, February 2005.

Slye, Ronald C. "Amnesty, Truth, and Reconciliation: Reflections on the South African Amnesty Process." In *Truth v. Justice*, edited by Robert I. Rotberg and Dennis Thompson (Princeton, NJ: Princeton University Press, 2000).

Slyomovics, Susan. *The Performance of Human Rights in Morocco.* Philadelphia: University of Pennsylvania Press, 2005.

Snyder, Jack, and Leslie Vinjamuri. "Trials and Errors: Principle and Pragmatism in Strategies of International Justice." *International Security* 28.3 (Winter 2003/4): 5–44.

Southwick, Katherine. "Investigating War in Northern Uganda: Dilemmas for the International Criminal Court." *Yale Journal of International Affairs* 1 (Summer–Fall 2005).

Soyinka, Wole. *The Burden of Memory, the Muse of Forgiveness.* Oxford: Oxford University Press, 1999.

Stahn, Carsten, Mohamed El Zeidy, and Hector Olasolo. "The International Criminal Court's Ad Hoc Jurisdiction Revisited." *American Journal of International Law* 99.2 (April 2005): 421–431.

Staub, Ervin. "Justice, Healing, and Reconciliation: How the People's Courts in Rwanda Can Promote Them." *Peace and Conflict: Journal of Peace Psychology* 10.1 (2004): 25–32.

Staub, Ervin, and Laurie Anne Pearlman. "Healing, Reconciliation, and Forgiving After Genocide and Other Collective Violence." In *Forgiveness and Reconciliation: Religion, Public Policy, and Conflict Transformation*, edited by Raymond G. Helmick and Rodney L. Petersen, 195–217. Philadelphia: Templeton Foundation Press, 2001, http://restorativejustice.org/rj3/Reviews/Helmick/collectiveviolence.htm.

Stover, Eric, and Harvey Weinstein, eds. *My Neighbor, My Enemy: Justice and Community in the Aftermath of Mass Atrocity.* Cambridge: Cambridge University Press, 2004.

Sundar, Nandini. "Toward an Anthropology of Culpability." *American Ethnologist* 31.2 (May 2004): 145–163.

Taguieff, Pierre-André. *Prêcheurs de haine. Traversée de la judéophobie planétaire.* Paris: Mille et Une Nuits, 2004.

Teitel, Ruti. "Transitional Jurisprudence: The Role of Law in Political Transformation." *Yale Law Journal* 106.7 (May 1997): 2009–2080.

———. *Transitional Justice.* New York: Oxford University Press, 2000.

———. "Transitional Justice Genealogy." *Harvard Human Rights Journal* 16 (Spring 2003).

Theidon, Kimberly. "Justice in Transition: The Micro-Politics of Reconciliation in Post-War Peru." *Journal of Conflict Resolution* 50.3 (June 2006): 433–457.

Thompson, Janna. *Taking Responsibility for the Past: Reparation and Historical Justice.* Cambridge, MA: Polity, 2002.

Torpey, John, ed. *Politics and the Past: On Repairing Historical Injustices.* New York: Rowman and Littlefield, 2003.

Trebak, Abderrazak. "Les auditions publiques: un moment historique de réconciliation." Rabat: MAP, 2004.

———. "2004: une année de réconciliation et d'actes pour clore la page du passé." Rabat: MAP, 2004.

Trial of the Major War Criminals Before the International Military Tribunal. Nuremberg: International Military Tribunal, 1947.

Tutu, Desmond. *There Is No Future Without Forgiveness.* New York: Doubleday, 1999.

United Nations. *Report of the World Conference Against Racism, Racial Discrimination, Xenophobia and Related Intolerance.* Durban, 31 August–8 September 2001.

United Nations Commission on Human Rights. "Civil and Political Rights, Including the Questions of: Disappearances and Summary Executions." *Report of the Working Group on Enforced or Involuntary Disappearances.* Geneva: Office of the High Commissioner for Human Rights, 21 January 2004.

———. Forty-ninth Session. *The Realization of Economic, Social and Cultural Rights: Final Report on the Question of the Impunity of Perpetrators of Human Rights Violations* (E/CN.4/Sub.2/1997/20/Rev.1). Geneva: Office of the High Commissioner for Human Rights.

United Nations Fact Finding Mission on the Gaza Conflict, Human Rights Council, 12th session, Agenda item 7, A/HRC/12/48, 25 September 2009, http://www2.ohchr.org/english/bodies/hrcouncil/docs/12session/A<->HRC-12.

United Nations Security Council. *Report of the Secretary General on the Rule of Law and Transitional Justice in Conflict and Post-Conflict Societies.* S/2004/616, 23 August 2004.

———. Resolution 808. New York: UNSC, 22 February 1993.

———. Resolution 827. New York: UNSC, 25 May 1993.

U.S. Congress. Senate. Bill 3930, Military Commissions, Act of 2006 (as passed by Congress), S.3930, September 22, 2006.

U.S. Congress. Senate. Committee on Foreign Relations. *Priorities in the Middle East and North Africa: Hearing Before the Committee on Foreign Relations Concerning Foreign Assistance Oversight.* 108th Cong., 1st sess., 26 March 2003.

van Zyl, Paul. "The Challenge of Criminal Justice: Lessons Learned from International, Hybrid and Domestic Trials." In *Dealing with the Past and Transitional Justice: Creating Conditions for Peace, Human Rights and the Rule of Law,* 21–23. Bern: Swisspeace, 2005.

Vuckovic, Nadia. "Qui demande des réparations et pour quels crimes?" In *Le livre noir du colonialisme, XVIe–XXIe: de l'extermination à la repentance,* edited by Marc Ferro. Paris: Robert Laffont, 2003.

Waltz, Susan. *Human Rights and Reform: Changing the Face of North African Politics.* Berkeley: University of California Press, 1995.

Walzer, Michael. *Just and Unjust Wars: A Moral Argument with Illustrations*. 3rd ed. New York: Basic Books, 2000.

———. *Thick and Thin: Moral Argument at Home and Abroad*. Notre Dame, IN: University of Notre Dame Press, 1994.

Washington Conference on Holocaust-Era Assets, http://www.state.gov/www/regions/eur/wash_conf_material.html.

Weissman, Fabrice, ed. *À l'ombre des guerres justes*. Paris: Flammarion, 2003.

Wendt, Alexander. "Anarchy Is What States Make of It: The Social Construction of Power Politics." *International Organization* 46.2 (Spring 1992): 391–425.

———. "Constructing International Politics." *International Security* 20.1 (Summer 1995): 71–81.

———. *Social Theory of International Politics*. New York: Cambridge University Press, 1999.

Wievorka, Annette. *L'ère du témoin*. Paris: Hachette, 2002.

Wievorka, Michel, and Jacques Derrida. "Le siècle et le pardon." *Le Monde des Débats* 9 (December 1999): 10–17.

Zartman, I. William, and Victor Kremenyuk, eds. *Peace Versus Justice: Negotiating Forward- and Backward-Looking Outcomes*. Lanham, MD: Rowman and Littlefield, 2005.

Zeghal, Malika. *Les islamistes marocains: Le défi à la monarchie*. Paris: La Découverte, 2005.

Ziman, John. "The Massacre of the Innocents." *International Security Information Services* 81 (February 2002).